THE POWER OF RUDRAKSHA

A Guide to the Holy Bead and its Healing Properties

KAMAL NARAYAN SEETHA

JAICO PUBLISHING HOUSE

Ahmedabad Bangalore Chennai
Delhi Hyderabad Kolkata Mumbai

Published by Jaico Publishing House
A-2 Jash Chambers, 7-A Sir Phirozshah Mehta Road
Fort, Mumbai - 400 001
jaicopub@jaicobooks.com
www.jaicobooks.com

THE POWER OF RUDRAKSHA
ISBN 978-81-7992-844-8

First Jaico Impression: 2008
14th Jaico Impression: 2022

Printed by
B.B. Press, Noida, U.P.

This book is dedicated to the all powerful Lord Shiva, who is the reason of all reasons.

DISCLAIMER

While neither the publisher nor I make any claim for the remedies or the benefits mentioned in this book, I hope this compilation will be treated as a database and a starting point to move forward.

— **Kamal Narayan Seetha**

CONTENTS

ACKNOWLEDGEMENTS

I acknowledge with sincere thanks the good work done by Dr Archana Juvekar, Professor of Pharmacology, Institute of Chemical Technology Mumbai, and her team of research scholars.

I wish to thank my publisher for making this book a reality.

PREFACE

R *udraksha* has fascinated people across the world due to its mystical properties. It is amazing that a seed of a fruit grown on trees has gone on to receive so much attention and created interest worldwide. Apart from Hindu religious saints, its users and worshippers vary from artisans, housewives, academicians to businessmen. *Rudraksha* has crossed the created boundaries of religion and nationalities.

Rudraksha is known and has been in use from time immemorial. Its origin is traced to Lord Shiva, one of the Trinities of the Hindu religion. From ancient times, Shiva's images and idols are shown wearing these beads.

A lot of mysteries are associated with *rudraksha*, which is not uncommon in the case of such rare and naturally occuring products. If one evaluates *amber, agar, shwetark, shaligram, gorochan,* or other similar products there is mysticism surrounding all these.

Primarily *rudraksha* is a symbol of spirituality. It is worn singly or in multiples in the form of *malas* (rosary). When *sadhus* wear them, they believe to have attained special powers and it is almost like a trademark for devotees of God. Many people wear *rudraksha* for its good omen, maybe as a talisman or just for good health. There are others who wear it as an ornament without knowing its virtues.

During the British rule of India, gold ornaments embedded with *rudraksha* used to be exported to England where these ornaments were said to be favourites of British women, including members of the royalty. This potential of *rudraksha* exists even today.

Rudraksha has not received wide publicity or acceptance on scientific basis, as having healing properties or mystical powers. This is not surprising, because many of the items of traditional and cultural importance to one specific religion (in this case for Hinduism) becomes a matter of faith and even superstition. Another reason could be the diversity of opinion on the benefits of *rudraksha* usage and its efficacy.

There have been no research or organised studies carried out on this bead, either for assessing its medicinal or healing properties and also its para-psychic or divine effects. Although as *Elaeocarpus* species, these trees are found across the globe, its spiritual significance is of interest only to those who believe in its divine aspects. Since the beads are identified more as a Hindu religious symbol it did not attract special attention of the Western commercial world.

The purpose of writing this book is to create an interest in the fertile minds of the people to look at these beads in an objective and dispassionate manner so that proper research can be carried out to unfold the mysteries surrounding them and come out with correct practices and usages for the beads as well as the other parts of the *rudraksha* tree. Apart from the bead, the outer skin of the fruit and leaves and bark of the tree can be used in making useful herbal products. There is also a passibility to study the properties of seeds belonging to different species of *Elaeocarpus*.

I had come across people who had mentioned several benefits from the use of *rudraksha*. I had also read about the bead and its efficacy in various publications and Ayurvedic references. The benefits ranged from achieving material successes to overcoming physical ailments or attaining calmness of mind. Many times, such an experience could be just coincidental, yet because of a large section of people conclusively asserting their views in favour of its good effects, I was motivated to continue with the studies.

The non-clinical tests conducted during the period, Feb 2005 till August 2007 at the Department of Pharmacology, University of Mumbai, (now Institute of Chemical Technology) on *rudraksha* and its benefits look quite promising. The summary of the findings of the tests is being published for the first time in this book.

I strongly believe this bead is worth much more than what is generally perceived. It could possess curative properties for many diseases that affect humans, for example, the unprecedented exposure of body cells to electro-magnetic waves created by cell phones, the electronic gadgets and processes or the changing lifestyles in terms of food, work schedules and stress. It can offer a protective shield to the human body. As such, there is a need for studying this product with dedication, devotion, confidence and patience to exploit its full potential.

There is another aspect to wearing *rudraksha,* which relates to its use as an ornament. Traditionally, wearing a necklace is the most common form of body decoration for the humans. Necklaces are most often embedded with beads made of precious metals, gemstones, bones, shells and several other natural and synthetic materials. To me, in all these stones and other materials – including pearls and diamonds, gold or platinum – there is nothing on this planet that matches *rudraksha* in its natural wild beauty, full of energy and usefulness both for body and mind. *Rudraksha* is a true bio-jewellery, beautiful and power-packed. Its aura and glow, whether you see them during day or night, are divine, impressive and mesmerizing.

As I have mentioned earlier, Hindu scriptures associate *rudraksha* with Lord Shiva, the greatest among the Hindu Gods. He is known as Mahadev and it is believed that *rudraksha* trees originated from his tears. In Sanskrit, *Rudra* means Lord Shiva and *aksh* means tears or eyes. Many believe and as scriptures declare, the blessings of Lord Shiva should be sought to get the maximum benefits from these beads. Had this book been written considering *rudraksha* merely as a product and without referring to its spiritual significance, I would not have done justice to theses beads. For generations, the mere utterance of the word *rudraksha* creates emotions and vibrations touching the soul and bring you closer to God.

The most important property of these beads as per experience is to make a person fearless. *Shakti* (Goddess of power) unites with Lord Shiva to provide this basic property of *rudraksha*. Each and every property of such divine products cannot be easily explained scientifically.

There are several approaches to understand the power of *rudraksha*, the most appealing is its adoption by Lord Shiva as an ornament.

He uses ornaments having symbols of power, which have serenity and beauty in their own sense. For example, He wraps snakes around His neck and arms, uses the intoxicating flowers of *dhatura* and wears tiger's skin to cover His body.

He applies ash (*bhasm*) from cremation ground on His body. Further, there is Moon over His head, river Ganges flowing from His locks of hairs and He holds the *damru*, a musical instrument. The Moon and Ganges are known for their vastness and might, while the *damru* is considered as the creator of Sanskrit language by unifying the sounds of 14 *Pratyahars*. Twelve *jyotirlingas*, representing His divine light forms, are situated in the most scenic locations in India, in difficult terrains but in magnificent natural surroundings. His permanent abode is in Mount Kailash in the Himalayas, which can impress any mortal in any way he/she would like to look at it. No other God could match His unique ways. Temples dedicated to Him can be found in practically all villages and towns in India where He is worshipped either in the *Linga* (phallus) form, or as the dancing Nataraja or together with consort Parvati and members of His family — sons Lord Ganesh and Kartikeya, and his vehicle Nandi (a bull). In short, for the Indian believers anything that is unusually blissful, beautiful, powerful or indicating vastness and depth is usually associated with Lord Shiva. It may be death, destruction, annihilation, poison, inebriation, the unapproachable Himalayas, *tantric* practices or the highest form of *yogas* and *tapasyas*, music, dance, language or anything, which is mystical.

Shiva is omnipotent and He exists in atoms and cosmos. He controls the cycle of birth and death. The more one tries to define and measure Him, the more dimensionless He becomes. He is responsible for creation of languages, art, dance, music, yoga, ayurveda and herbal medicines. By far, He is the most worshipped God in India and even finds mention in the inscriptions in many ancient temples in China, Japan and Indonesia.

Since Lord Shiva is considered the creator of *rudraksha*, it becomes a symbol of spirituality, fearlessness and a source of power for health, peace and prosperity. Most Hindu, Jain and Sikh homes in India have *rudraksha* either as loose beads or in rosary form. Unfortunately, even after having these beads for generations, hardly anyone seems to know their genuineness or the true value or how exactly they have to be used and in what numbers and how to maintain them. Usually, people who trade in these beads hide many facts and for commercial reasons do not share their views.

Following reasons could be attributed to the lack of knowledge about these beads among people:

1. Absence of proper literature or published information. Most of the books or articles available in the market contain irrelevant information. There are books, one for example, titled "Secrets of *Rudraksha*", which contains no relevant information on *rudraksha* but is full of details on worshipping methods and rituals associated with the bead. Some of these books have been written by traders and retailers of *rudraksha* and other *puja* items and information is presented in a manner best suited to their interests.

2. Several restrictions imposed by way of rituals and customs or ways to wear *rudraksha*. For example, in many families, women are forbidden from wearing *rudraksha,* while men can wear only one. In one of the religious sects, there is a practice of a person being allowed to wear a single *rudraksha* at a young age and every year knots are tied on the thread that holds the bead so that by the time the man reaches the age of 50, the bead virtually touches the throat. Some people (particularly priests from South India) encase it with silver or

gold in box form and wear it around their neck in a chain.

3. Complex rituals and perceived negative effects. People in certain societies consider wearing *rudraksha* as a very complex ritual and are often discouraged to do so fearing negative effects, without any evidence. Some sects advise on the need for *tantra sadhana* to obtain the full benefits from *rudraksha* (for example, going to a crematorium at night and doing the *suddhi* of *rudraksha*). A Bollywood movie of 2004, titled "*Rudraksha*", highlighted several untrue and unrealistic aspects about this bead and hypothetically created a new variety called *Ravan Rudraksha,* claiming to possess mysterious powers. Such instances only make these look like magical product and create superstition.

4. Inhibitions prescribed in scriptures. A few of the great scriptures, if one reads them carefully, give differing views, particularly on regimens like vegetarianism or abstinence from alcohol, as well as on the size of the beads, *mantras* to be chanted or the number of beads to be worn or the part of the body where they are to be worn. These restrictions have to be accepted in a constructive manner, instead of trying to read in between the lines, and in the true spirit of the history of the scriptures and their passing from generation to generation without any blatant control or religious intolerance.

5. Presence of a large number of fake beads in the market. Spurious beads in the market have shaken the confidence of people and this is one of the important reasons that inhibit its usage. Offering single-faceted (one *mukhi*) round beads in different handcrafted forms or crafting them from other seeds or carving additional lines on the beads have all become

part of a roaring business for many.

In these circumstances, there is an absolute need for joint efforts to popularize this bead and bring out its true qualities and benefits.

In ancient India, as a result of the efforts of great *rishis* and other learned people, sciences like astrology, ayurveda, yoga, languages, music and dance have come to be evolved to great heights. There could be a good enough reason to assume that these ancestors were not ordinary humans but were endowed with capabilities to explore and make great discoveries. We can only guess the extent of efforts required to discover and assign properties for a bead like *rudraksha*. In this modern age, with resources of all types, including satellite-assisted mapping and exploration facilities, the question is whether we can invent something basic like *rudraksha* again?

Today, we are trying to find scientific explanation for everything that was acclaimed as a useful product or practice ages ago – be it neem, tamarind, bitter gourd, mustard, the time-tested ayurvedic drugs, or practices like yoga, *pranayam*, or meditation or rituals like offering water to the rising Sun or blowing of a conch shell. Surprisingly, most of the products or practices are getting scientific approval today. Because of this, appreciation of older principles and traditions are now becoming prominent and increasingly followed in this and other places in the world. It is the emergence of old values supported with scientific facts that is leading people more and more towards spirituality, yoga or ayurveda.

The new age gurus and learned orators like Shri Morari Bapuji, Sri Sri Ravishankar, Ma Chidvilasanand (Muktanand

Ashram), ashram chiefs like Swami Avadheshanandji, Swami
Satyamitranandji of Bharat Mandir, Haridwar, Swami
Chidanand of Parmartha Niketan, Rishikesh, Shri Pranav
Pandyaji of Shanti Kunj, Haridwar, Swami Punyanandji Giri
of Sanyas Ashram, New Delhi, Swami Vishweshwaranand
Giri of Sanyas Ashram, Mumbai or for that matter, most
members of Hindu religious institutions, *sanyasis* and
astrologers wear *rudraksha*. Shri Morari Bapu wears a
rudraksha mala and does not believe in gems or any other
superstitious rituals. The yoga and *pranayam* teacher and the
outspoken Swami Ramdevji is against all superstitions, gems,
stones or *yantras*, but respects the virtues of *rudraksha* and
offers *malas* as his blessings to his followers. When I had the
met Swami Ramdevji in the year 2005 I told him about the
benefits of wearing *rudraksha (especially* while doing *pranayams)*
and had requested him to initiate some research on *rudraksha*
in his ayurvedic research project at Haridwar.

In order to understand the properties of *rudraksha*, there is
need for pool of experts from fields like digital biology,
magneto therapy, Kirlian or other bio-field photo imaging,
X-ray/CT scanning and botany, along with researchers in
pharmacology, medicine and physics. As such, a project of
this scope and nature can be undertaken only at a corporate
level or by the government.

Today, there are efforts to popularize the usage of
rudraksha and to remove several misconceptions about it.
Institutions like Rudra Life in Mumbai and Rudra Centre in
Nagpur/Mumbai organise exhibitions throughout the
country and abroad, which have been attracting large crowds.
People who attend the exhibitions discuss about *rudraksha*

xvi   The Power of Rudraksha

selection and seek clarifications for their doubts. In their interactions with several thousands of people, the organizers have found that by and large people accept *rudraksha* as a powerful and divine bead but generally have doubts on availability of genuine beads and on the identification procedure. In fact, many were found to be so obsessed with the efficacy of *rudraksha* that they were against any scientific exploration or research work to be carried out. They claim the beads are "self proven" and have powers of God and should not be subjected to scientific investigations.

It was in the year 1997 that I felt the need to share my experience and knowledge about *rudraksha* with others. I did it in a modest manner through an exhibition at Nagpur, which was appreciated by the visitors. This prompted me to take it on a wider scale all over the country and also overseas. Besides India we have held exhibitions in Malaysia and Singapore and had the opportunity to interact with thousands of people about their experiences of using *rudraksha*.

I must say that people wearing *rudraksha* get positive results either for their health-related issues or for aspirations like prospering in life, getting married or for removing negativities. I believe the good results have not been properly monitored or documented. Rudra Life, which is located at Mumbai, started conducting scientific studies in association with recognised laboratories to understand more about *rudraksha*, its structure, physical and medicinal properties.

In the meantime, I felt it necessary to summarize and present the status of the work carried out so far in the form of a book so that it can be taken up from here by people from different vocations and areas of study. I hope this book will give the preliminary information about *rudraksha* and the areas where further work is needed.

Rudraksha is for self-empowerment and for bringing about positive changes from within. It has been generally found that people suffering from hypertension, diabetes, cardiac problems, stomach disorders, stress, arthritis and fear get beneficial results by wearing *rudraksha*. Even disorders like asthma, insomnia and hypertension get cured or controlled by wearing *rudraksha* alone in some cases and along with natural therapies or herbal medications in other cases. Such therapies can be yoga, *pranayam*, sun therapy and use of other alternate healing methods.

However, more work needs to be done in this respect. A new beginning is to be made by conducting basic research in all seriousness so that the full potential of this wonder bead can be exploited. I have no doubt that *rudraksha* can help to make the world disease, stress, and fear-free. It can easily become the low-cost treatment as well as preventive therapy for various physical and mental disorders. However, I see a long journey between these beliefs and reality.

I welcome suggestions from readers to improve the contents and presentation of the book.

Om Namah Shivaya!

Kamal Narayan Seetha

RUDRAKSHA – THE BEADS 1

Rudraksha is a genus of large evergreen trees with more than 360 species distributed in the tropical and subtropical regions of the world. The scientific classification of *Elaeocarpaceae* to which *rudraskha* belongs to is as follows:

Kingdom: *Plantae*

Division: *Magnoliophyta*

Class: *Mangoliopsida*

Order: *Oxalidales*

Family: *Elaeocarpaceae*

Genus: *Elaeocarpus*

Type: *E. serratus Linn, Eganitrus, Roxb, etc.*

These species are distributed in Madagascar, India, Sri Lanka, Nepal, Sikkim, Bhutan, Myanmar, Tibet, Thailand, Malaysia, Indonesia, northern parts of Australia, New Zealand, New Caledonia, Fiji, Philippines, Southern China, Japan and Hawaii. The islands of Borneo and New Guinea have a large concentration of the species.

In the late nineteenth century a botanist, Dr. William Roxburgh, had classified the most popular variety of these trees found in Nepal while studying the flora of India and Nepal in his capacity as Director, Indian Botanical Garden, Kolkata. He is considered as an authority on ***Elaeocarpus ganitrus*** Roxb. commonly called *rudraksha*, which match the broad specifications given in our old religious texts. The above species of *rudraksha* are mostly found in Nepal and Indonesia as of now, as at other places there has been no organized plantation work.

It is interesting to note that fossilized remains of *rudraksha* have been recently discovered from Upper Siwalik sediments (Kimin formations) of Arunachal Pradesh by Dr Subir Bera and others from the University of Kolkata. It appears they are carbonized fruits resembling modern taxon **Elaeocarpus lanceaefolius** Roxb. Occurrence of these fruits indicates a sub-tropical to temperate, broad-leaved to evergreen forest in the area at the time of deposition and also the fact that these trees appear to be originally from the Indian subcontinent. **E. angustifolius** is a relatively fast-growing tree, most common in secondary forests. It grows wild in tropical forests in Queensland, New Guinea, Malaysia and southern Nepal. It may have been introduced by Hindu missionaries and traders in some of these areas.

In Greek, **elaei** means 'wild olive' tree and **carpus** means 'fruit' and therefore the seed of fruit from wild olive-like trees have been classified as *Elaeocarpus*. In Sanskrit, Hindi and Marathi it is known as *rudraksha*, in Kannada, *rudrakshi*, in Tamil *aakkam*, in Telugu *rudraksha halu* and in Bengali *rudrakya*.

These trees may be 14.60 metres to 29.20 metres tall **(Fig. 1-A)** depending on area (Nepal *rudraksha* trees are over 20 metre tall) and have trunks up to 1.22 metre in diameter.

Its leaves are like mango tree leaves having length of around 17.78 cms and width of 2.54 cms to 4.45 cms. The leaves are light green in colour in the beginning and turn deep green at maturity and change to yellowish red before turning grey (coffee colour) and falling. This cycle of leaves continues all over the tree throughout the year. **(Fig. 2)**

Flowering takes place in mid-November and bunches of white flowers grow from old leaf axils. **(Fig. 3)**

The flowers enhance the beauty of the tree and they seem to have a mild aroma similar to *raat rani* flowers. The length of the flower bunch is smaller than that of the leaf. After nearly a month of flowering, fruits start appearing but this occurs only when the tree is seven to eight years old. Younger trees flower, but do not produce fruits. The fruits are 2 cms to 4 cms in diameter and green in colour. After maturity, the colour starts turning blue and then bluish-violet, **(Fig. 4)** then deep brown and finally black. The size of the beads varies according to the area where trees are located. For example, fruits of the Nepalese variety are largest in size and Indonesian variety the smallest.

Rudraksha is the fruit (stone) of the **E. ganitrus** Roxb. The stony endocarp or the bead can be seen on removal of the outer epicarp and fleshy middle mesocarp. The outer skin of the fruit has several medicinal values and normally the local people of the area where these trees grow, make use of these by boiling them in water and drinking the water in case of fever, cough or cold. The leaves have antibacterial properties and are used in treating wounds. They are also taken orally to cure headache, migraine and mental disorders and for the treatment of epilepsy.

Inside the fruit is the stony endocarp, or bead, which is attached to the stem from the base of the stone. The bead has very hard rough surface **(Fig. 5)** having uneven grooves and a long cavity in the centre from the point where it remains attached to the stem. The bead contains seed/s inside and receive their nourishment from the central cavity. From this central cavity vertical clefts remain attached. While each cleft has separate compartment having one internal seed, the joint of these clefts protrude outside the body of the seed. This joint, visible from outside, is known as **mukhi** or **dhari** (facet). To understand it in a simple manner, a five *mukhi* bead will have five clefts having five internal seeds **(Fig. 6),** a nine *mukhi* bead will have nine clefts and nine seeds, etc. The number of internal clefts should be the same as the number of *mukh* in any *rudraksha*. This is a good test to recognize a *rudraksha* having several facets (*mukhi*). However, in this procedure, the bead usually gets destroyed. And in many beads, particularly those beyond six *mukhi*, it has been observed that the seeds often get overlapped or in a few cases some of the seeds do not attain complete growth. A lot of practice and closer examination through x-ray are required in order to do a perfect job of seeing the compartments and counting the internal seeds. It is, however, certain that the number of clefts inside remains equal to the number of facets. Details regarding this aspect and X-ray studies are given in Chapter 4. A combination of internal study and outer examination of the surface should be employed to determine the number of facets or *mukhis*.

The protrusions are thorny when the bead is unripe and as it starts maturing, the thorny surface becomes smoother. Seeds tend to be lower in density if plucked before maturity. *Rudraksha* up to 21 *mukhis* **(Fig. 6)** have been found, and documented. In the crop of the year 2005, some higher *mukhi* beads like 22, 23, 25, and 29 *mukhis* have been obtained. This has happened after a long time. In Indonesian varieties, higher *mukhis* beyond 21 are common and in some instances beads up to 38 *mukhis* have been obtained. Older texts like Shivapuran mention upto 14 mukhis only.

Some of the beads get joined on the trees naturally if the seeds grow side by side they are known as *Gaurishankar rudraksha* (Twin Beads) **(Fig. 6)**. In some extremely rare cases, even three beads get joined and such unique bead is called *Trijuti* or *Gauri-Path* or *Brahma-Vishnu-Mahesh* **(Fig. 7)**. Only a few natural *Trijutis* are found in a particular season in different shapes and sizes. A balanced *Trijuti* with nearly equal spacing and uniform bead size is an absolute rarity.

Any *Gaurishankar* and *Trijuti* beads should be subjected to tests to bring out any artificially created joints, which may not be noticed even by using magnifying glasses. The technique of joining has been improvised so much that traditional tests like boiling the beads in water for a few hours do not separate these glued pieces. However, some skilful tests described in later chapter may establish the authenticity of the beads.

One *mukhi rudraksha* from Nepal (round in shape) is mythical and many resourceful people, are willing to bet for its existence. Some traders whose family business is *rudraksha* for the last few generations have also not seen a perfect eye shaped* one *mukhi rudraksha* from Nepal. This subject has been discussed in detail in Chapter 4. One *mukhi rudraksha* from Indonesia is also rare but it is available. However, care should be taken to procure it from a good source. One *mukhi rudraksha* from Indonesia is 8 mm to 10 mm in length and 4 mm to 7 mm in central diameter. It is elliptical in shape.

---

* According to some people, one mukhi round rudraksha from Nepal should be having the shape of an eye. Its appearance has to be closer to 2 mukhi from Nepal.

There are naturally grown *rudrakshas* having different shapes and looks and such *rudrakshas* are named according to their looks and shape. One such bead, which is considered very auspicious, is **Sawar (Fig. 7)**. It is a twin-bead like *Gaurishankar* but it differs in that one of the beads has only one complete *mukh* while the other is a normal bead with number of *mukhs*, mostly four to seven. *Sawar* in Hindi means a rider (one *mukhi* riding over another). Many people cut out the one *mukhi* joined seed from *Sawar* and wear it or use it as one *mukhi rudraksha*.

Although the cutting damages the bead, the faith is important, as the bead is considered as divine.

The special *rudraksha* (including *Gaurishankar*, *Trujuti*, etc.) may not have any reference in ancient epics, but people regard them as auspicious because all *rudrakshas* have the blessings of the Gods. There are beads having no lines at all over the entire surface and these have been given the name of *Gupta Mukhi* (Hidden Facets).

The fruits of *rudraksha* are green in colour and are nearly round in shape for the common varieties (5, 6, and 7 *mukhis*). Its pulp, tasting sour, is eaten by the birds, when green. It turns to blue and then dark brown with aging. With such deep blue-(sometimes violet-) coloured fruits all over, the tree looks magnificent. It is often called **"Blue Marble Tree"**. Corner has reported in his article, "Wayside Trees of Malaya", that the brilliant blue colour of the fruit is caused not by a blue pigment but by the structure of the cuticle, which reflects blue light; thin pieces of skin are green in transmitted light. The blue colour is normally caused by anthocyanins, modified by their association with metals or other flavonoid pigments. However, no such anthocyanins were extractable in acidic methanol from *rudraksha* fruits, suggesting that the basis for the presence of the colour may well be structural. Three physical observations produce colour in animals — thin film interference, Tyndall scattering and diffraction. The basis of the blue iridescence in *rudraksha* fruits also appears to be thin film interference. The blue colouration of the fruits is not reduced by immersion in water; if anything, the intensity enhances. Colourations in fruits are generally regarded as an adaptation to promote dispersal by animals, particularly birds. Ripe *rudraksha* fruits fall on the ground; the colour persists even after the cortex decays; and the persistent colour may attract frugivore dispersers. While the iridescent blue colour is most striking in the fruits of *rudraksha*, the blue colour is prevalent in *Eleaocarpus* throughout its distribution. In classical cultures of the world, the medicinal and sacred values of plants are frequently associated with the remarkable appearance of the plant — what is generally known as "the doctrine of signatures". For instance, the medicinal benefits of the ginseng and mandrake plants are suggested by the limb-like lateral roots. It is tempting to speculate that the spiritual significance of *rudraksha* fruits is associated with the striking blue colour of the wall. As Lord Shiva is blue-throated (*Neelkantha*), it will be an interesting study to compare properties (specially its medicinal values) with other fruits having identical colour. David W. Lee has done remarkable work to study the colour of *rudraksha* fruits and leaves and some of the observations given here are from his article published in "Current Science" Vol.75, No.1, July 1998. **(Ref. 37)**

Elaeocarpus trees are planted for ornamental purposes as bunches of blue fruits all over the tree give a very scenic look. After maturity period of a month or so, it turns nearly black. The fruit falls off on its own in the ripened stage. Many times, planters pluck the fruits much earlier, particularly when they notice that the bead is of higher *mukhi*s. In such cases the inner seeds remain underdeveloped and the stone may have lower density.

Rudraksha's outer skin is hard to remove. The seeds are buried inside the earth along with cow dung and table salt for couple of weeks for the skin to become soft. The beads can then be taken out easily. The farmers adopt different practices to remove the outer skin and for cleaning the *rudraksha* seed. For example, in some cases, the seeds are boiled in water and then allowed to get fermented so that the skin becomes soft, however, by this method the beads become darker.

The trees give fruits during winter (around November) and after their cleaning and processing, the new crop reaches markets around January. In certain varieties, particularly in trees grown in the Sahyadri ranges and in Maharashtra, flowering takes place in February or March and the yield comes by October to November. There are species, which give two crops in a year. The July crop yields higher quality compared to the one, which comes in January. This phenomenon is specific to certain species and areas only and not to all plants.

The wood of tree is off white or grey in colour and is used for furniture making and as fuel. Due to this reason and since there is no protection from local governments in Nepal or Indonesia, the trees are felled mercilessly. Their numbers are dwindling. The good news, however, is that in the recent past, several farmers and big traders are into planting on a large scale and in organised manner in Nepal and North-East India

(Bengal, Assam etc.) and in the coming years this will yield results – both in quantity and quality. I have visited a plantation (having 42 grown up trees) near Cochin and a few trees are also found scattered across the country.

The family of *Elaeocarpaceae* has six important taxa

(1) ***Elaeocarpus ganitrus*** *Roxb*, which are found in Nepal, Malaysia, Indonesia and in smaller numbers in northern Bihar, Assam, Bengal and Arunachal Pradesh. Primarily, these are the *rudraksha* beads used in the making of *malas* and other wearable articles. These are the ones described as pure and authentic in our ancient scriptures. The flowers of these varieties are white, in dense racemes arising mostly from old leaf axils, the drupe deep or bluish purple and obovoid (12.5 to 25.40 mm in diameter) enclosing a hard longitudinally tubercled, normally 5-celled stone. Most of the usefulness and description of cultural attributes mentioned in this book pertains to this type.

(2) ***E. floribundus*** *Blume*: The bark of these trees is used to counter diseases of gums.

(3) ***E. Oliongus*** *Mast.*: Its fruit is used as an emetic and in the treatment of ulcers, rheumatic pneumonia, leprosy and piles. It is a large tree with smooth bark, found in Western Ghats ascending to 2000 metres. Leaves are broadly elliptic or ovate, coriaceous, often tinged with red flowers, white in auxiliary racemes, the drupe oblong, containing 1 or 2 seeded stone. The wood is suitable for making match boxes.

(4) ***E. petiolatus*** *Wall*: The juice of its leaves is used in Malaysia as a cure for sunstroke. The roots are used to cure fever.

(5) ***E. serratus*** *Linn*: In Bengali, it is known as *Jalpai*, in

Kannada *Perinkara* and Tamil *Ulanga-kerei*. The leaves are used
in rheumatism and as an antidote to poison. It is a moderate-
sized tree found in eastern Himalayas up to 1000 meters and
in evergreen forests of North Kanara and the western coast.
Leaves are ovate or obovate, serrate, acuminate and
coriaceous. Flowers are white in auxiliary racemes. The drupe
is ovoid, 25.40 mm to 40 mm, containing a much tubercled
one-seeded stone.

(6) *E. tuberculatus Roxb*: In Tamil, this variety is known
as *Rutthracham* and in Kannada *Dandele*. The bark of the tree
is used to cure haemetemesis and indigestion, while the seed
is used as a remedy for typhoid fever and epilepsy. The tree is
found in south Kanara through Western Ghats in Coorg,
Mysore and also in Nilgiris, Palani and Annamalai. This
variety produces the elliptically-shaped beads, which have
become popular particularly for the one *mukhi* **Chandrakar**
(half moon-shaped) type. Leaves are obovate, serrulate,
crowded about the ends of branchlets, while flowers are
white in copious racemes aggregated below the leaves. The
drupe is smooth and ovoid, and contains one or two seeds,
with two-valved and deeply tubercled stone. The nuts are
used in rheumatism, typhoid and epilepsy. The beads are
increasingly used for wearing because of its spiritual
attributes and in the absence of Nepali one *mukhi rudraksha*
and the great rarity of one *mukhi* Indonesian beads. It is
however, improper to classify the above half-moon shape as
rudraksha, except as driven by commercial advertisements.

In addition to the above, these trees produce fewer two,
three or four *mukhis*. No five *mukhis* are found on such trees.
The end portion of these beads is smooth. Following are also
such trees types: *E. prunifolius, E. glabrescens, E.*

amoenus. The shape of the bead is, however, not round; it could be half-moon-shape (*Chandrakar*). These are not considered to be *rudrakshas* finding mention in the epics.

There are trees which give two *mukhi rudraksha*: **E. polystachyus, E. rugosus,** and **E. pendunculatus.**

The following three types of trees give only five *mukhi rudraksha*: **E.parvifolius, E.nitidus and E.stipularis**

The following types give three *mukhi rudraksha*, mainly found in Malayasia: **E. cuneatus, E. floribundus and E. cyanocarpa.**

Trees of the following types give *rudraksha* with unclear lines or only a few clear *mukhs* and such *rudraksha* is used for carving out additional lines and make fake beads. **E. paniculatus, E. sikkimensis, E. obvatus, E. subvillous.**

Some of the popular varieties of *Elaeocarpus* flowers, fruits and seeds are shown in **Fig. 1-B**.

The above description has been given to enable the readers to know that a large range in *rudraksha* exists; but in the scope of present book we are mainly concerned with **Elaeocarpus ganitrus** Roxb., which meets the definition given in the ancient scriptures. This has been discussed in detail in Chapter 2.

There is another species known as *Bhadraksha,* originating from trees known as *Koenigii, Goodeniaceae, Scaevola Fruitescens, Lanceaefolius and Sikkimensis.* The seeds of these varieties are flat, light in weight and not so thorny. Mostly available as two *mukhi*, they do not possess any natural hole. Some people use these beads for doing *Japa* and they also find mention in certain scriptures, but it is generally believed that these types are of inferior quality. Mostly used as religious offering or as a

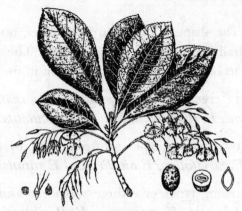

Elaeocarpus oblongus Gaertn

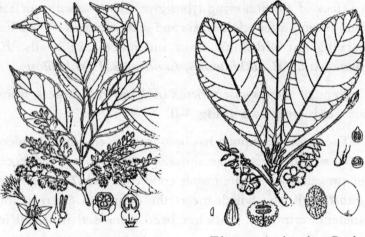

Elaeocarpus aristatus Roxb   *Elaeocarpus tuberculatus* Roxb

Fig. 1-B: Different Elaeocarpus leaves and fruits

mala with selective limited purposes, these two *mukhi Bhadrakshas* are used rampantly to make fake one *mukhi rudraksha* in which one line is left out as it is while the other side is carved for making symbols of snake, *shivling* or other religious motifs.

The following table gives details of some species of *Elaeocarpus* and the regions where these are found.

Sr. No.	Latin Name	Local name		Regions where found
1.	ELAEOCARPUS GANITRUS E. SPHAERICUS	Hindi & Marathi Bengali Kannada Tamil Telugu English	: Rudraksha : Rudrakya : Rudrakshi : Akkamrudrakai : Rudraksha Halu : Woodenbegar : Utrasumbeek	Assam, Bihar, U.P., Kerala, Tamil Nadu, Madagascar, Sri Lanka, North Australia, The Philippines, Nepal, Singapore, New Zealand and China
2.	E. SERRATUS E. CUNEATUS E. INTERGRIFOLIUS E. LACUNOSUS	Tamil Kannada English	: Ulung, Kaaeri : Bijandmara : Dhandadamba : Ceylon Olive	Bihar, Assam, Bengal, Nepal, Java, Sumatra, Borneo and Singapore
3.	E. FLORIBUNDUS E. GROSSA E. LOBBIANUS E. RIGIDUS E. RAMOSII	Bengali Assamese Manipuri Nepali	: Jalpai : Belfoe : Charpai : Koving	Sikkim, Assam, Bengal, Java, Sumatra, Kashi Hills, Singapore and Thailand

Sr. No.	Latin Name	Local name		Regions where found
4.	E. ROBUSTUS E. TECTORIUS E. ECRASOEDUM E. LEPTOSTACHYUS	Kannada Malayalam Oriya Tamil Assamese	: Hinnaltodi : Kattakara : Malamkara : Nardhampa : Panasiya : Bikki : Perang : Selang	East Himalayas, Sikkim, Assam, Maharashtra, Bengal, Tamil Nadu, Karnataka, Kerala, Andaman & Nicobar, Bramhadesh, Malaysia, Sri Lanka and Singapore
5.	E.SIKKIMENSIS	Assamese Nepali	: Selang : Bhadras	Sikkim, Bhutan and Assam
6.	E. WALLICHII E. ACCUMNIATUS			Assam, Meghalaya, Orissa, Bramhadesh, Java and Indo- China
7.	E. LANCEAEFOLIUS E. LANCEIFOLOUS E. SERRULATUS			Darjeeling, Kashi Hills, Garo Hills, Bhutan, Java, Indo-China

Sr. No.	Latin Name	Local name		Regions where found
8.	E. OBLONGUS	Kannada	: Hanaltodi	Tamil Nadu (Nilgiris,
	E. GLANDULOSUS	Tamil	: Khattakaeri	Annamalai), Karnataka
	E. ADENOPHYLLUS	Marathi	: Kaas	and Borneo
	E. PERIMKARA		: Kasava	
	E. ANGUSTIFOLIOUS	Nilgiri	: Baikmara	
9.	E. ARISTATUS	Assamese	: Garela	Assam, Bihar, Gara Hills,
	E. MONOCERA	Bihar	: Garela	Andaman & Nicobar,
	E. ROXBURGHII		: Sopa	Bramhadesh and Nepal
			: Garali	
			: Nanini	
			: Garali	
			: Nanini	
		Nepali	: Dalchivari	
10.	E. TUBERCULATUS	Kannada	: Bhutadi	Tamil Nadu (Nilgiris) and
	E. SERRULATUS		: Dandemara	Maha. (Mahabaleshwar)
	E. MONOCERA	Tamil	: Ruthrachan	
	E. TYBERCULATA	Malayalam	: Pilaibagyra	
		English	: Deccan Olive	

Sr. No.	Latin Name	Local name		Regions where found
11.	E. ROGOSUS E. APICULATUS	Assamese Garo Hills	: Gattonga : Fulchampa : Borchampa : Aashimaifak	Tamil Nadu (Nilgiris) Hills of Bramhadesh, Bihar, Garo Hills
12.	E. FERRUGINEA E. MONOCERAFER E. RUGINEA E. RECORVATUS E. OBTUSUS E. MONOCERA	Assamese	: Patisopa : Phutkuli	Tamil Nadu (Nilgiris), Maharashtra (Konkan), Kerala, Manipur, Assam and Bramhadesh
13.	E. GRANDIFLORUS E. MONOCERA E. GRANDIFLORA			Bengal, Java and Indo- China islands.
14.	E. VERUNNA E. FUNLAYSONIANUS	India Nepali	: Bhadrak : Bhadraksha : Bhadras	Uttaranchal (Kumaon Hills) Sikkim, Nepal, Sayam, Bramhadesh

Sr. No.	Latin Name	Local name	Regions where found
15.	E. PRUNIFOLOUS E. MONOCERA PRUNIFOLIUS		Kashi Hills, Assam and Manipur
16.	E. APICULATUS		Malaysia and Indo-china islands
17.	E. PUNIFOLIUS		Cilvet, Kashi Hills and Garo Hills
18.	E. PANICULATUS		Malaysia, Indo-china islands, Singapore and Sri Lanka
19.	E. ACRONODIA		Malaysia, Java, Borneo, Indo-china islands and Singapore
20	E. OVALIFOLIUS		East Himalayas (up to 2000 feet), Sikkim, Kashi Hills, North and South Karnataka, Brahmadesh, Malaysia and Sri Lanka,

G/S	Distribution	Drupe	Uses	Ref
E. ferrugineus (Jack) Steud.	Nilgiris, Palani, Annamalai Travancore Hills	Smooth, **ovoid**, nut with rugged shell	Wood used as timber	WOI
E. ganitrus Roxb. **E. sphaericus (Gaertn.)K. Schum** UTRASUM Bead tree	Nepal, Bihar, Bengal, Assam, M.P. and Bombay, Victoria garden, Amboli, S. Konkan, Hirva	Deeper bluish purple, globose, **obovoid**, 1.27 cm to 2.54 cm in diameter, hard longitudinally grooved, tubercled normally 5-celled	Stones used as beads for rosaries, fewer/higher than 5-cell fetch higher prices; stone used in epileptic fits	WOI FOM
E. lanceaefolius Roxb.	Eastern Himalayas, Hills of Assam up to 2438.28 m	Greenish, **ovoid**, containing longitudinally grooved, 1-seeded stone	Timber for working, fruits edible, stones as beads	KB WOI
E. oblongus Mast. Non Gaertn. E. glandulosus Wall.	Western Ghats up to 1828.71 m Mahabaleshwar, Panchgani	Drupe **oblong**, containing 1- or 2-seeded stone, 2.5-4 cm long, narrow at both ends	Emetic, rheumatism, pneumonia, ulcer, piles, leprosy and dropsy; wood used for match boxes	WOI FOM

G/S	Distribution	Drupe	Uses	Ref
E. robustus Roxb.	North-eastern parts of India 609.75 m, Andaman Islands	Drupe **ovoid**, 2.54 -3.18 cm long enclosing a deeply furrowed rugose stone	Timber for wood to good finish	WOI
E. serratus Linn.	Eastern Himalayas up to 914.36 m, Evergreen forests of North Kanara and Western Coast down to Travancore	Drupe **ovoid/oblong** 2.54 – 3.81 cm/2.5 – 4 cm long, smooth greenish containing a much tubuercled. 1 seeded stone	Timber for lining; leaves in rheumatism; antidote for poison; leaves has vitamin C 257 mg/100gm. Fruits in dysentery/diarrhea	WOI FOM
E. tuberculatus Roxb.	Kanara southwards through Western Ghats in Coorg, Mysore, Travancore, common in Nigeria, Plain, Anomaly Hills	Drupe 4 – 5 cm stone compressed, tubercled on the flattened sides with thick margins.	Wood comparable to teak wood	WOI

G/S	Distribution	Drupe	Uses	Ref
E. *petiolatus* Wall. Synonmy *E. integer* Wall.	Assam, Sylhet, Burma, Malay Peninsula, Great Nicobar islands	Fruit not observed	Preparations of root given in fever; bark is bitter, fruit sour, juice of leaves for application in sunstroke.	WOI FOM
E. *varunua* Buch.-Ham. E. *floribundus* Blume E. *prunifolius* Wall.	Eastern Himalayas and Assam	Yield edible fruit	Infusion of bark and leaves of *floribundus* used as mouth wash for inflamed gums	WOI
E. *aristatus* Roxb.	Eastern Himalayas, Assam, southern part of Deccan peninsula, Andaman, Talkat Ghat, Konkan	Fruit of size and shape of olive, stone **oblong**, pointed at ends, somewhat rugose(nottubercualte), 1 or (rarely) 2-celled.		FOM
E. *grandifolius* Kurz.	Assam (Lahkipur, Pegu Yomah, Tennasserim in Burma	Drupe **oblong**, 3-5 cm in diameter, pyrene one boney, deeply lacunose-wrinkled somewhat compressed.		FOM

Following is a list given by Wealth Of India and Flora Of Maharashtra, which mentions species along with details of drupe (seed) and popular end-uses of the tree. Some of the species are repeated but the information can be used objectively:

The following is another list of the species, which is reproduced from Botanical Survey of India and Kew Bulletin (U.K.):

- *E. aberrans*
- *E. acrantherus*
- *E. acuminatus:* India. Endangered.
- *E. acutifidus*
- *E. aemulus*
- *E. affinis*
- *E. alaternoides*
- *E. alatus*
- *E. alnifolius*
- *E. amboinensis*
- *E. amoenus:* Sri Lanka
- *E. amplifolius*
- *E. angustifolius:* **(syn. *E. grandis*)** Blue fig, blue marble tree, blue quandong. Queensland, Australia.
- *E. apiculatus*
- *E. bifidus*
- *E. biflorus*
- *E. blascoi:* India. Endangered.
- *E. castanaefolius*
- *E. colnettianus*
- *E. coorangooloo:* Queensland (Australia)
- *E. coriaceus:* Sri Lanka
- *E. crassus:* New Guinea

- *E. debruynii:* New Guinea
- *E. eumundii*
- *E. floribundus*
- *E. ganitrus* (rudraksha tree)
- *E. gaussenii:* Southern India. Endangered.
- *E. graeffii*
- *E. grandiflorus*
- *E. grandis*
- *E. hartleyi:* New Guinea
- *E. hedyosmus:* Sri Lanka
- *E. hookerianus:* Pokaka. New Zealand.
- *E. japonicus*
- *E. johnsonii*
- *E. kaalensis*
- *E. kirtonii*
- *E. mastersii*
- *E. miegei:* New Guinea, Bismarck Archipelago, Solomon Islands, Aru Islands and Melville Island.
- *E. montanus:* Sri Lanka
- *E. moratii*
- *E. munronii:* India. Endangered.
- *E. neobritannicus:* New Guinea, Bismarck Archipelago
- *E. oblongus*
- *E. obovatus*
- *E. obtusus*
- *E. petiolatus*
- *E. photiniaefolius:* Ogasawara Islands.
- *E. pruifolius:* India. Endangered.
- *E. recurvatus:* India. Endangered.
- *E. reticulatus:* **(syn. *E. cyaneus*)** blueberry ash. Australia.

- **E. serratus:** Southern India, Sri Lanka.
- **E. sphaericus**
- **E. stipularis**
- **E. subvillosus:** Sri Lanka.
- **E. taprobanicus:** Sri Lanka.
- **E. timikensis:** New Guinea.
- **E. tuberculatus:** Southern India, Sri Lanka
- **E. variabilis:** Southern India.
- **E. valetonii**
- **E. venosus**
- **E. venustus:** India. Endangered.
- **E. verruculosus**
- **E. verticellatus**
- **E. viscosus**
- **E. whartonensis**
- **E. xanthodactylus**
- **E. zambalensis**

Rudraksha is known to be used for religious purposes for approximately two millennia. The genus ***Elaeocarpus ganitrus*** Roxb. is considered as *rudraksha*. It is difficult to ascertain the natural distribution of *rudraksha* because of the commercial aspect. It is probably assumed that Hindu missionaries and traders were responsible for introducing these trees in tropical forests of Queensland, New Guinea, Malaysia and Southern Nepal. It is also interesting to note that some small-sized Indonesian beads, which are imported into India and which fetch good prices (as the size gets smaller, the price increases) are subjected to special agro techniques developed by farmers in Java and Bali.

Our knowledge of genus ***Elaeocarpus*** is incomplete since even today revision of this remarkable taxon is undertaken.

Zmarzty (2001) has recognised nine species from Southern India and Sri Lanka, including three new species namely *E. hedyomus* Zmarzty, *E. variabilis* Zmarzty and *E. taprobanicus* Zmarzty and one new variety *E. serratus* Linn. var. *weibelii* Zmarzty. Similarly Coode (2001) has described two new species of genus *Elaeocarpus* i.e. *E. crassus* Coode, *E. timikensis* Coode from New Guinea. The confusion around the taxonomic treatment of the genus is still being solved. For example, the typification of *E. decipiens* and its new variety from Taiwan (China) has been brought out by Hui and Ya (2006). **(Ref. 38)**

There are some popular varieties of *Elaeocarpus,* which grow outside India and Nepal, in Australia, New Zealand, and Malaysia. They are also found in the Andaman & Nicobar islands. These trees are often planted in gardens.

While details of *rudraksha* beads of *Ganitrus* Roxb variety are discussed in Chapter 4, a few major points are being mentioned herein. Some of the broad parameters given in our ancient epics, particularly *Shiva Puran, Shrimad Devibhagwat* and *Padma Puran,* are useful and relevant even today.

As per **Shiva Puran (Ref. 1),** *rudraksha* of the size of *embolic myrobalan* (*Dhatriphal or Amla*) is the best and the one having size of fruit of jujube tree (*Badriphala*) is of medium quality. The meanest (inferior) variety of the bead is the one having the size of a gram. *Rudraksha* of even size, glossy, firm, thick and with many thorn-like protrusions yield the desired results. Six types of *rudraksha* are to be discarded: those defiled by worms, are cut and broken, have no thorn-like protrusions, have cracks and are not round. The one having a natural hole is the best and the one in which it is to be bored through human effort is of medium quality. (In this epic there is one statement that smaller the *rudraksha*, the more powerful it is and a reduction in weight of one tenth is considered as the most fruitful. This statement is not clear and consistent with the previous one and is best taken as a later addition by some interested party. The statement is given below:

"The size of *amla* (myrobalan) is the best and size like that of jujube (*Ber*) is of medium quality. Size equal to gram (*chana*) is worst. *Rudraksha* of jujube (*Ber*) size is a giver of happiness and good luck. The one of *amala* size removes all bad omens. The one having the size of *gunja phal* is good for everything. Smaller the size of the *rudraksha*, better it is in effectiveness. The one having one tenth's of size smaller than the previous one will be more effective."

Shrimad Devibhagwat (**Ref. 2**) states: "A *rudraksha* with the size of *embolic myrobalan* is highly meritorious and is the best of all. A *rudraksha* bead of the size of *ber* (Jujube fruit) is of medium quality and the one the size of a gram is of mean quality. Lustrous and thorny *rudraksha* of equal size are the best ones. Thornless, worm eaten, uneven, non-spherical beads are forbidden. *Rudraksha* having natural hole is the best and the one which requires human effort for making a hole is of medium quality. *Rudraksha* should be of spherical shape and if rubbed against any rough surface it should leave a gold-coloured streak."

Rudrakshajabalopanishad (**Ref. 3**) mentions that *rudraksha* the size of *Amla* (*embolic myrobalan*) is the best. The one having the size of jujube (*Ber*) is of medium quality and the smallest the size of a gram (*chana*) is the worst.

Therefore, one may conclude that the bigger-sized beads

are better than smaller ones. It is clear from these three ancient epics that only round variety of *rudraksha* having large size like that of *amla* (15 mm to 30 mm in diameter) are better and they should have a natural hole. Its surface should be thorny, hard and glossy.

The only variety that fits into this definition is **Elaeocarpus ganitrus** Roxb, presently grown only in Nepal with scattered trees found in north-east India. The medium types (which are not fakes) like the Haridwar/Dehradun varieties, require drilling to make holes in its centre.

The smaller-sized Indonesian and Malaysian varieties, used in making of *mala*s, have beads with diameter of 4 mm to 12 mm. Opinions differ with regard to the effects of these small-sized beads. As these are usually worn in larger numbers, the acupressure and touch effect is higher and this aspect more than compensates for the smaller size. It is also not clear whether the smaller-sized beads mentioned in *Shiva Puran* or other ancient scriptures refer to beads from the same area or whether it is a comparison between the Nepali and Indonesian varieties. The possibility that the ancient wisdom has compared Indonesian variety with Nepali or Himalayan variety is remote, hence it is suggested to treat Indonesian beads independently.

Larger-sized beads get preference because of the psychological impression they have good appearance and clarity of lines. When we discuss about efficacy of *rudraksha* beads, it is necessary to understand (a) the type and source of *rudraksha* that is being worn, (b) their numbers, (c) duration of wearing per day, and (d) precautions that are being taken to maintain the beads.

Details on these aspects are given in later chapters.

Mukh or facet of *rudraksha*

A *mukh* is a complete dividing line running from top of the seed unto its bottom. Generally in two, three four, five and six *mukhi rudraksha,* these dividing lines are more or less equally spaced (there could be several exceptions). In the higher *mukhis*, the *mukh* may be spaced unequally although the better-looking ones are those having nearly equal distribution of surface. Mostly, the lines or *mukh* is on the raised mountain portion of *rudraksha* body and not on the ridges. This is an important point to remember while identifying genuine rudraksha from the fake ones.

This feature makes it slightly difficult for people manipulating the beads by creating extra lines. It is a matter of wit between nature and man's greed. There are unscrupulous people, who very cleverly study the free space availability and shape before creating the extra line and this makes it difficult for an ordinary customer to identify the bead. These people insert a full section of *rudraksha* having multiple *mukhis* into another *rudraksha* with counter space to create a higher *mukhi* bead. This is done usually for 12 and higher *mukhi* beads. An expert can discover the manipulation by just seeing such *rudraksha*.

About 70% of all *rudraksha* beads from nature are five *mukhis*, 20% of four *mukhis* and six *mukhi*s and the balance 10% makes for lower *mukhis* (1, 2, 3) or higher *mukhis* (7, 8, 9 and upwards). *Rudraksha* of 16 *mukhis* and upward are really rare and only few pieces are found from nature in an entire year. Only one or two pieces of 20 or 21 *mukhis* and one or two *Trijutis* occur in nature each year. *Gaurishanker* (two beads joined naturally on the trees and having one common shell outside) is also a rare variety. Hence, buyers of such extremely rare varieties should be extra careful while procuring them.

Rudraksha up to 29 *mukhis* have been reported from Nepal. There are higher *mukhi* beads in the Indonesian variety. Such beads are an extremely rare feature of nature.

In ancient epics like *Shiva Puran, Padma Puran, Shrimad Devibhagwat* or *Skand Puran rudraksha* up to 14 *mukhis* are mentioned. There is no reference to those beyond 14 *mukhis*, possibly due to extreme rarity of such beads. Though not covered in these epics, some rare *rudrakshas* like *Gaurishankar* are very popular since olden times as they are used by saints and priests for meditation and religious rituals. Higher *mukhi* beads have been popular among princely families, rich business families and saints. I have seen old collections of some royal families, which comprise the entire range of one *mukhi* to 21 *mukhis*, *Gaurishankar* and *Trijuti* dating back to 12th and 14th centuries, all in good condition and preserved using oils and camphor. Reference of beads higher than 14 *mukhis* is found in *Katyani Yantra* and some other old scriptures written some eight or nine centuries ago.

Colour of *rudraksha*

Rudraksha seeds are in colours of white, red, yellow and black as per *Pauranik* versions (belonging to **Elaeocarpus ganitrus** Roxb). This classification depends entirely on nature (maturity/type and location of the tree). Practical difficulties are experienced while classifying *rudraksha* according to colour as there are no standards of colour and often the shades are overlapped. Further, in none of the scientific studies, the results have been categorized according to colour. It appears that *rudraksha* of any colour may give similar results and after wearing for say four or five months, all varieties age and turn black or deep brown due to reaction with body oils and sweat. Hence any categorization depending on the colour is best ignored. Those who believe strongly in this type of classification, as it is mentioned in the epics, may continue to do so as it is not interfering with someone else's ideology. Wearing of "white" *rudraksha* by Brahmins, "red" by Kshatriyas, "yellow" by Vaishyas and "black" by Shudras has been recommended but there is no wide support for this due to various reasons. On practical grounds this classification has very few takers.

The internal structure

Rudraksha seeds differ in structure according to their sources. Nepali and Indonesian beads (*E. **ganitrus*** Roxb) have one compartment for each *mukh* in the vertical segment. Each compartment may have a seed inside, brown or blackish in colour from outside and off-white/white from inside. The number of compartments (clefts) in a *rudraksha* should be equal to the number of its *mukhs*. A seven *mukhi* will have seven compartments and 12 *mukhi* 12. And same is the case with a one *mukhi* or two *mukhi* beads. This is a crucial test to establish the genuineness and authenticity of a *rudraksha*.

However, this may not be applicable to Dehradun/ Haridwar *rudraksha* as all *rudraksha* from one to four *mukhs* have only one seed inside. **(Fig 10)** It is, therefore quite easy to make a fake one *mukhi* bead from say either two, three or four *mukhi rudrakhsa* of this variety because it will show only one hole/seed. However, it should not be presumed that all one *mukhi rudrakshas* of Dehradun/Haridwar variety are fake, although it will be of 'medium' quality. One should be able to recognise the fake beads by close examination and finding out that extra lines have been erased. Therefore, the luster, hardness, density and surface characteristics must be determined first to fix the source and type of species – whether it is from Nepal or Haridwar/Dehradun and then apply the above principle.

Indonesian *rudraksha* has the same characteristics as Nepal variety as far as internal structure is concerned. As we know, the power of *rudraksha* emanates from the internal seed. Therefore, it is very important to understand this conclusion. A one *mukhi rudraksha* from Indonesia has one seed inside, (or one cleft or compartment) **(Fig. 8)** 2 *mukhi* has two seeds, 3 *mukhi* three seeds and so on as in the case of Nepali beads and there is no confusion **(Fig. 9)**. A one *mukhi* from Indonesia is thus a natural *rudraksha*. The kaju- (cashew) shaped one, two and three *mukhi* beads also follow the same pattern like Haridwar/Dehradun types whereby there is only one hollow slit inside these beads, irrespective of the number of *mukhs*. **(Fig. 10)**

Non-destructive test methods have also been studied like X-ray, CT scan, etc., (it is not necessary to cut and destroy the bead to check the internal sections) to count the *mukh*. The difficulty arises as all seeds are not uniformly developed. **(Fig. 11 X-ray images)** and only compartments can be seen.

Some of the commonly followed methods of establishing the genuineness of *rudraksha* are:

1. It should sink in water
2. It should rotate if held between two copper coins and
3. If boiled in milk, the milk will not get spoiled even after a week of storage.

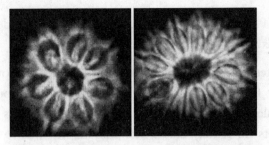

Fig. 11: X-ray of Rudraksha Beads

These methods do not hold good on several counts.

Sinking in water: A ripe *rudraksha,* plucked from tree will have density higher than water. It will, therefore, sink in water. However, if it is externally tampered with and lines altered or two beads glued together, they all will sink. Also, if a bead made of light wood or if a low density berry is cleverly impregnated with a pint of heavy metal or say glass (we have come across such cases), the bead will sink in water. Hence this is not a foolproof test.

The specific gravity of *rudraksha* is higher than 1.00 and as such the bead should sink in water in most cases. Therefore, it is not wrong to assume this test as an important parameter, but it is not enough and other aspects must be clearly understood. Many people try this test on *rudraksha mala* of Indonesian beads. They try to dip the entire *mala* along with the thread used in connecting the beads in water. Normally, because of the thread, the *mala* may not sink initially. But, once the thread gets soaked in water, it becomes heavy and the whole *mala* will sink. It is not wise to dip the *mala* with a thread. Ideally, the beads should be taken out and dipped in water separately. The Indonesian small-sized seeds sink only when these are of high quality and having higher specific gravity. If they float, it must be presumed that the density of the beads is low and they are not necessarily fake.

The test is not effective in another instance. If you have a perfectly formed bead with a larger hole, it will not sink in water unless all the trapped air inside the bead vents out and water gets in. It may take a few minutes for this to happen, but by this time people will conclude that since the bead did not sink, it is fake.

An old and dry bead will also not sink in water. Similarly, a genuine bead plucked unripe or sourced from low-density species, also will not sink.

Therefore, this test, mostly popularized by traders, is not a foolproof method for all *rudrakshas*. At best, it can be used on a genuine *rudraksha* just to confirm that it is from a ripened fruit and it is of proper density.

Copper Coin rotation: Any round object having protrusions like those found on *rudraksha* shall rotate if held between two coins due to the mechanical force applied on a pivoted surface. Even if a seed of berry (*Ber*) is taken, it may rotate if mild pressure is applied because of its protrusions. The electromagnetic power of *rudraksha* has no role to play and it cannot physically rotate the bead.

The pendulum test is a similar method of testing. Many people, who are experts in the art of healing by controlling energy levels, try to apply the same technique on *rudraksha*. Many use their palm or a Pendulum **(Fig. 12)**.

The healers judge the extent of energy fields over hand or pendulum rotation and then feel the vibrations through their minds and concentrate. The healers have their own skills, but such tests are not used commonly to determine the genuineness of a *rudraksha* by experts worldwide.

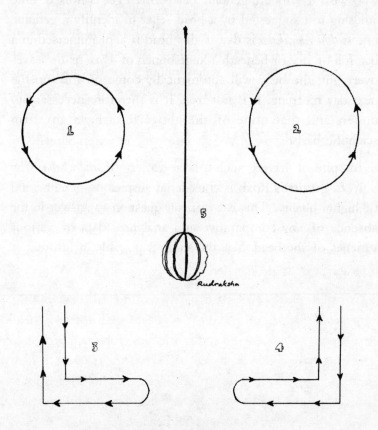

Fig. 12: Pendulum of rudraksha *and bi-directional rotation*

Boiling in milk: There is no scientific basis to prove that milk can be preserved for a longer period of time if it is boiled with a *rudraksha*. True, the bead may increase the electrical charge in milk and it may have some property in curing some of the mind-related diseases and also in improving memory.

There are several other gimmicks and unfounded methods employed by traders and other interested parties that people who wish to procure genuine beads often get confused. One amusing test suggested by a bead seller to identify a genuine one *mukhi rudraksha* is that if this bead is kept immersed in a bag full of rice or beneath a huge bunch of *Pipal* or *Bel* leaves overnight, the bead will automatically come on the top the next day morning. It is not true. It is therefore necessary to understand that none of the above tests have any firm scientific basis.

In spite of having such a large variety of *rudraksha*, why only **E. ganitrus** Roxb is considered auspicious, genuine and of higher quality? This is a difficult question to answer in the absence of any comparative and analytical data of various varieties of the bead. Yes, the study is possible in future.

MULTIFACETED *RUDRAKSHA* 2

A *mukh* or facet (referred to as 'channel') on *rudraksha* bead is a line traveling from one end of the *rudraksha* to the other end as depicted in **(Fig. 13)**.

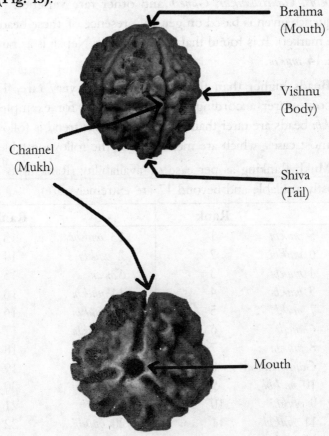

Brahma
(Mouth)

Vishnu
(Body)

Channel
(Mukh)

Shiva
(Tail)

Mouth

Fig. 13: Rudraksha; mouth, body and tail

The rudraksha bead has a top portion from where the lines (*mukh*) originate and this is called *Brahma*. The middle portion having the largest diameter is known as *Vishnu* and the bottom portion where the lines end is known as *Shiva*.

Over 70% of all available *rudraksha* (from Nepal) are 5 *mukhis*, another 18% are 4 and 6 *mukhis* and the balance 10% comprise 2 *mukhis*, 3 *mukhis*, 7 *mukhis*, 8 *mukhis*, 9 *mukhis*, 10 *mukhis*, 11 *mukhis*, 12 *mukhis*, 13 *mukhis*, 14 *mukhis* and 15 *mukhis*. The remaining 2% are beads with more than 15 *mukhis*, *Gaurishankar*, *Ganesh* and other rare varieties. (The sequence given is based on general presence of these beads in the market). It is found that the two *mukhi* Nepali is as rare as the 14 *mukhi*.

Beads higher than fourteen *mukhis* are very rare. They become rarer according to their *mukh* — for example 21 *mukhi* beads are rarer than 20 *mukhi* and this trend is followed in most cases, which are mentioned in the following table:

Mukh Ranking as per ease of availability (Rank upto 7 is mostly available and beyond 17 are extremely rare).

	Rank		Rank
5 *mukhi*	1	13 *mukhi*	13
6 *mukhi*	2	2 *mukhi*	14
4 *mukhi*	3	*Sawar*	15
3 *mukhi*	4	14 *mukhi*	16
7 *mukhi*	5	15 *mukhi*	16
Ganesh	6	16 *mukhi*	17
8 *mukhi*	7	17 *mukhi*	18
Gaurishankar	8	18 *mukhi*	19
10 *mukhi*	9	19 *mukhi*	20
9 *mukhi*	10	*Trijuti*	21
11 *mukhi*	11	20 *mukhi*	22
12 *mukhi*	12	21 *mukhi*	23

The above ranking is based on market response and information from the trade and applies only for the Nepal variety of beads. Indonesian beads are comparatively easily available, especially the five *mukhi* beads used in *mala* form. The higher *mukhi* beads are also available easily due to lesser demand today.

Those with 22 *mukhis* and above are historic occurrences. The two beads that are joined naturally on the trees get produced similar in numbers as 10 or 11 *mukhis* and these are known as *Gaurishankar*. Three beads joining naturally on the trees is a rare phenomenon and its occurrence is similar to that of 19 *mukhis* and above (three to four pieces per year in each season). This three-bead variety is known as a *Gauri-Path*, *Trijuti*, *Tribhagi* or *Brahma-Vishnu-Mahesh*. *Gaurishankar rudraksha* having one, two or more *mukhs* on one bead and on the other one *mukhi*, is known as *Sawar* (*Sawar* in Hindi means 'rider' and here one *mukhi* is termed as a rider, riding on the other bead, which can be a *rudraksha* of any *mukhi* — generally four, five, six or seven *mukhis*). Many people cut this bead out of the twin *Gaurishankar* and use it as one *mukhi* separately with great reverence. The one *mukhi Sawar* bead also has one natural hole and therefore if some people accept this as one *mukhi* from Nepal, it is the individual's choice. The fact remains that it is not an independent bead and is part of a twin bead.

It is mentioned in Chapter 4 that the cut-and-identify test (x-ray test) is applicable to only **ganitrus** Roxb variety (also known as Nepal beads) and not to Haridwar or South Indian varieties. However, all Indonesian *rudraksha,* including the tiniest ones, follow the same principle like Nepali beads. In the non-destructible tests like those done through X-rays and

CT-scanning, the clefts inside a *rudraksha* can be seen clearly. In beads with higher *mukhs*, it becomes a bit difficult due to the overlapping of the seeds. It is also noted that some seeds do not get developed well. In most cases, the number of only 50 to 70% seeds are formed and seen.

The *Bhadraksha* variety mostly comprises two *mukhs* and in very small numbers three *mukhs*. These flat beads do not find extensive and popular use as compared to *rudrakshas*.

The description for *rudrakshas* of various *mukhs* given below are based on facts mentioned in ancient epics like *Shiva Puran*, *Shrimad Devibhagwat*, *Padma Puran*, and *Skand Puran* as also from several of the recent books acknowledged in the bibliography. Some of the properties of the beads are given based on experiences of several persons contacted by an experts' team in the last few years during the interaction with several thousand persons. It is, therefore, important for those undertaking future studies to consider these views and then pool and analyse the available information.

Shiva Puran states that *rudraksha* neutralises the sins committed by a person. As such, this power can be bestowed only on such an object, which is the purest of the pure. While reading about *rudraksha*, we sometimes get confused whether by wearing *rudraksha* one gets absolved of all the sins committed. It is necessary to understand that these scriptures have seen long cycles of history and there have been some changes carried out, which could be variants of the original beliefs. Therefore, the best course left for us is to look at and accept good things from the past.

ONE *MUKHI RUDRAKSHA*

The one *mukhi rudraksha* is the most auspicious of all

rudrakshas but it is the most misunderstood among all *rudrakshas*. If someone compiles the anecdotes on this variety, a full book can be written on it. I am narrating some of my observations on this. Readers must realise that the properties mentioned are of the genuine one *mukhi rudraksha* from Nepal or Indonesia.

Shape and Size

The one *mukhi rudraksha* from Nepal, if at all found, shall be similar in shape but smaller compared to the two *mukhi* variety, also from Nepal. (It will be oval in shape and slightly flat and having the shape of an eye (or fish) when viewed from the sides). It may be 10 mm to 15 mm in length. It shall not be round in shape as per the natural configuration discussed and summarised in chapter 4. On the contrary, it may be slightly elliptical, but should not be confused with the *Chandrakar* variety. The beads of the Nepal variety shall have a natural hole in the centre. On the shape, a variation is not ruled out. Round bead having one face only may he due to undeveloped and such *rudraksha* is available from some trees. Although x-ray study reveals more than one compartment, still some people accept these as "genuine" one mukhi.

The Indonesian one *mukhi rudraksha* is very small, 5 mm to 12 mm in length and 3 mm to 6 mm in diameter **(Fig. 6)**. It has the shape of a thick rice grain. One *mukh* is complete on one side and on the other side there is a partial closure line just near the mouth. Only one seed occurs inside the Indonesian one *mukhi rudraksha*, which is almost similar in looks to the Indonesia variety of two *mukhi rudraksha,* the only difference being that in one *mukhi* only one line is complete, while in two *mukhi*, one can clearly see two complete lines. One *mukhi* is slightly smaller in size, slightly flatter and shorter than the two *mukhi*. This passes the x-ray test.

One mukhi Chandrakar **(Fig. 14)** belongs to E. tuberculatus Roxb variety is just an alternate to *Rudraksha*. It is now widely used with many species finding way in the market. Fakes, wood-plastic molded and cut-paste types are also being sold and therefore one should be careful about this alternate also.

Fig. 14: One mukhi Chandrakar

Properties

The one *mukhi rudraksha* is blessed by Lord Shiva Himself. In Chapter 12, you will know more about this mighty Hindu God who is entirely lovable and worshipped in mythology as the most powerful of the Gods, the creator of language, music, dance and Ayurveda and as the lord of love and responsible for the cycle of birth and death. In fact, Hinduism and its philosophy and thoughts cannot be understood fully without understanding the Shaivite principles.

One *mukhi rudraksha* washes away the sins as serious as 'brahman hatya' (killing of a Brahmin). It enhances knowledge about the Supreme (*Brahma Gyan*) and the wearer is known to win over his senses. He then engages himself in *Para-Tatva*

(*Shiva Tatva*). It is also known to give eternal bliss and *nirvana* (*moksha*) after death. At whichever place this *rudraksha* is worshipped, Goddess Lakshmi (Goddess of Wealth) bestows Her presence. It is the most auspicious *rudraksha* among all beads and not only does it bring the wearer or worshipper closer to Shiva (spirituality and kindness) but also fulfils all his or her desires in the material world. The wearer also gains powers of concentration and enjoys inner peace.

As per *Shiva Puran*, one *mukhi rudraksha* offers worldly pleasures and salvation and therefore has a unique place among all the *rudrakshas*. It gives leadership qualities and skills to cope with stressful situations and hence is a preferred choice for those who assume leadership roles or head any organisation.

The controlling planet of this *rudraksha* is Sun. All negative effects posed by this planet on a person are got over by wearing this *rudraksha*. Its use is said to cure headache, eye defects, piles and diseases of the liver and skin.

As per recounts of various experiences by people, if a person has any addiction (specially vices like smoking, drinking, drug abuse, tobacco chewing, over eating, excessive talking and the like), wearing a one *mukhi* (in these cases Indonesian *rudraksha* can be used) helps him or her in overcoming such habits. A full transformation takes place as the wearer quits these vices or habits with little efforts and the lifestyle gets changed permanently.

Who should wear?

All adult persons can wear this *rudraksha*. It can also be kept in a *puja* room or altar, where regular worshipping can be done. Those who are addicted to habits or particular lifestyles, which are not conducive to their physical and mental well-being, can wear the one *mukhi* Indonesian *rudraksha* to come out of the predicament. If one wears more than one bead, it is believed to be proportionately more effective.

One *mukhi* in *Chandrakar* form is a symbolic *rudraksha* especially for invoking the blessings of Lord Shiva and hence it can be worn by all or kept in a *puja* room. Unfortunately, in advertisement campaigns on TV channels and in sales propaganda about *Chandrakar*, its source and type are not fully revealed and it is equated with the original one *mukhi rudraksha*, which is not fair. The benefits are often exaggerated. *Chandrakar* is not **E. Ganitrus** Roxb, but is an alternative for one *mukhi rudraksha*. As already mentioned earlier it belongs to E. *Tuberculatus* Roxb variety.

Fake one *mukhi rudraksha* is made either from two *mukhi Bhadraksha* or from the round Dehradun variety or from five *mukhi rudraksha* of other regions. It is advised that once you know that a *rudraksha* is fake, it is better not to wear it or even keep it in your home as it may increase negativities in the mind, particularly after you have known about it. Even if such a fake bead has been given as a gift or as a blessing by a guru or a spiritual person (who may give it out of ignorance), it is advisable to discard it in a river, sea or put in a pond/well.

A one *mukhi* bead is worn by persons requiring favour of Sun as a planet or to remove its malevolent effects, or those seeking devotion to God, minimising attachments to the worldly things and ultimately hoping to attain *nirvana*.

Mantras to be recited for one *mukhi rudraksha*

Om Hreem Namah (Shiva Puran)

Om Om Drushaan Namah (Mantra Maharnava)

Om Rudra (Padma Puran)

Mahamrityunjaya Mantra (Brahajjalopanishad)

Om Namah Shivaya

TWO *MUKHI RUDRAKSHA*

The descriptions given here pertain to the Nepal or Indonesian variety of two *mukhi rudraksha* having a natural hole. Beads from Haridwar/Dehradun, where the hole is manually drilled, are of medium quality.

The shape of two *mukhi rudrakshas* from Nepal is flat, slightly tapered and the surface is smoother and hard. Its size may be up to 15 mm long and 10 mm in width and 8 mm thick. *Rudraksha* from Haridwar/Dehradun is oval in shape, has a rough surface and is of lighter density. It will be bigger, say up to 20 mm in length and average diameter of 15 mm. It has an oval shape with slightly flatter look. There will be only one cavity. The Indonesian two *mukhi rudraksha* is small, having a length of 10 mm and diameter of 5 mm to 6 mm, but it has a natural hole in it. Its density is also higher than the Haridwar variety and has a smooth surface. There are two seeds inside this bead compartment similar to the Nepal bead. **Fig. 6** shows all the three types of *rudrakshas*.

The price of Nepal two *mukhi rudraksha* is several folds higher than that of the Haridwar variety – sometimes even up to 100 times.

Properties

The two *mukhi rudraksha* is blessed by the *Ardhnareeshwar* form of Lord Shiva, representing Shiva and Shakti **(Fig. 15)**. According to the epics, a demon named Adi, assuming the form of Parvati, tried to entice Shiva who realizing the ruse, killed him. However, the real Parvati, as she saw Shiva with another woman, became furious. Firstly, she cursed Nandi, Shiva's vehicle, who was supposed to have guarded and kept a watch so that no one enters her sanctum sanctorum. As a result of the curse, Nandi became a heartless cold stone forever. Thereafter, Parvati, still in great rage, tried to commit suicide, but was stopped by Brahma, who took away her dark form of anger and fierceness as incarnated in Goddess Kali. Then Parvati gained her poise and her golden complexion. She is known in this avatar as Gauri. Lord Brahma also blessed her saying "You and your husband shall be staying so close that you will melt into each other, becoming one person, and will be known as *Ardhnareeshwar* (half man, half woman). A mighty lion born of her rage became her new mount on which she would ride as *Durga* to fight against demons throughout the universe.

Fig. 15: Ardhnareeshwar

The epics mention that in our world, female and male qualities exist in the same body and procreate from within themselves. *"Agnishomatmakam jagat"* is a hymn from the Vedas. Fire (*Agni*) is the male principle and is present in the menstrual flow of the female. The Moon (*soma*) is the female principle and is present in the sperm of the male. *Kam* (desire) is the unifying force for the two. Without Shiva's unity with the Divine Energy (*Shakti*), no creation is possible. In the *Adwaita* philosophy, *Maya* (illusion) is not renounced but is fully accepted as a power or energy of the *Brahm*. Hence, the permanent union of Shiva and Shakti is considered as Adwaitism. The right half side of Shiva is feminine. In this form, the potential of feminine and masculine qualities are equal, hence it is described as *"shaktya sahitaha shambhu"* or Shiva with Shakti.

Wearing two *mukhi rudraksha* frees one from the sin of cow slaughter. As per *Padma Puran*, this *rudraksha* is blessed by Fire God (*Agni*) also, and hence absolves the wearer from any type of sin. The wearer or worshipper is also known to get such benefits, which are normally attained through *yajnas* and *homas* or *Agnihotra*.

This *rudraksha* is useful for good family life, good relationships with all people and to get married. In fact, it is known to bring in unity of all kinds — between friends, husband and wife, father and son, or buyer and seller. It is used for material gains as well as to attain *nirvana* and *moksha*. It is also known as *Dev-Dev* in view of its spiritual and material (dual purpose) characteristics.

Who should wear?

Those who are single and facing difficulty in getting the

right match or those having relationship problems should wear this *rudraksha*. Also, people seeking happiness and material gains as well as those spiritually inclined and aspiring for *moksha* should either wear it or worship it. It is also useful in begetting children.

Mantras to be recited for two *mukhi rudraksha*
Om Namah (Shiva Puran)
Om Om Namah (Mantra Maharnava)
Om Khum (Padma Puran)
Om Shreem Namah (Skand Puran)
Mahamrityunjaya Mantra
Om Namah Shivaya

THREE *MUKHI RUDRAKSHA*

In describing the properties of three *mukhi rudraksha*, the Nepal variety is referred to. While the Haridwar/Dehradun variety may be less effective, no qualitative difference is known. Indonesian three *mukhi rudraksha* may be effective either at similar levels or slightly lesser than that of the Nepal beads. **(Fig. 6)** This aspect as well as the number of beads to be worn should be kept in mind while reading about bead properties.

The three *mukhi rudraksha* represents *Agni* (Fire) **(Fig. 16)**. Like *Agni,* which burns and consumes everything, yet remains pure and full of power, three *mukhi rudraksha* purifies a person from all sins committed in the past. Those suffering from inferiority complex or fear or those experiencing self-

Fig. 16: Lord Agni

hatred or mental strain should use this *rudraksha*. It is also effective in removing laziness and making a person energetic.

As per *Shrimad Devibhagawat*, this *rudraksha* condones the sin of performing an abortion. Being *Agnisambhoot* (produced from fire), it is useful in making the soul pure and enables one to live a life without guilt.

Padma Puran assigns this *rudraksha* to *Brahm* (the Supreme Lord) and it helps in solving all problems in life and brings in success.

Three *mukhi rudraksha* is used in disorders like blood pressure, diabetes, ailments of the stomach, fever, defects of eyes and even cancer. If a child suffers from repeated occurrence of fever or is very weak, three beads of three *mukhi rudraksha* should be worn around the neck to get relief. For children below six years, even wearing one bead may help. Three *mukhi rudraksha* is commonly used for all types of diseases and several experiences of its benefits have been recorded. It is also believed that it counters the ill effects of Mars, like land disputes, blood poisoning and accidents.

According to the old epics, the whole of universe is controlled by the power of three, particularly by the three-stage philosophy of *Shaivagam*. Three *mukhi rudraksha* is the symbolic seed for this aspect.

Who should wear?

People suffering from any diseases, weakness, laziness or inferiority complex should wear three *mukhi rudraksha*. It has been found to be particularly effective against skin diseases, stomach disorders, or defects of eyes and in controlling stress and in gaining self-confidence. While children below six years can wear one bead, those above this age may wear three beads. Adults can wear nine beads of the Nepal or Indonesian variety. A *mala* with 54+1 beads of the Indonesian variety being smaller in size is also very popular for such usages.

Mantras to be recited for three *mukhi rudraksha*

Om Kleem Namah (Shiva Puran)
Om Om Namah (Padma Puran)
Om Dhum Dhum Namah (Skand Puran)
Mahamrityunjaya Mantra
Om Namah Shivaya

FOUR *MUKHI RUDRAKSHA*

Four *mukhi rudraksha* of Nepal **(Fig. 6)** is easy to obtain and is one of the most commonly used *rudrakshas*. Indonesian four *mukhi* beads are smaller in size and are used in *mala* form. From four *mukhi rudraksha* down wards, the size and shape of the bead start changing towards oval instead of being round, both in the case of the Nepalese as well as the Indonesian varieties.

The four *mukhi rudraksha* is blessed by Lord Brahma, one of the Gods of the Hindu Trinity and is responsible for creation. **(Fig. 17)** He is the abode of knowledge and creativity. Brahma is also known as

Fig. 17: Lord Brahma

Prajapati, Hiranyagarbha, Brahmanspati or Vishwakarma. He took birth from the lotus flower evolved from the naval of Lord Vishnu.

As per *Mahabharata*, Brahma is the creator of the Universe. It is said that one who wears four *mukhi rudraksha* attains the level of *dwij* (twice born), transforms himself to a totally new personality and assumes a new and better role in life. The *dwij* concept is the essence of Hindu caste system, which has been totally misunderstood by most people. People bent upon dividing the masses on

Fig. 17(a): Saraswati – the Goddess of knowledge

caste lines never allow truth to prevail and even after knowing these great principles, no one presents it in a correct perspective. Caste system (varnashram dharma) is based on principles of work type and personality and not entirely on lineage. This division of human race as brahmin, kshatriya, vasihya or shudra is natural and created by God for Social stability however, it is based on natural virtues and not by birth.

A person wearing a four *mukhi rudraksha* is known to get shining intelligent eyes and a balanced mind and he or she can use the power of speech to his/her advantage. This *rudraksha* also absolves the person from various sins including sins like killing of humans or animals. I must mention here that the epics talk about the aspect of "absolving from the sin of killing" for *rudrakshas* of all *mukhs*. I believe that although laws were in existence at all times to punish the guilty and they had taken their own course, the *rudraksha's* property is to purify the mind, to create a consciousness and to make the person repent truly for the mistakes. Like the "confession" among Christians, *rudraksha* is used as a tool to make the soul pure after repentance. A person committing a murder gets punishment and is sentenced to death or life imprisonment. This punishment does not necessarily purify his or her soul. This is possible only after he or she truly repents having committed the wrongful act. Using *rudraksha,* one can absolve oneself of the sins and make sure to get justice from the almighty.

The four *mukhi rudraksha* gives fame in all the four *dishas* (directions) and is suitable for all the four stages of human life (celibacy, family life, detachment from family or worldly life and finally renunciation of the world itself — *Brahmacharya, Grahasth, Vaanprasth* and *Sanyas*).

Children can wear this *rudraksha* to improve their concentration in studies and for better memory. Excellent testimonials have been received for this *rudraksha* from students, teachers and those engaged in mental and skilled work. It can be worn to gain success in areas of *dharma* (duties), *arth* (wealth), *kaam* (leisure/pleasure) and *moksha* or *nirvan* (eternal freedom from the cycle of birth and death). Four *mukhi rudraksha* has proved to be very effective in curing diseases related to the mind (loss of memory, epilepsy etc.) It is effective in controlling or curing diseases of the nose and gall bladder and paralysis.

Who should wear?

Students, teachers and all those engaged in mental work

should wear this *rudraksha*. In fact, today there is hardly any work that is based on static knowledge. Constant and continuous upgrading of the mental setup is required to sustain and survive the challenges of contemporary lifestyles and needs.

While it can be used as a single *rudraksha* in case of children below six years, it is used along with six *mukhi rudraksha* for better learning and good performance. A total of three beads are usually be worn.

A crown made of four *mukhi rudrakshas* along with five *mukhi* and/or six *mukhi rudrakshas* and consisting of up to 550 beads is used in Crown Therapy. The crown is put over the head of the person for treatment of any mental disorders or to control stress.

Malas of small beads of four *mukhi rudrakshas* from Indonesia (basically for comfort while wearing in view of the small size) is highly effective in making a person calmer and healthier. This variety can also be used in any number with any combination of *rudraksha.*

The four *mukhi rudraksha* (Nepal) is also used by boiling it in milk for 10 to 15 minutes and then drinking the milk in order to cure memory loss or any mental disorder.

Three beads of four *mukhis* can be soaked in a glass of water for about 12 hrs. and this water can be safely given daily for improving memory. Dry the beads and repeat the soaking each day.

Mantras to be recited for four *mukhi rudraksha*
Om Hreem Namah (Shiva Puran*)*
Om Hreem (Padma Puran*)*
Om Hreem Hoom Namah (Skand Puran)

Mahamrityunjaya Mantra
Om Namah Shivaya

FIVE *MUKHI RUDRAKSHA*

Five *mukhi rudraksha* is the most common *rudraksha* and constitutes about 60% to 70% of total production. Indonesian five *mukhi* beads are smaller in size (from 4 mm to 15 mm in diameter). The Nepalese beads are bigger than the Indonesian variety (from 15 mm upwards up to 30 mm in diameter). Beads found in Pali area of Nepal are considered to be the biggest in size. **(Fig. 6)**.

Five *mukhi rudraksha* is blessed by Lord Shiva Himself **(Fig. 18)** in the form of Kalagni *Rudra*. Wearing this *rudraksha* removes sins of various types committed through forbidden acts. In *Padma Puran,* it is said that wearing five *mukhi rudraksha* is most important for all as it is blessed by Vaamdev (Shiva). A wearer is honoured by the Gods themselves for a long period. This *rudraksha* is like *devguru* (Guru of the Devas) as it is controlled by the planet *Vrihaspati*

Fig. 18: *Panch Mahadev*

(Jupiter). In Shrimad Devibhagawat, it is said that *Panchvaktraha swayam rudraha kalagnirnamatah; Agamyagamanam chauva tatha chabhayabhakshanam; muchyate naatra sandeham panchvaktraha dharanaat.* (Five *mukhi rudraksha,* known as

Kalagni Rudra, removes the sins committed under forbidden laws in case of eating or in sex life).

It is believed that by wearing three large five *mukhi* beads, one can avoid accidental death.

Shiva in Mahadev form brings in benefits to the mankind. He has three eyes on each face except on the one facing north. He has thick locks of hair and a crescent moon over the head. The fifth face points upwards towards spiritual progress.

Creation, preservation, destruction, detachment and obligation are the five deeds we see in everyday life and the five *mukhi rudraksha* symbolises these deeds. The *Pachakshari Mantra (Namah Shivaya)* evolved from this five-face form of Lord Shiva and the *Pranava Om* came as a companion. Therefore, the five *mukhi rudraksha* assumes importance in any *sadhana* or meditation.

The five forms of Lord Shiva — *Sadyojaat, Ishaan, Tatpurush, Aghor* and *Vaamdev* — live in five *mukhi rudraksha.* Some describe this *rudraksha* as *Rudra-Kalagni* also.

Normally, when *rudrakshas* are used in combinations, they will essentially have at least one five *mukhi rudraksha.* Most of the *malas* we see are of five *mukhi rudrakshas.* In fact, the word *rudraksha* signifies five *mukhi rudraksha* unless specified differently. Some botanists opine that all other facets or types of *rudraksha* are "freaks of nature" and only five *mukhi* is basic however we do not agree with this view.

Five *mukhi rudraksha* gives fame and mental peace. With respect to its medicinal values, it is widely used to control blood pressure and diabetes. It is also used for diseases of the ears, thighs and kidney. Three beads of raw (untreated by

color or oil) five *mukhi rudraksha* are used by several families
in India for water therapy, wherein these beads are soaked in
water at night, stored preferably on a copper vessel. The
soaking time should not be less than 8 hours. This water
should be taken daily, preferably empty stomach, for
controlling blood pressure, diabetes and stomach disorders,
or even as a general health guard against all diseases. The
beads should be taken out of the water every day, dried in the
air for an hour or so and then used again.

There are divergent views on how long these beads will be
effective when used in water therapy — one month, a year or
more. Experience, has found it to be effective for upto one
year. Thereafter, the beads should be replaced. In fact, all
medical — non-clinical or clinical — trials have been
conducted using five *mukhi rudraksha,* as these are available
easily.

Who should wear?

Any person can wear this *rudraksha* in specified numbers
(usually not less than three). Those who wish to have first
hand experience about the efficacy of *rudraksha* should wear a
mala of *rudraksha* (7 mm to 10 mm in diameter, which are
usually available at low costs) or three numbers of large five
mukhi rudrakshas. Beads lower than 7 mm are mostly
ornamental in nature.

Usually, five *mukhi rudraksha* available in standard shops
will be genuine as it is available in plenty. *Malas* should be
27+1, 54+1 or 108+1 in numbers. The last 1 in all the *malas*
is a *meru* bead, generally used in *Jap Malas* to show the end of
the counting. This is used in wearable *malas* too. Some users
recommend 81+1 combination as it is also a multiple of 27

basic beads. However, this is to be used only when there is no option while adjusting the length of the *mala* or because the beads are not available. Bear it in mind that a combination of three and more in any odd number can be worn.

The five *mukhi Kanthas* having bigger five *mukhi* beads in 27+1, 32 or 36 in numbers are very common. It is an excellent item to wear for overall health, to ward off fear and for meditation purposes. In case you have excess of five *mukhi* beads through collection or got by way of gifts, it is best to select the best of the beads and dispose off the damaged ones in water (well, lake, river etc.). Make a *Kantha* of 27+1 or 32 beads either in wool or in silver or any metal, and start wearing. It can also be given gifts or donated to a temple with specific request to offer them in a garland to adorn the deity of Lord Shiva. It can also be put on a photograph of a God or Goddess. It is advisable to make use of the beads in any manner possible than just keeping them in a locker and allowing them to dry and get destroyed. Usually this happens only with the *five mukhi rudraksha* and hence the suggestion

Mantras to be recited for five *mukhi rudraksha*

Om Hreem Namah (Shiva Puran)
*Om Hoom Namah (Mantra Maharnava/*Padma Puran*)*
Om Hreem Hoom Namah (Skand Puran)
Mahamrityunjaya Mantra
Om Namah Shivaya

SIX *MUKHI RUDRAKSHA*

Six *mukhi rudraksha* is found easily and is a low-priced variety. Beads from Nepal are similar in size to five *mukhi rudraksha*, while the Indonesian variety is slightly smaller (usually 8 mm to 10 mm in diameter.) **(Fig. 6)**

Shrimad Devibhagwat assigns the six *mukhi rudraksha* to Kartikeya and *Nirnaya Sindhu*, calls it *Guhasangyak* (meaning hidden knowledge) and *Jabalopanishad* assigns it jointly to Kartikeya and Ganesh (both sons of Lord Shiva). It is known for refining wisdom, improving power of expression and increasing willpower. Using this *rudraksha* also pleases the Goddess of wealth, Mahalakshmi. It is also good to improve oratory skills and the wearer can influence any assembly or group of people. He remains brave like Skand. It is also known to purify a person from serious sins committed. Goddess Parvati also blesses the one wearing six *mukhi rudraksha*.

In *Rudra Samhita* (*Kumar Khand*), it is mentioned that Kartikeya **(Fig. 19)** was born to Ganga and was raised from infancy by six women. He had six heads for each of these mothers. Lord Shiva brought him for killing the demon, Tarakasur and He and Parvati gave him several lessons in martial arts, weapons,

Fig. 19: Lord Kartikeya

power of mind and knowledge. Parvati also gave her enormous wealth and luxury and made him to live eternally, while Goddess Lakshmi gave her wealth and a beautiful necklace and Goddess Saraswati all sorts of knowledge. Kartikeya killed Tarakasur using the power of *Kantimat Shakti* in one stroke.

Wearer of six *mukhi Kartikeya rudraksha* gets blessed with wealth, health and happiness. The controlling planet is Venus, which signifies luxury, pleasure and comfort in life.

It is worn along with four *mukhi rudraksha* in order to excel in education.

As for its medicinal values, it is good for the eyes and can control sexual diseases, diseases of the mouth, urinary problems, neck-related diseases and dropsy. Childless couples use it along with *Gaurishankar* (or Nepalese two *mukhi rudrakshas*) to get children. Wearing six *mukhi rudraksha* of either Indonesian or Nepal variety in numbers exceeding three is said to cure all kinds of mental diseases, cancer and failure of any organ. It can also be worn on the right hand (either wrist or arm) singly or in combination with beads of other *mukhs*. It can be of help to people with speech defects like stammering.

I believe any future research work should focus on this bead along with three, four and five *mukhi rudrakshas* as these are easily available and affordable by most people.

Who should wear?

Students, teachers, artists, writers and scientists engaged in learning and mental work should wear this *rudraksha*. Leaders and actors who have to perform and give speeches, etc. can derive benefit by wearing this bead.

Six *mukhi rudraksha* is also an alternative to 13 *mukhi rudraksha*.

In South India, this *rudraksha* is used by people from young age. It is also extensively used by Lingayatas and priests.

In order to gain full advantage of its medicinal values, it should be used under the guidance of a knowledgeable person.

Mantras to be recited for six *mukhi rudraksha*

Om Hreem Hoom Namah (Shiva Puran)
Om Hoom Namah (Mantra Maharnava)
Om Hroom (Padma Puran)
Om Hreem Namah (Skand Puran)
Mahamrityunjaya Mantra
Om Namah shivaya

SEVEN *MUKHI RUDRAKSHA*

Seven *mukhi rudraksha* is nearly round in shape. The Indonesian variety is smaller in size (8 mm to 10 mm in diameter). Though it is rarer than six *mukhi rudraksha,* it is available easily **(Fig. 6)**.

This *rudraksha* is assigned to the seven *Martrikas* (seven mothers), Sun, *Saptarshis* (seven great sages), *Mahasen (Kartikeya), Anang (Kamdev), Ananta (Vaasuki,* the king of snakes) and *Nagrata (Nagraja).* Most popularly, it is assigned to *Ananta*, meaning the supreme Lord (Brahm), who is dimensionless.

As per *Brahma Puran,* which is dedicated to explain the origin of the universe, Lord Vishnu created a lotus out of His navel as desired by Lord Shiva. It was huge, multi-stem structured and beautiful, having yellow color of the *Kaner* flower. From His right side, Lord Shiva produced Brahma (called Hiranyagarbh) and put him inside the lotus stem. Hiranyagarbh took birth from the lotus. The four-headed Hiranyagarbh wanted to know about himself and hence started moving inside the lotus stem but could not trace the origin even after hundreds of divine years. Lord Shiva Himself advised him to meditate and after 12 divine years of penance, Lord Vishnu appeared before him. As the two debated the origin, Lord Shiva appeared Himself in the form of *Jyotirlinga* (phallus with an aura) and said, "Both of you are having great powers and extensive knowledge, but you are not able to find the end or beginning of this universe. Therefore, call it *Ananta*" (dimensionless).

This connotation of *Ananta* given to seven *mukhi rudraksha* indicates that it is a very useful bead offering several powers to the wearer.

As per *Padma Puran*, the following divine snakes live in the seven *mukhs* of this *rudraksha*: Anant, Karkat, Pundareek, Takshak, Vashoshiban, Karoash and Shankhchud. It is, therefore, assumed that a person wearing the seven *mukhi rudraksha* is not affected by poisoning of any kind. It also removes sins resulting from committing crimes like theft, adultery and drug abuse.

A person wearing this *rudraksha* can find hidden treasure, get increased attention from the opposite sex and destroy enemies.

As this *rudraksha* is also assigned to *Saptamatrikas*, it is considered to please Goddess Mahalakshmi. The seven mothers are: *Brahmi, Maheshwari, Kaumaari, Vaishnavee,*

Vaaraahee, Indraanee and Chaamunda.

As it is blessed by several powerful Gods and Goddesses, this *rudraksha* brings fame, wealth and progress in life and removes bad luck. The wearer also gets the divine blessings of Goddess Mahalakshmi. **(Fig. 20)**.

As per *Jabalopanishad*, seven *mukhi rudraksha* resembles *Sapta Brahmi* or *Sapta Rishi* (seven great sages created by Lord Brahma out of his thought) and it provides health and wealth. These great seven sages are: Marichi, Atri, Angira, Pulatsya, Pulaha, Ritu and Vashishtha. In every Manvantar (cycle of universe), there are

Fig. 20: Goddess Mahalakshmi

different *Saptarshis*. They are also visible in the skies like seven stars in the constellation, known as *Saptarshi Lok*. It is said that pious people who do *Sandhya Vandanam* (a daily ritual of prayer with special mantras) and recite *Gayatri mantra* go to the *Saptarshi Lok*.

The controlling planet of seven *mukhi rudraksha* is Saturn. In *Matsya Puran*, Saturn in human form is described as "dark complexioned, having a 'dand' (a rod to give punishment),

Rudrakshamala in the other hand and the entire body is covered by veins. He is ready to cure all the diseases of the one who prays for it.

As per experience, seven *mukhi rudraksha* has been found to be very useful in controlling pain caused by arthritis. It is also effective against muscular pain and useful in treating all kinds of sexual diseases (including impotence), heart problems, throat diseases and leukaemia.

Who should wear?

Seven *mukhi rudraksha* can be used by people involved in all types of professions or businesses to gain wealth and prosperity. It is preferable to use eight *mukhi* (Ganesh) *rudraksha* also along with seven *mukhi rudraksha*; however, seven *mukhi* itself is very powerful. Some families keep it in the altar for worshipping or in the cash box.

Those suffering from diseases of the bone or arthritis shall find it very useful to control the disease and to reduce pain. One must wear at least five pieces of large Nepalese *rudraksha* or a full *mala* of 54+1 or 108+1 Indonesian beads.

Mantras to be recited for seven *mukhi rudraksha*

Om Hum Namah (Shiva Puran)

Om Hrah (Padma Puran)

Om Hreem Namah (Skand Puran)

Om Hreem Shreem Kreem Soam

Mahamrityunjaya Mantra

Om Namah Shivaya

EIGHT *MUKHI RUDRAKSHA*

Eight *mukhi rudraksha* is a rare bead and it is available in lesser numbers than seven *mukhi rudraksha*. In the year 2000, the crop of eight *mukhi rudraksha* was very poor and there was great shortage of this bead.

The shape of the Nepalese variety is slightly elliptical **(Fig. 6)**. It is observed that from this bead upwards, the shape tends to become oval. The Indonesian variety is smaller in size (9 mm to 15 mm in diameter). The cost of eight *mukhi rudraksha* is almost 10 to 20 times that of seven *mukhi rudraksha.*

Eight *mukhi rudraksha* is blessed by Lord Ganesh, the remover of obstacles, (*Vighnaharta*) **(Fig. 21)**. As per *Shrimad Devibhagwat, Padma Puran* and *Mantra Maharnava*, this *rudraksha* is assigned to Kartikeya and Ganesh. As per *Rudrakshajabalopanishad*, it is a form of eight mother goddesses, eight Vasus and Ganga and all the three give their blessings to the wearer. It improves intelligence and health. It also gives the wearer an analytical mind,

Fig. 21: Lord Ganesh

great understanding and good writing skills. Sins committed while telling lies get condoned by wearing this. It is also known to bring in fame, excellence in art, leadership qualities and prosperity.

From medical viewpoint, it may cure diseases of the nervous system, prostrate and gall bladder.

Who should wear?

Usually, eight *mukhi rudraksha* is worn along with seven *mukhi rudraksha*. People, who confront obstacles in life and get failures, should wear this *rudraksha*. It can also be used to propitiate *Shani Bhagwan* and people having *Shani Dosha* should wear it along with seven *mukhi rudraksha*.

Mantras to be recited for eight *mukhi rudraksha*

Om Hum Namah (Shiva Puran)
Om Sah Hoom Namah (Padma Puran)
Om kam vam namah (Skand Puran)
Mahamrityunjaya Mantra
Om Hreem Greem Leem
Aam Shreem
Om Namah Shivaya

NINE *MUKHI RUDRAKSHA*

Nine *mukhi rudraksha* is among the rare beads found both in Nepal and Indonesia. The shape is flatter than eight *mukhi rudraksha* and tends towards oval **(Fig. 6)**. Its price is higher than that of eight *mukhi rudraksha*.

Nine *mukhi rudraksha* is blessed by *Durga* **(Fig. 22)**, the Goddess *Shakti*, who took birth on Earth nine times in different forms to protect her followers. These nine goddesses — *Sheilputri, Brahmacharni, Chandraghanta, Kosshmanda, Skandmata, Katyayani, Kalratri, Mahagauri* and *Siddhidatri* — are worshipped during the festival of *Navaratri*. As per *Padma Puran* and *Shrimad Devibhagawat*, Lord Bhairav

Fig. 22 Goddess Durga

blesses this *rudraksha*.

Sins committed by a person get condoned by wearing this *rudraksha*. It also makes a person fearless and stress-free. Wearing it is like getting one's conscience purified through fire. It also makes the wearer powerful and self-confident.

As per *Rudrakshajabalopanishad*, there are nine types of power in this *rudraksha*. It protects the wearer from untimely death, as it is blessed by Bhairav, also known as Kal Bhairav. Yamraj, the God of Death, is known as Kal and therefore both Kal and Kal Bhairav protect the person wearing nine m*ukhi rudraksha*. For this reason, it is said to remove the fear of time from the mind of the person. It is ruled by planet *Ketu* and nullifies all the negative effects of this planet.

Who should wear?

Persons having fear of any kind, including that of death, should wear nine *mukhi rudraksha*. In combination with 10 and 11 *mukhi* varieties, it becomes a powerful tool for protection. It is also known to bring in wealth. Housewives who remain tense due to problems related to family life and are concerned about their husbands and children and working women should wear this *rudraksha* either singly or in combination with other varieties.

Mantras to be recited for nine *mukhi rudraksha*

Om Hreem Namah (Shiva Puran)

Om Hum Namah (Mantra Maharnava)

Om sum (Padma Puran)

Om Hreem Veing Yun

Raim Laim

Mahamrityunjaya Mantra

Om Namah Shivaya

10 *MUKHI RUDRAKSHA*

Ten *mukhi rudraksha* is among the rare varieties, however its price is lesser than nine *mukhi rudraksha*. It is available in round/oval shape. **(Fig. 6)**

It is blessed by Lord Vishnu **(Fig. 23),** according to *Nirnaya Sindhu, Mantramaharnava* and *Shrimad Devibhagwat*. As per *Rudraksha-jabalopanishad*, it is blessed by Yamraj **(Fig. 24)**, the God of Death, and by Dashdigpal, the controller and guardian of ten directions. It eliminates sufferings caused by the influence

Fig. 23: Lord Vishnu

of the nine planets, *Betals* and *Brahmarakshas*, and thus protects the wearer from black magic and evil eye and averts untimely death. Fear of ghosts and fear of apparitions (that

someone is behind you) get eliminated. As this *rudraksha* has blessings of several gods — Vishnu, Mahasen (Kartikeya), Yamraj, Dashdigpal and Dashmahavidya — it is considered very powerful.

Fig. 24: Shri Yamraj

This *rudraksha* is also used to correct *Vaastu dosh* (directional faults), which could adversely impact running a business. It is also very helpful in facing and solving court cases, disputes and acts of enmity.

It is interesting to know that this *rudraksha* brings the *Vaishnavaite* and *Shaivaite* sects of Hindus together in using the powers of the two mighty Gods in ridding human misery caused by unexplainable problems like ghosts, black magic and ill effects of jealousy.

Who should wear?

A *Narayan Kawatch* made of 10 nos. of 10 *mukhi rudraksha* and 1 no. of one *mukhi rudraksha* is a powerful tool to win over any adversary, in a legal dispute. A *Dosh Nivaran* combination of one 10 *mukhi rudraksha* can be used for correction of *Vaastu dosh*, removing negativities and protecting oneself from black magic, etc.

Those suffering from insomnia, instability of mind and those who fail to find a direction in life and profession can also derive help from this powerful *rudraksha*. It can also be kept at the place of worship to get combined blessings of *Hari-Har*.

Mantras to be recited for 10 *mukhi rudraksha*

Om Hreem Namah Namah (Shiva Puran)

Om Hreem Namah (Mantramaharnava)

Om Ksheem (Padma Puran)

Mahamrityunjaya Mantra

Om Namah Shivaya

11 MUKHI RUDRAKSHA

Eleven *mukhi rudraksha* **(Fig. 6)** is blessed by Shri Hanuman **(Fig. 25)**, who is also called *Ekadash Rudra*. As per *Padma Puran*, the wearer of 11 *mukhi rudraksha* is known to be bestowed with the virtues of Shri Hanumanji, like oratorial and negotiation skills, self-confidence, intelligence and physical and mental power. He

Fig. 25: Shri Hanuman chanting name of Lord Ram

or she will also not get the pangs of rebirth in this universe. This *rudraksha* has the power to control the physical senses, make one fearless and it is therefore recommended for meditation purposes and to secure devotion to the God.

Lord Indra **(Fig. 28)** also blesses this *rudraksha* and as such it brings good luck and fortune and confers leadership qualities and the power to gain control over all the 11 senses (Five physical, five sensory and one of heart or *mana*). Eleven *rudras* are said to reside in the 11 mouths of this great *rudraksha*. The epics say it should be worn on the topknot — *Shikha* though it is a difficult proposition. It can also be worn around the neck like other *rudraksha*. The wearer is expected to get the benefit of performing thousands of *aswamedha yagnas* (sacrificing horses) and donating hundred thousand cows (*pasu dana*) to *brahmins*. One acquires happiness, protection, longevity and victory by wearing this *rudraksha*. It protects the wearer from all types of accidents and prevents untimely death. In *Skand Puran*, Lord Shiva says that 11 *mukhi rudraksha* is his own form of 11 *rudras*. The 11 *rudras* are *Kapali, Pingal, Bheem, Viroopaksha, Vilohita, Shasta, Ajpaad, Ahirbudhanya, Shambhu, Chand* and *Bhava*. (There are many other forms of 11 *rudras* quoted elsewhere).

In *Rudra Samhita*, it is mentioned that after the *Devas* were defeated by the *Asuras* (demons), they ran away from Amaravati and reached the hermitage of sage Kashyap for shelter. Taking pity on them, the sage went to Kashi (Banaras) and prayed to Lord Shiva through rigorous penance. Shiva then appeared before him and assured him that He will protect the *Devas*. Kashÿap got 11 *rudras* as his offsprings through Surabhi. These 11 *rudras* then defeated the demons and offered total protection to the *Devas*.

For adverse phase of Saturn for any Zodiac sign *rudraksha* brings great relief.

It is believed that the power of these 11 *rudras* is present in this *rudraksha.*

From medicinal point of view, it is considered good for stomach disorders, acidity and liver and breast diseases. It can also be worn by people to cure heart ailments, diabetes and blood pressure.

For those engaged in yogic or *tantric* practices, this *rudraksha* is very beneficial as it takes care of health and helps in *hathyog, mantrayog, yam niyam, aasan, shatkarma* and several *tantric* activities.

Who should wear?

This *rudraksha* offers protection and a wearer can become fearless in life and gain prosperity. It is also good for meditation and practice of yoga.

Mantras to be recited for 11 *mukhi rudraksha*

Om Hreem Hum Namah (Shiva Puran)
Om Shreem Namah (Mantra Maharnava)
Om Shreem (Padma Puran)
Om Room Moom Yoom Aum
Mahamrityunjaya Mantra
Om Namah Shivaya

12 MUKHI RUDRAKSHA

Twelve *mukhi rudraksha* **(Fig. 6)** is blessed by Sun **(Fig. 26)**. It is also called *Dwadahsh-Aditya*. According to *Padma Puran*, a wearer of this *rudraksha* can free himself from the fear of fire and diseases; he can acquire wealth and happiness. He will never experience poverty. He is freed from the sin of killing

Fig. 26: Surya (Sun God)

(or getting them killed) animals like elephants, horses, cats, rats, rabbits, tigers, bears, foxes and even men (in wars or in self-defence).

Shrimad Devibhagwat mentions that 12 *mukhi rudraksha* dispels fear of armed men, horned animals and lion. The wearer never suffers from physical and mental pain. It makes the person fearless and trouble-free.

Rudrakshajabalopanishad mentions about Lord Vishnu blessing this bead. According to experience of many this *rudraksha* has the power to cure several diseases. It also provides quality of leadership and control over people. It makes the wearer radiant like the Sun and gives inner strength to rule. It helps to remove all types of doubts from the mind and makes a person happy from within.

As per *Atharvaved*, Sun removes weakness of heart and cures skin disorders including leprosy and diseases of the eye. Twelve *mukhi rudraksha* has all these virtues.

The wife of Sun is *Chhayadevi* (shadow Goddess) and sons are *Kaakvahan*, *Shani* and *Yam*. Sun is the controlling lord of sapphire (*Manikya*), the precious gem. All herbs get their properties from Sun and the ill effects of Saturn and Yam can be corrected by the blessing of Sun. The Veda trinity of *Rik, Riju* and *Saam* belonging to Lord Vishnu are embodied in Sun and gives it the heating power. Aditi was the mother of all *Devas*, Diti was the mother of *Daityas* (criminals) and Danu the mother of *Danavas* (demons). While *Devas* started losing the battle with *Daityas*, Aditi prayed to the Sun for the welfare of her sons and then the Sun blessed her saying he will take birth as Aditi's son, named Sahastranshu, and then destroy the *Daityas*. Thus was born Martand, who killed all the *Daityas*. Our great epics are full of stories about the Sun and his powers.

Lord Krishna's son *Saamb* was extremely handsome and charming but he got infected by leprosy as a result of committing a sin. He worshipped Sun and was cured of the disease. In *Markandeyapuran*, it is said that anyone wearing 12 *mukhi rudraksha* will be free of all types of problems.

The wearer of 12 *mukhi rudraksha* should take care to adhere to the following routine for better results:

- wake up before sunrise
- offer water to Sun and look towards Sun through the water (after bath)
- recite any sun *stotras* (with Sun's 21 names or 108 names)
- perform *hawan* and recite *Gayatri Mantra* on Sundays
- give up eating salt, oil and ginger on Sundays
- touch eyelids and surrounding area of eyes with this *rudraksha*

From medicinal viewpoint, 12 *mukhi rudraksha* is considered as suitable for curing diseases of the eyes, mental disorders, bone diseases, indigestion, blood pressure, diabetes and problems of the intestine.

Who should wear?

All persons who can obtain this *rudraksha* should wear it, as it is an effective tool to remain healthy and prosperous. Administrators, businessmen, politicians and senior professionals should wear this *rudraksha* to gain authority and power.

It is also used as a remedy for *Vaastu* defects (directional faults) and for countering any kind of black magic.

Mantras to be recited for 12 *mukhi rudraksha*

Om Kroam Kshoam Roam Namah (Shiva Puran)

Om Hoom Hreem Namah (Mantramaharnava)

Om Hreem (Padma Puran)

Om Hreem Kshoam Ehranih Shreem

Mahamrityunjaya Mantra

Om Namah Shivaya

13 *MUKHI RUDRAKSHA*

Thirteen *mukhi rudraksha* **(Fig. 6)** is blessed by Kaamdev (Cupid) **(Fig. 27)**. It is known to fulfill all the desires including perfection in alchemy, research work and medicine. The wearer gets everything to enjoy life to its full. A person who wants to accomplish and enjoy *sudha-rasayan* (luxuries of life) and those who are dedicated to synthesise something through research get the desired results by wearing this *rudraksha*. It removes the sin of killing close relatives like father, mother, brother, sister and guru (in the context of those who have committed such deeds, but are remorseful

Fig. 27: Kaamdev

and seek pardon). As per *Padma Puran*, the wearer of this bead is endowed with good luck and accomplishes the nectar like elixir, alchemy and the impression of the feet of a deity or a holy person. He or she is also known to attain heaven after this life.

Thirteen *mukhi rudraksha* is also blessed by Lord Indra **(Fig. 28)** and as such the wearer gets the blessings of all the Devatas. It gives spiritual attainments as well as all materialistic successes. After getting rid of all the sins, the wearer can seek death of his choice (*Ichhamrityu*).

Many consider 13 *mukhi rudraksha* as blessed by Goddess Mahalakshmi. She is the daughter of Maharshi Bhrigu and Khyati. She has two brothers, namely Dhata and Vidhata, and she is the wife of Lord Vishnu. It is also said that she is one of the 14 jewels produced after the churning of the ocean by the *Devas* and the *Asuras*.

Fig. 28: Lord Indra

She is always portrayed as sitting on a lotus and holding a lotus flower in hand.

In *Shrimad Devibhagawat*, it is said that wherever a *Shivaling* is worshipped and *Shankh* (conch), *Shaligram* and *Tulsi* are present and serviced, Lakshmi remains in her full glory.

When Lord Vishnu took the form of a sunlamp, she was born as *Padma* (lotus); when He took the incarnation as Parasuram, she was born as Earth, as Ram she became Sita and as Krishna she became Rukmani.

It is said that Lord Indra was able to regain his kingdom by wearing 13 *mukhi rudraksha* on advice by his chief priest Vrahaspati and Lord Brahma.

A person wearing this *rudraksha* gets multifold benefits by offering prayers to Goddess Mahalakshmi (like reading of *Lakshmi Sukt* or *Mahalakshmi Stotra*).

From medicinal viewpoint, 13 *mukhi rudraksha* is used for psychiatric illnesses and as a cure for sexual disorders.

Who should wear?

All performing artists, actors, leaders and politicians, top executives and those in marketing profession should use this *rudraksha*. People seeking wealth should use this *rudraksha* as per guidance given above.

Mantras to be recited for 13 *mukhi rudraksha*

Om Hreem Namah Namah (Shiva Puran)

Om Kshaam Chaum Namah (Mantramaharnava)

Om Kshaum (Padma Puran)

Om Kshayem Staum Namah (Skand Puran)

Om Eem Yaam aap Aum
Mahamrityunjaya Mantra
Om Namah Shivaya

14 *MUKHI RUDRAKSHA*

This *rudraksha* is blessed by Lord Shiva Himself and is known to have been directly produced from His eyes. Therefore, it has a special status **(Fig. 6)**. It is known as controller as *Ajna Chakra* (Medulla Plexus), which is located between the two eyebrows. One who wears this *rudraksha* on the forehead **(Fig. 29)** is worshipped by Devas and *brahmins* and finally gets *nirvana* (freedom from cycles of birth). It helps in opening of the *Ajna Chakra* and thus improving visualisations power. It is like the third eye of Lord Shiva and helps people to protect themselves and make correct judgment in every action they plan. The *Ajna Chakra* has the shape of lighted two-leaf white lotus, has the word *ham*, *ksham* residing in it, its *beej tatva* (seed element) is *Om*, the *Loka* is *Tap*, *Yantra* is like *Linga* (phallus) and the ruling deity is Lord Shiva.

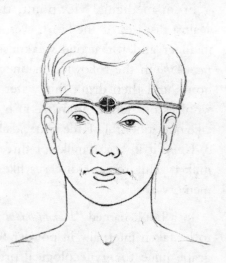

It is said that the wearer of 14 *mukhi rudraksha* gains *Shiva-shakti-pind*, meaning he or she will imbibe *Shakti Peeth* and *Jyotirlinga*. The wearer purifies the ancestors and brings

Fig. 29: Wearing 14 mukhi on forehead

fame and purity to the forefathers. This *rudraksha* not only improves the present, but sets right the past and makes the future completely foreseen and positive.

To get the best results from this bead, the wearer should touch the *Ajna Chakra* located on the forehead with the *rudraksha* for a few minutes. It is also considered as having a form of Hanuman. Lord Shiva took birth as Hanuman to help Lord Ram in search of Seeta and to defeat the demon Ravan. As son of mother Anjani, Hanuman went to the Sun and learnt from him all the arts and practices. As a form of Rudra, Hanuman's total life is dedicated to the welfare of good people and for the destruction of evil forces. He is totally devoted to Lord Ram. He is also full of intelligence and is a forceful orator and an effective ambassador of Lord Ram. A wearer of 14 *mukhi rudraksha* gets all good blessings from Lord Hanuman. This *rudraksha* also helps in increasing secretions of the eight *chakras* (*Vishnu chakra*).

From medicinal viewpoint, this *rudraksha* is effective against diseases of the heart, eyes, skin, womb and mind and in ulcer and for sexual weakness. People have used this *rudraksha* in the following manner: 1. Dip in water for few hours and then drink this water for solving problems of wrinkles on skin; 2. Immerse in honey for 24 days and then take one spoonful of the honey daily for sexual disorders; and 3. Keep it in cow's milk for three hours and then give the milk to children for diseases like fever and for improving memory etc.

In a book named "*Vanaushadhi Kataksha*", it is prescribed to be taken internally in powder form (0.25 mg) along with grape juice for gynecological problems. It is also said to correct stammering.

However, all these claims need to be confirmed through clinical trials.

Who should wear?

This *rudraksha* is also known as *Maha Shani,* and those affected by planetary positions of Saturn (*Shani Dasha*) should wear it. Those who are involved in share trading or any speculative business will find it very useful. Professionals engaged in human resources management will find this *rudraksha* helpful in judging people in a better and effective manner. People in import-export business too can carry out their business effectively through proper judgement of their associates even without having to meet them personally.

Mantras to be recited for 14 *mukhi rudraksha*

Om Namah (Shiva Puran)

Om Namo Namah (Mantramaharnava)

Om Nraam (Padma Puran)

Om Dum Maam Namah (Skand Puran)

Om Aum Hasphrem khaphrem

Mahamrityunjaya Mantra

Om Namah Shivaya

RARE *RUDRAKSHA* (*GAURISHANKAR, TRIJUTI, GANESH* AND 15-to-21 *MUKHI RUDRAKSHA*)

There are several varieties of *rudraksha,* which do not find mention in the old scriptures but are referred to in later writings. In *Katakana Yantras,* it is claimed that these rare varieties have several mystical powers. Of these, *Gaurishankar rudraksha* is very popular among common users as well as among saints and priests for its properties that help in meditation. Properties of other rare varieties are not exactly known as very few people can afford these rare beads. However, based on experience and information available, some of their salient features are given below.

GAURISHANKAR RUDRAKSHA

Two naturally joined *rudrakshas* are called *Gaurishankar*. It is regarded as a unified form of Shiva and Shakti. Some people call this variety *Ardhnareeshwar rudraksha*. It is known to possess the properties of two *mukhi rudraksha,* though its effects are slightly different from those of two *mukhi rudraksha*, particularly in aspects like relationships. A *Gaurishankar rudraksha* can be worn in order to improve the relationships between husband and wife, father and son and between friends. **(Fig. 7)** Those aspiring to get married or couples desirous of having children wear this *rudraksha.*

Sometimes, this bead has different shapes and configurations and these are described below:

1. *Sawar. Sawar* in Hindi means rider and in this case, one of the beads rides – essentially a one *mukhi* – over the other bead, which can be of any *mukh*. In a *Sawar rudraksha*, one of the beads will always be a one *mukhi* and it is considered to be next only to the original and rare one *mukhi* round *rudraksha* in virtues. Some people even cut the one *mukhi rudraksha* from the twin bead and use it separately. However, experts feel this will not be a pure one *mukhi rudraksha*. Natural holes exist in both the beads.

2. *Gaurishankar* with different *mukhis*: The most common *Gaurishankar rudraksha* varieties will have a total of 9, 10 or 11 *mukhs*. There are some *Gaurishankar* varieties, which have up to 21 *mukhs* as also one *mukh* in each of the beads. There are

differences of opinion on whether counting the total *mukhs* is the correct way of determining the number of *mukhs*. Logically, counting can be done together as in higher *mukhis* many times twin characteristics can be found. In other words, in several higher *mukhi* beads – 11 *mukhi* to 14 *mukhi* – there will be two holes on the bead. As such, the number of *mukhs* should be counted on both the beads to arrive at the total number of *mukhs*.

A *Gaurishankar rudraksha* can be worn around neck. In many families, the tradition is to keep this *rudraksha* in the puja room (at the altar). From medicinal viewpoint, its properties correspond to the number of mukhs it will have – if it has nine *mukhs*, it will have properties of a nine *mukhi rudraksha*.

3. Garbhgauri: A twin bead in which one of the beads is much smaller than the other is worn by women for getting conceived. It has the name of *Garbhgauri*.

Who should wear?

A *Gaurishankar Kantha* having 32 beads is not to be worn by a married person as it is ideally meant for people who observe celibacy like *sanyasis*. It can be kept at the worshipping place by anyone and not worn. Why this restriction on this variety cannot be explained except that the energies emanating from a 32-bead *Kantha* will be too high for an ordinary person to absorb and may affect the body *chakras* adversely with a feeling of renunciation coming in strongly. This *rudraksha* can be worn singly or even in higher numbers to achieve desired results in improving relationships and/or for meditation. In all *malas* used in meditation, *Gaurishankar rudraksha* is usually one among the combination of the beads used. It is also one of the most common *rudraksha* for which there are ample number of fakes. Usually, such beads are made by artificially joining two lower *mukhi rudrakshas* (mostly five or six *mukhis*). Adequate care should be taken while examining this *rudraksha* and identifying its genuineness before one acquires it. (Chapter 4)

Mantras to be recited for *Gaurishankar rudraksha*

Om Namah Shivaya

Mahamrityunjaya Mantra

Om Aim Hreem Yugal rupanye Namah

Om Gaurishankarabhyam Namah

15 *MUKHI RUDRAKSHA*

Fifteen *mukhi rudrakshas* have similar qualities as 14 *mukhi rudrakshas* and therefore the prices of the two varieties are more or less the same. Fifteen *mukhi rudraksha* is blessed by Lord Shiva in his incarnation as Pashupati. It has all the virtues of 14 *mukhi rudraksha* and additionally offers luck in acquiring wealth **(Fig. 6)**.

Lord Shiva has 1008 names out of which *Pashupati* (lord of animals) is one of the most common. As *Pashupati*, He provides life to humans and animals and takes it back at His free will. Lord Shiva is also called Sharva, "the hunter". His hunting weapon is *Trishul* (Trident) with the auspicious number of 3 at its tips. Trishul is considered very holy and it is offered to the Lord as a token of love for Him and to get His blessings. At many places, where Shiva temples are located over mountains or at great heights, the devotees carry *Trishul* manually, often very heavy, as offering to Him. One such temple is at Bhairrogarh at Pachmarhi in Madhya

Pradesh. As Pashupati, He carries some of the oldest forms of weapons like axe (*parasu*), hand drum (*damru*), stick (*yog dand*), arrow (*pinaka* and *ajagava*), spear (*paupata*), sling or noose (*pasa*) and the divine rod (*khatwang*). He is seen as wearing a *rudraksha mala*, carrying a skull, a lotus flower, a discus and a sword.

The famous Pashupatinath temple is located in Kathmandu in Nepal and is revered by all Hindus.

Mantras to be recited for 15 *mukhi rudraksha*

Om Shreem Manovaanchitam Hreem Om Namah

Om Hreem Namah

Mahamrityunjaya Mantra

Om Namah Shivaya

16 *MUKHI RUDRAKSHA*

This *rudraksha* **(Fig. 6)** is called *Jai* (victory) *rudraksha*. Its supernatural powers protect the wearer against any theft or cheating and render him victorious against his/her adversaries. It is dedicated to Lord Ram **(Fig. 25)** and therefore is endowed with great human virtues like good family relations respect and fame. It is also regarded as having the blessings of *Mahakaal*, which remove the fear of time and therefore death in wearers. It is also helpful to people whose birth signs contain unfavourable planetary positions. Whenever a person is in a situation where he or she is afraid of losing his/her beloved one, or is likely to be blamed for some acts, or is about to get married, or has to compromise on his or her principles or is afraid of death, this *rudraksha* offers inner strength to overcome such situations.

Shiva assumed the *Mahakaal* form as soon as He heard of Sati's (His wife Parvati's) demise and became an angry and ferocious God. To please the Mahakaal Shiva, *Mahamrityunjaya Mantra* (conceived by sage Shukracharya) was the most appropriate mantra. As per *Markandeya Puran*, it was this *mantra* that saved sage Markandeya from death. Even today, people chant this mantra in order to overcome fear of death, or for any other fear.

Who should wear?

Sixteen *mukhi rudraksha* can be worn singly or in numbers, if necessary, along with other beads. It can be worn in order to overcome adversaries and to win over fear of death or for other reasons.

Mantras to be recited for 16 *mukhi rudraksha*

Mahamrityunjaya Mantra
Om Haum Joom Sah
Om Hreem Hoom Namah
Om Namah Shivaya

17 *MUKHI RUDRAKSHA*

Seventeen *mukhi rudraksha* is a popular bead because of its several properties **(Fig. 6)**. It is believed that this *rudraksha* can make the wearer rich in a short span of time.

It represents Lord Vishwakarma **(Fig. 30)** who is an expert in crafting and creativity. The wearer not only gets sudden wealth, but spiritual powers too. Wealth can come in the form of sudden rise in the share prices, in the value of property, unexpected inheritance or through games of chances. As per *Katyayani Yantra*, 17 *mukhi rudraksha* represents Goddess

Katyayani. This *rudraksha* gives all the four attainments of life – *dharma, arth, kaam* and *moksha.*

Fig. 30: Lord
Vishwakarma

Women wearing this *rudraksha* can expect to have all their desires – good marital life, children, happiness and a prolonged life for husband – fulfilled.

Following are the mantras for Katyayani Devi:

Vande vaanchitam manorathartha chandrardh krit shekhram,
Simharudha chaturbhuja katakana yashswaneem;
Swarnavarna ajnachakra sthitaam shastham durga trine tram,
varaabheet karaam khaddar padmadharaam katyayan sutaa
bhajaami.

Woman desiring to get married should chant the following mantra:

Katyayani mahamaye mahayoginya dheeshwari
Nandgopsutam devi patim me kuru te namah.

Women, who wear 17 *mukhi rudraksha* and offer prayers to Katyayani Devi, will get Her blessings. For others, it may bring in sudden wealth.

Mantras to be recited for 17 *mukhi rudraksha*

Mahamrityunjaya Mantra
Om Namah Shivaya

18 *MUKHI RUDRAKSHA*

Eighteen *mukhi rudraksha* **(Fig. 6)** represents Bhumi (Earth) **(Fig. 31)**. The wearer of this *rudraksha* remains wealthy and free of all diseases.

Old scriptures say Earth was
born from the sweat of Madhu and
Kaitabh, the two powerful demons.
It is said that their sweat got
dehydrated as a result of the heat
of the Sun. Hence, Earth is also
known as *Medani*. As Earth (also
called *Pith* and *Avani*) offers
motherly affection to one and all –
be it plants, animals or the matter
on it – it is called *Avani*. One of its
greatest virtues is to give pardon to
all irrespective of the sins
committed. This brings the name
Kshamadhatri. When a person
donates part of the earth he owns,
he earns the blessings of all the
Gods. It is a sin to take away

Fig. 31: Bhumi (Earth)

another person's land without legal sanction. It is not
advisable to do farming on land meant to grow feed for cows,
or to construct a water tank or well or road.

One should not keep *Shivling*, statue of Goddesses, conch,
shaligram, flowers, *tulsi*, camphor, sandalwood, *rudraksha mala*,
kusha grass, *gorochan*, books and *yantras* on Earth without
offering some support. It is a sin to dig Earth at the time of
eclipse or earthquake. Earth is called *Bhumi* as residential
buildings (*bhuvan*) can be constructed on it.

Eighteen *mukhi rudraksha* is recommended for those who
are launching major projects, new works of any type or
making a change in the business line. Those engaged in

Gayatri Sadhna will find it very useful to meditate and to get concentration. Females who face abortions very often get relief by wearing this *rudraksha*. It is also good for the health of small children.

This *rudraksha* can be worn singly. However, it is advisable to keep a *mala* with all beads up to 18 *mukhs* in the house for proper progress in life and for purposes of protection.

Who should wear?

Persons launching major projects or looking for making a change in their line of business should wear this *rudraksha*.

Mantras to be recited for 18 mukhi rudraksha

Om Hreem Hoom Eakatva Rupe hum Hreem Om
Om Hreem Shreem Vasudhaye Swaha
Mahamrityunjaya Mantra
Om Namah Shivaya

19 MUKHI RUDRAKSHA

Nineteen *mukhi rudraksha* **(Fig. 6)** represents Lord Vishnu **(Fig. 23)** whose abode is *Ksheersagar* (ocean of milk). It is known to fulfill all materialistic desires. It also offers clarity to a person as to how he or she has to carry out a business. One can undertake any work — whether business, serving mankind, politics or social activity – without having to undergo much stress.

In many epics like *Shrimad Bhagawat, Shilpratna* and *Vishnudharmottar Puran*, Lord Vishnu is depicted as taking rest in *Ksheersagar*, on the great snake Sheshnag. Goddess Lakshmi is with Him on one side. Wearing a great ornamented crown, He has the *Shree Vats* on His chest, *Kaustubh Mani* and

Vanmala (two extremely precious gems) around His neck, has
a conch shell in His right hand, three *valays* in the second
hand, *gada* in another hand and a *chakra* in the fourth. *Nand,
Sunand, Sanak Sanatan,* etc., several rishis, Brahma, Shiva and
many Devas are praying to him. Goddess Lakshmi, Pushti,
Saraswati, Kanti, Kirti, Tushti, Urja Samvit and Maya etc. are
at His service. One of His legs is on the lap of Lakshmi and
other on the seat of Sheshnag. One of his four hands extends
up to the knee and other up to the naval. His one hand
supports the head from below and the fourth has
Santanmanjari. From his navel, a lotus stem is coming out over
which Lord Brahma is seated. Madhu and Kaitabha, the
demons, live near the lotus stem. This is the description of
the Lord of the Universe, responsible for the life of all the
living beings and plants and it is He who blesses the 19 *mukhi
rudraksha.* A wearer, therefore, gets generous blessing of Lord
Vishnu and enjoys all luxuries, all the wealth and success in all
actions.

It is also mentioned in some epics that this *rudraksha*
facilitates one to live a stress-free life.

Mantras to be recited for 19 *mukhi rudraksha*
Om Hreem Hoom Namah
Om Vam Vishnave Ksheershayayanye Swaha
Mahamrityunjaya Mantra
Om Namah Shivaya

20 MUKHI RUDRAKSHA

Twenty *mukhi rudraksha* is an extremely rare bead **(Fig. 6)**.
In one entire season in Nepal, there can be just four or five in
a whole year. Even the Indonesian beads of this variety are
found in lesser numbers. Normally, it is difficult even to see

this *rudraksha* in its pure form at most shops. Most of the time one sees only fake ones as the real ones are only sold through personal contacts.

Twenty *mukhi rudraksha* represents Brahm (Not just Brahma, the creator, but the Hindu Trinity consisting of Brahma, Vishnu and Shiva). It is said to derive energy from various sources and is full of divine powers. The powers of nine planets, ten *Digpals* and the power of the Trinity are all converged in this *rudraksha*. **(Fig. 32)**

According to Hindu teachings, the nine planets are Sun, Moon, Mars, Mercury, Jupiter, Venus, Saturn, Rahu and Ketu (the last two shadow planets). Agni, Indra, Varun, Soam, Vishnu, Vrahaspati, Vayu and Kuber are the eight *digpals*, who are the lords of the

Fig. 32: *Akshar Brahm – Om*

directions. There are variations in their classifications in different scriptures.

The Trinity of Gods is Brahma, Vishnu and Shiva. The power of these 20 centers is concentrated in the 20 *mukhs* of this *rudraksha*. It is a rare *rudraksha* and if one is able to get it, one should handle it with great reverence while wearing it or worshipping it.

Mantras to be recited for 20 *mukhi rudraksha*

Om Hreem Hreem Hum Hum Brahmane Namah

Mahamrityunjaya Mantra

Om Namah Shivaya

21 MUKHI RUDRAKSHA

Twenty one *mukhi rudraksha* **(Fig. 7)** represents Lord Kuber **(Fig. 33)**. The wearer of this *rudraksha* gets enormous wealth. He or she does not lose his or her fortunes as long as the *rudraksha* remains with him/ her. All luxuries of life, whether physical or materialistic, are available to him/her

Fig. 33: Lord Kuber

and the wearer always remains protected from all evil forces or legal tangles.

It is also said that the person remains untouched by any tantric effects or evil's eye.

Kuber is the lord of treasury. He is also called Vitteshwaraye (God of finance). Without his consent, even Goddess Lakshmi, the Goddess of Wealth, cannot bestow her blessings on a person. Lord Shiva always blesses Kuber and he is the *gana* chief and king of Yaksha. Brahma's son is *Pulastya*, who gave birth to Vishrawa who in turn gave birth to

Kuber. Kuber worshipped Lord Shiva intensely and then got to reign over Alkapuri, the magnificent city created by Vishwakarma.

Once, after his great *tapasya* (deep penance/meditation), Kuber opened his eyes and he could not bear the shining form of Shiva and when Shiva gave him the power to see the divine light, he saw Parvati next to Lord Shiva by keeping his eyes wide open. Parvati did not like his way of looking at her and her anger led to Kuber losing one of his eyes. Pleased with his hard work and *tapasya*, Shiva made him in-charge of the treasury. He is also called Pingalnetri (one-eyed).

Kuber also means one having enmity (He had kept a menacing eye of enmity towards Parvati). In fact, all those who have been fortunate to earn money through their hard work or by luck have to encounter several persons who are jealous of their achievements. This *rudraksha* is as rare as the one *mukhi* round Nepalese variety and people should procure this bead with the greatest care. There is one example of a fake 21 *mukhi rudraksha* supplied by a source, which apparently made it from a wild berry (in another case from wood) with great precision. One should know that the size of 21 *mukhi rudraksha* is not abnormally big. It is almost the same size as that of 16 or 17 *mukhi* round *rudraksha*. Only on rare occasions does a large, round 21 *mukhi rudraksha* gets produced. In the *Gaurishankar* form also, 21 *mukhi* is considered genuine provided the number of lines are clear and well demarcated.

In case of Indonesian 21 *mukhis rudraksha*, the lines are so close to each other that even after having a size of less than 25 mm, all 21 lines can be clearly seen. There are less chances of getting an Indonesian fake 21 *mukhi rudraksha*. However, care should be taken to examine and count the lines, which usually remain on the surface without any deep grooves.

Mantras to be recited for 21 *mukhi rudraksha*

Om Hreem Hoom Shivamitraye namah

Om Yakshyaye Kuberaye Vaishrawanayae Dhandhaanyadhipataye Dhan Dhanya Samraddhi me Dapay Dappay Swah

Mahamrityunjaya Mantra

Om Namah Shivaya

TRIJUTI

Trijuti is a wonder of nature. Three *rudraksha* beads get joined on the tree itself. In other words, it is a *Gaurishankar* with a third *rudraksha*. Although there are several *Trijuti* types, one having the three beads in equal shape and size and uniformly stuck to each other is a rarity. Such beads are produced only once in several years. **(Fig. 7)**

The market has several numbers of crafted *Trijutis* and one should be extremely careful while buying this bead. Normally, people crafting a *Trijuti* take a genuine *Gaurishankar* and another bead, matching it in color and contours, and join them with great precision and using high quality adhesives. As a *Trijuti* can fetch lakhs of rupees, high level of craftsmanship is used in creating the fakes. Earlier, the bonded beads could be separated if boiled in water for one to two hours, but newer types of adhesives and newer techniques make it difficult to identify the fake beads. Even now, one can boil the bead in water for two to three hours and there could be discolouration of one or more beads, if they are bonded. If the bead is genuine, the colour should be almost uniform across the entire surface of the bead.

A *Trijuti* is also known as *Tribhagi, Gauri Path* or *Brahma-Vishnu-Mahesh* and represents the Trinity. It is symbolic of all the basic characteristics of the universe. It is a auspicious *rudraksha*. It represents the complete personality and gives the wearer total control over difficult situations. It can be a very useful tool in leadership and in achieving total success.

A *Trijuti* can have any number of *mukhs* although in most cases this aspect is not given any weightage. For example, 14, 19, 20 and 21 *mukhi Trijutis* are considered extremely rare and possess highest qualities. A *Trijuti*, in which one of the beads is one *mukhi*, is also very rare and known to possess high qualities. I have so far not come across one such *Trijuti*. Some wearers of *Trijuti* have experienced strange feelings for first few weeks of their wearing including experiencing weird dreams. They are advised not to be afraid and reach wrong conclusions. It is the mystic power of this divine bead, which takes time to get synchronized with the body system of the wearer.

Mantras to be recited for *Trijuti*

Mahamrityunjaya Mantra
Om Namah Shivaya

GANESH RUDRAKSHA AND OTHERS

If a *rudraksha* of any *mukh* gets a protrusion on its body similar to the trunk of an elephant, this *rudraksha* is called a Ganesh *rudraksha* **(Fig. 7)**. Only in recent times this *rudraksha* has received wide popularity. The bead resembles Lord Ganesh with his trunk. In view of high prices commanded by eight or 11 *mukhi rudraksha*, which are also blessed by Ganesh, traders sell this *rudraksha* as a cheaper alternative.

Depending on the *mukh*, the beads also should be effective and all the respective blessings may be there. Eight *mukhi* or eleven *mukhi* Ganesh has special significance and are considered very auspicious.

Ganesh rudraksha is used alternatively with other beads in a *Siddha Mala* to make up for the numbers to 27 (1 to 14 *mukhi* beads will require 13 *Ganesh rudraksha*). Thirty two beads of *Ganesh rudraksha* are strung together to make a *Kantha*, which people keep at worshipping place to protect them and to remove any obstacles in life. Some people even wear such a *Kantha* regularly.

Some people get obsessed with the image of Ganesh in *rudraksha* to such an extent that they look for the contours on the surface of any *rudraksha* resembling Lord Ganesh. There are books written on this issue and the whole approach looks intriguing and questionable. Practically, only such *rudraksha* is called *Ganesh rudraksha*, which has a trunk-like elevation on its body.

In addition to the above varieties, there are possibilities of getting several other varieties since it is a product of nature. For example, *Sawar*, which is a *Gaurishankar rudraksha* with one bead having only one line and another bead a normal *rudraksha* of four to seven *mukhs*. This has been explained in Chapter 1. Then there is *Nandi rudraksha*, which has two trunk-like protrusions on two sides of the bead. Some call this bead *Dwi Ganesh*.

All these varieties and others not explained and available from nature are revered by people who use them in the hope of deriving benefits. No authentic information is available about specific properties of these beads. If one wishes to use such *rudraksha,* it should be done with full devotion and the wearing procedure shall be the same like other *rudraksha* and *mantra* of *Om Namah Shivaya* should be chanted.

Mahamrityunjaya Mantra

The *mantra*:

Om Tryambakam Yajaamahe Sugandhim Pushti Vardhanam
Urvaa rukmiva Bandhnaan Mrityormuksheeya Mamrataat

Its meaning is as follows:

"O Lord Shiva, you are a three-eyed Trayambakeshwar and as you can see and change future destiny, I pray to you as per the following: Please make me physically and mentally strong and full of good qualities so that I as a body and soul become a symbol of good human qualities and spread good virtues (*sugandh*) and strong will (*pushti*).

"As I mature and become older, I may ripe and face death so naturally and painlessly, the way a water melon detaches itself from the plant after it gets ripened (in terms of taste and flavour) without even letting the leaf next to it, knowing about it. After death, I should get the *Nirvana* or *Moksha* so as to get out of the cycle of birth and death. This way, I shall get the nectar of eternal peace."

THE SCIENCE OF *RUDRAKSHA* 3

Rudraksha has been known for a range of benefits like spirituality, health, prosperity and resolution of psychological issues, fear or problems involving emotions. Its efficacy has been explained in the *puranas*. In fact, *Shiva Puran, Shrimad Devibhagwat,* etc. are full of worthy mentions about these beads. As one wears *rudraksha,* all types of sins, including acts of murder, eating of prohibited items or bad deeds like cheating, get condoned and the sinner gains purity of thought and deed. Removal of fear is the basic characteristic of these beads. It is mentioned that Lord Shiva, as he witnessed the agony that mankind has been going through generations after generations, questioned Himself and Lord Brahma as to "why we play the game of producing and destroying human race, which suffers endlessly". As He searched for a satisfactory explanation, tears started rolling down His eyes and wherever these tears fell, *rudraksha* trees are said to have grown. The message that is conveyed in this anecdote is that the *rudraksha* beads have a purpose to achieve, that is, to care for the sorrows of the mankind.

It is experience of many that wearing *rudraksha* brings in health, happiness, calmness and prosperity. However, the emphasis laid in related epics is on the aspect of deliverance from sins. To pursue any spiritual path, the body, mind and heart should be devoid of past thoughts. For meditation practices to be effective, one should forget the past, the present and the future. *Rudraksha* has been found to be an

Tree

Flowers

Raw fruits

Ripe fruits

Seeds as Rudraksha

Fig. 1A

Fig. 2: Progressive stages of leaf (This is one of the leaf that turns to orange then brown)

Fig. 3: Flowers in full bloom

Fig. 4: Dried fruits and The Seed (Rudraksha)

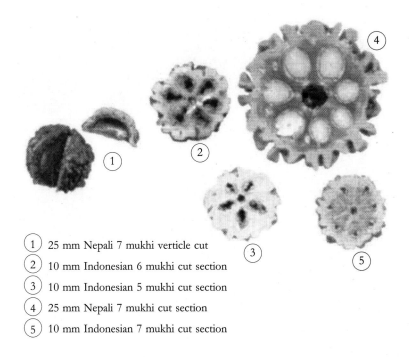

1. 25 mm Nepali 7 mukhi verticle cut
2. 10 mm Indonesian 6 mukhi cut section
3. 10 mm Indonesian 5 mukhi cut section
4. 25 mm Nepali 7 mukhi cut section
5. 10 mm Indonesian 7 mukhi cut section

Fig. 5: Cut sections

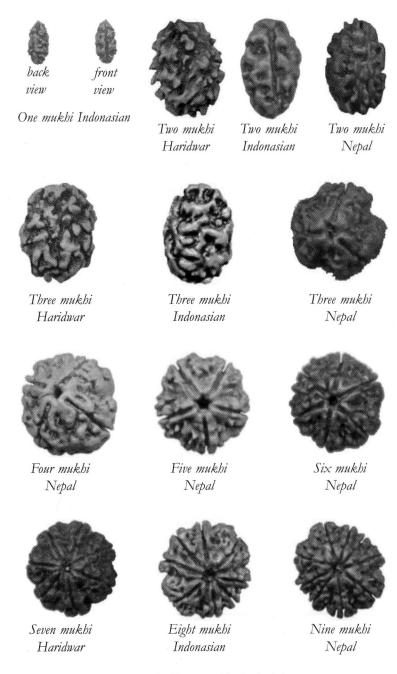

back view   front view

One mukhi Indonasian

Two mukhi Haridwar

Two mukhi Indonasian

Two mukhi Nepal

Three mukhi Haridwar

Three mukhi Indonasian

Three mukhi Nepal

Four mukhi Nepal

Five mukhi Nepal

Six mukhi Nepal

Seven mukhi Haridwar

Eight mukhi Indonasian

Nine mukhi Nepal

Fig. 6: Different mukhi Rudraksha

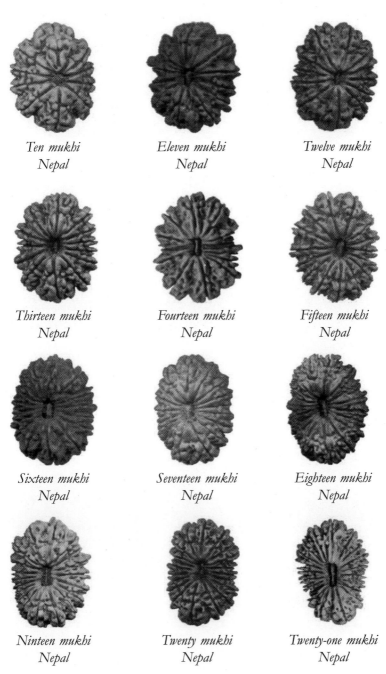

Ten mukhi
Nepal

Eleven mukhi
Nepal

Twelve mukhi
Nepal

Thirteen mukhi
Nepal

Fourteen mukhi
Nepal

Fifteen mukhi
Nepal

Sixteen mukhi
Nepal

Seventeen mukhi
Nepal

Eighteen mukhi
Nepal

Ninteen mukhi
Nepal

Twenty mukhi
Nepal

Twenty-one mukhi
Nepal

Fig. 6: Different mukhi Rudraksha

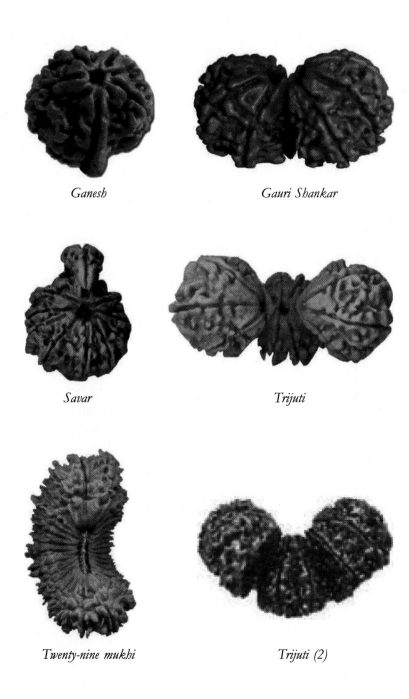

Ganesh

Gauri Shankar

Savar

Trijuti

Twenty-nine mukhi

Trijuti (2)

Fig. 7: Some Rare Beads

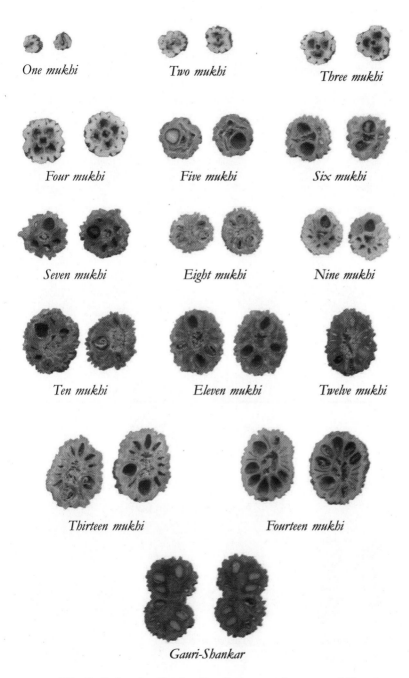

One mukhi

Two mukhi

Three mukhi

Four mukhi

Five mukhi

Six mukhi

Seven mukhi

Eight mukhi

Nine mukhi

Ten mukhi

Eleven mukhi

Twelve mukhi

Thirteen mukhi

Fourteen mukhi

Gauri-Shankar

Fig. 8: Indonasian Beads : Cut Sections one-fourteen mukhi

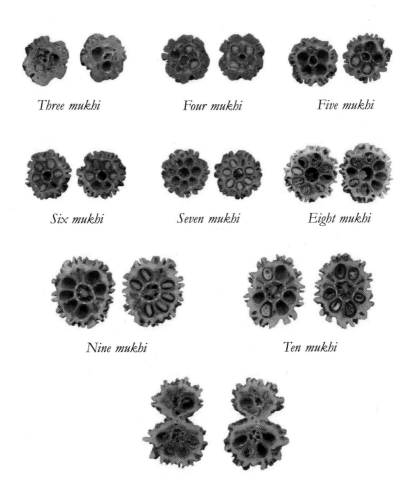

Three mukhi   Four mukhi   Five mukhi

Six mukhi   Seven mukhi   Eight mukhi

Nine mukhi   Ten mukhi

Gauri-Shankar

Fig. 9: Nepal Beads : Cut Sections

One mukhi
Chandrakar

Two mukhi
Haridwar

Three mukhi
Haridwar

Fig. 10: Other Cut Sections

श्री केदारेश्वर

श्री मल्लिकार्जुनेश्वर

श्री हटकेश्वर

श्री गोमुखेश्वर

श्री सोमनाथ

श्री त्र्यम्बकेश्वर

श्री रामेश्वर

श्री विश्वनाथ काशी

श्री ओंकारेश्वर

श्री भीमशंकर

श्री मंगेश्वर

श्री वैद्यनाथ

Fig. 11: Twelve Jyotirlinga

Lord Shiva

Lord Shiva

Shankar, Parvati and Family

Dosh Nivaran (10)

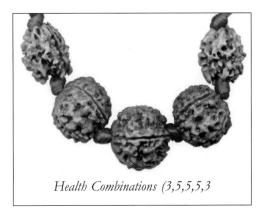

Health Combinations (3,5,5,5,3

Saraswati (4,6,4)

Surya Pendant (12)

Business Growth (7,8,12)

Ajna Chakra (14)

Fig. 37: Rudraksha Power Combinations

Rudraksha Coral
Sphatik Mala

Coral Mala

Dhyan Yog Mala

Raksha Pendant

Siddha Mala – Gold Caps

Durga Shakti
Bracelet

Protection Combination

Fig. 37: Rudraksha Power Combinations

Fig. 39: Siddha Mala

Fig. 40: Indra Mala

Rudraksha Kandha

Fig. 41: Meditation Dress

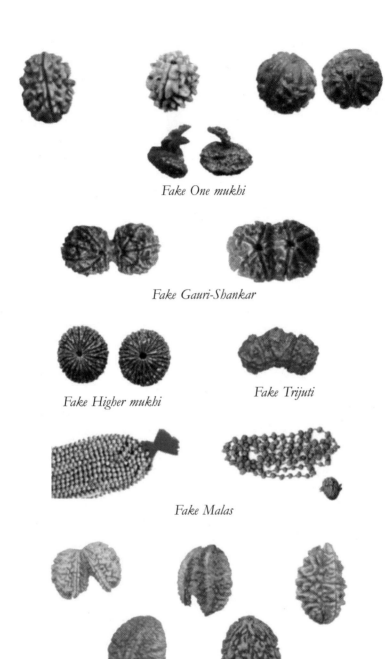

Fake One mukhi

Fake Gauri-Shankar

Fake Higher mukhi

Fake Trijuti

Fake Malas

Bhadraksha and different berries

ideal tool for this as it is known to purify the thoughts and to make man worthy of embarking on a spiritual path. One can restart life with renewed confidence.

It must be clarified that mere wearing of *rudraksha* is not a licence for one to commit any sinful deeds. It has a great virtue to give strength and purity to one's inner feelings. As one wears the bead, one tends not to repeat the mistakes committed earlier.

Rudraksha is also useful as a medicinal herb, specifically for cardiac problems, blood pressure and mental disorders. It also improves intelligence. This aspect has been further described in Chapter 5.

It is not an ordinary seed or an herb. In India it is held in high reverence and is considered divine. People do not touch it without performing the required ablutions. It is always held in the right hand (as the left hand is considered impure!) and is accepted, when offered, with bare foot. There are several other auspicious gestures associated with it.

John Garret and Kerber Drory have reported many medicinal values of *rudraksha*. As early as in the year 1864, Dr. Abraham Jajuar had recorded that *rudraksha* could be used in mind-related diseases and for controlling stress. **(Ref. 13)**

It is also reported that injectible oils made from *rudraksha* are exported from Indonesia to China for treatment of undisclosed diseases. Research work at University of Cologne in Germany, International University at Florida (Miami-USA), as well by a pharmaceutical giant in Switzerland shall bring out new findings about the medicinal properties of this ancient bead. The work carried out by University of Mumbai from the year 2005 onwards initiated by Rudra Life of Mumbai has found the bead useful in cases of diabetes of cardiac ailments and inflammation and for memory enhancement. *Elaeocarpus* contains indolizidine alkaloids, which is reported as a promising constituent for the treatment of HIV/AIDS **(Ref. 40)**.

Oral administration of *rudraksha* in powder or paste form as a medicine is yet to be introduced, as toxicity studies are under way. Initial studies show that it is safe to take rudraksha powder.

Effectiveness of these beads when worn on the body is still under study. There is need for further evaluation of its surface topography, electro-magnetic properties such as capacitance, inductance etc., and its digital biological effects. Some work has been carried out at the Benaras Hindu University, India, but the study is inconclusive in terms of effects of different *mukhis* or correlation between oral/body intake and touch **(Ref. 13)**. This study, although preliminary, brings some interesting points. For example, it says, "*Rudraksha* beads in body contact as dielectric material in variable *Puranic* uses form capacitors of different types. Holding a *rudraksha* bead between a pair of fingers and receiving time-varying low voltage electrical signals can be electrically modeled as a simple capacitor having a vericon dielectric material between two parallel plates. Their rosaries, made either in cotton thread or in metal wires in other uses such as on shoulder, wrist, forehead, neck or hair, etc. represent free space capacitors, wherein each body organ provides time-varying and different electrical signals. As mentioned, these electrical signals result due to ionic currents in body functioning and are controlled by the neural processor in the human brain. In each use, the cause for different bio-effects seems due to their variable contact stimuli affecting electrical signatures of tactile sensory nerves and modulation of the latter by specific electrical properties of different *mukhi* beads.

"In different scriptural uses, the thorn of beads makes variable contacts with tactile nerves. Because of variable thorn surface features of *rudrakshas*, each *mukhi* would have different points of contact and hence, each *mukhi* would produce specific type of stimulus in use even on the same strength. The biomedical and spiritual effects of each *mukhi* thus may be attributed to the surface structures and electrical properties."

Whatever may be the results of these studies, it is accepted that the touch-effects of *rudraksha* surprise us. It may be wrong to assume that wearing of *rudraksha* was advised because of the scarce availability of the beads or due to the fact that these beads were available only in Nepal. In older times, it was not so easy to get the beads in large quantities if it was to be used as a medicine. It is possible that as the beads were powerful enough, it could have been advised to simply wear them to get the desired results. In all *pauranic* statements, only wearing has been specified. It is, therefore, recommended that detailed studies of this aspect of electromagnetic properties of *rudraksha* are further carried out.

The Kirlian photography (or aura imaging) is another approach, which may throw light on the power of these beads. In this process, the emanating energy from different organs of the body is photographed using a special camera and the aura is measured by the color of the surrounding waves. From the quantum and color of the radiating energy, one can determine the affected parts of the body system and treatment prescribed. The aura varies from person to person depending on the energy level. For example, a person having higher level of thoughts (alpha state of mind), will have larger and more radiant aura towards white color compared to an ordinary human being. Experiments have been conducted proving that after wearing *rudraksha*, the aura showed changes. However, a lot of work needs to be done to evolve standards and evaluation system for this specialized field. It is essential for aura testing to have a room with constant humidity and the comparative measurements should be done within the shortest possible time interval. For example, if you conduct a test at 9 a.m., then the reading on the same object may be different at 5 p.m. Therefore, the time differential factor should also be kept in mind. The bio-sensing mechanism is yet to be established as an authentic system to represent the energy level of any person.

From various experiences and several testimonials, it has been found that by wearing *rudraksha*, stress, mental disorders, fear, cold and throat-related diseases and blood pressure get controlled. It has been observed that primarily calmness of the mind is achieved and fear goes away by wearing *rudraksha*. There are other benefits too. How does this happen? There are various theories and the answer is usually not simple.

As we know, the hippocampus in the human brain is responsible for memory and spatial navigation. The sharpness of mind depends on speed of the nerve cells in hippocampus. There is a fluid known as synapse, which is present between two nerves and any message received by one nerve is transmitted to the other nerve through this fluid medium using bio-electrical energy. This is a cycle by which the messages are communicated from and to the brain. Memory is a pool of such bio-electrical messages. The heart or *mun* is formed at this stage although the correct interpretation of *mun* is not found yet. There is one *antahkaran*, or inner consciousness, which is derived from the merger of *mun*, *buddhi*, or intellect, *chiita*, or likes and dislikes, and *ahamkar*, or ego. This is also known as the four forms of *mun*, or the *man-chatushtaya*.

This *mun* gets its shape from the food we take and it decides the inclination of the mind – whether it is towards *saatwik* (pure thoughts, with eagerness to do good things only), *raajasi* (thoughts delving in luxury and a carefree way of life) and *tamasi* (bad thoughts full of ill will towards all). The food we take has a great role in the formation of *mun* – determining whether it is *saatwik* or *raajasi* or *tamasi*. The nervous system of the body is controlled by the autonomic nerves close to the heart and the *mun* is regulated by these nerves. These nerves are extremely small but they are spread all over the body and control the functions of heart, blood vessels, stomach, mind, eyes etc. The digestive system, control of blood pressure, sweating and functioning of various glands are all regulated by the autonomic nerves. *Rudraksha*, if worn close to the heart, impacts these nerves and thereby the entire body system. As the flow of electromagnetic currents through *rudraksha* gets only positive energies because of the chanting of *mantras* and purity of upkeep, the signals given by them are beneficial to the body and mind.

The Benaras Hindu University research paper **(Ref. 13)** gives a further interesting insight: "When a *rudraksha* bead of rosary is held between any finger pairs in chanting the *mantras*, the signal across it shall be bi-directional, whose instantaneous amplitude shall depend upon input signal amplitude and its interpretation by the neural network.

"In the light of body-brain electrical circuitry relationship, it may be indicated that the modulated signals by the receptor nerves, on reaching the brain, can in fact modulate the brain signals, which may give rise to psycho-physiological effects. The steady state of modulated signals, reaching from the chest region to brain can in turn induce the rhythm in the electrical signals of the heart, which in consequence may result into normal functioning of the heart. Besides these, the effect of modulated signals, in turn may trigger secretion of all necessary hormones and enzymes in the body and result in steady state of health conditions. Further, the rhythmic mechanical pressure by the beads on the soft tissue of the fingers (or heart) during use of rosary improves the peripheral circulation in the body. Because of resonance absorption of *rudraksha* at about 350 MHz, i.e., near the frequency band of human body resonant absorption, it may supplement the required energy to the body systems to maintain rhythm city of life process.

"Because of the difference in output signal frequencies, *rudraksha* of various *mukhis* are suggested to produce different bio-effects. The effects of different frequencies are already well established. Frequencies 0-5 Hz affect the sympathetic nerves, 0-10Hz affect the outstripped muscle, 10-15 Hz affect the motor nerves, 90-110Hz affect the sensory nerves and 100-150 Hz affect the parasympathetic nerves. Thus, various uses of *rudraksha* seem to cause bio-effects mediated through the stimulatory action on the nervous system.

"This study reveals that the biomedical application of *rudraksha* beads as described in the *Shiva Puran* is true to the best of scientific knowledge."

The study at least confirms that *rudraksha's* positive effects on health are not myth, but we need to understand "how".

Dr. Gode a research scientist proved in the year 1983 that rudraksha has sterol and polyphenolic compounds. Dr. S.P. Gupta, in the year 1985 had treated patients of high blood pressure by orally giving rudraksha powder for 10 days. The results were positive and curative powers were proved, with no side effects. **(Ref. 19)**

One research scholar Dr. V.I. Pande had conducted a survey of 1000 rudraksha users wearing it as a rosary and some of the observations are detailed below (although there are different methods, rituals and varied lifestyles of all people covered in the study, still it is an interesting survey):

Males wearing rudraksha malas: 95% Females 5%.
89% of all users were of age more than 35.
Out of these persons 43% were between 35 to 40 years of age, 28% were of age up to 50, and the balance started using rudraksha after they crossed 50 years.
35% of all people were using *rudraksha* for Blood pressure problems, 18% for mental diseases and the balance for spiritual or general considerations.
Out of the people who were wearing *rudraksha* for blood pressure control, 85% felt better after wearing rudraksha. Those wearing for mental disorders 71% felt better. **(Ref. 19)**

Do *rudraksha* have electrical power and if so, does it have useful effects on the body or mind?

Many products on this planet may have electrical charge or

magnetic power (One can use magnets directly!!) but what make rudraksha different is their dose and interaction with body cells. As per one study done by Shri Vasantrao Vaidya, of Sangli (Maharashtra) **(Ref. 19),** Rudraksha when dipped in water transmitted their electrical energy into the water. He used Electron Water Conductivity test to check the flow of ions from rudraksha by using distilled and aerated water (150 ml each at 50°C).

Experiment No. 1

Time duration after start	Distilled water	Aerated water
24 hours	396 micro millimhos	410 micro millimhos
48	611	623
72	724	710
96	746	780

Experiment 2

24 hours	421	510
48	610	650
72	745	754
96	772	785

We have also conducted several tests for electrical conductivity of rudraksha soaked in water using different mukhis and following are the observations:

5 *mukhi*

Time duration after start	Distilled water
24 hours	144 micro milli mhos
48	270

In fact all types of grains and seeds from vegetation have this characteristic. However, the type and rate may vary. It is recommended to soak rudraksha seeds for say 8 to 12 hours, the water get charged and if this water is taken in empty stomach in the morning, it offers several benefits as confirmed by many testimonials. It is also mentioned in some texts that this charged water should be taken while standing over a wollen mat or wooden plank or any insulation below the feet and not just standing on the floor, so that the charged ions are retained in the body. The rise in conductivity is due to electrolytes dispersing in water.

Rudraksha acts as a neutralizing source for any excessive harmful charge received by the body.

In todays' world, where we have millions of sound and radio/electronic waves around us due to explosive growth in communication (tv/telecom, mobiles), our body cells remain day and night exposed to these powerful waves. Today we may not be realizing but with passage of time it may be found that it is harmful for our brain or metabolism. Many countries are now going in for the "safe" mobile handset, with low electromagnetic radiation.

Therefore, a time may come when effects of sound and digital waves including thousands of television and other video transmitting data will be categorized as harmful and then some solution will have to be found to save the humanity from this catastrophe. Can rudraksha protect people from these radiation effects economically, without any side effect ? Without actual trials it is difficult to forecast. But as we have studied in references mentioned above that rudraksha work like capacitors and have the most appropriate electrical energy suitable for humans and therefore this aspect needs to be looked into seriously.

A recent private and independent study reveals that "rudraksha is capable of neutralizing all the harmful radio and communication frequencies on human body. It has also been noticed from experiments that rudraksha from Nepal/ Indian sub continent, have the highest power at the time of Sunrise (IST) and also nearly the same at the time of Sunset (IST). At mid day and mid night the frequencies are at their lowest. It could be the reason why it is recommended to do the morning meditation with rudraksha at the time of sunrise or at sunset. The so called "sleep cycle" of rudraksha starts nearly 2 hour after the sunrise and by mid-noon they totally sleep and again wake up in the evening." This study also needs to be studied further as no data was made available.

The experts in the fields of Digital Biology or Magneto Biology are conducting various research on these beads and their initial observations reveal an astonishing fact that rudraksha bead behaves like a living organism. It becomes unconscious if put on anesthesia and come back to normal behavior after some time and also change its performance cycle with time. May be in some years to come rudraksha will assimilate with human body and mind and take upon themselves all the negativities and thus will be an answer to many of the sufferings and will relieve stress, cure mind related diseases and give calmness so that people can lead a fearless life.

Electronic waves from mind

Rudraksha activates body cells and give electronic signals to the mind. This has been experimented in the laboratory and this is one aspect which needs to be thoroughly investigated. We can take advantage of latest gadgets available to map the mind after wearing rudraksha just as some studies have shown positive influence on mind after doing yoga or meditation or both. **(Ref. 14)**

The body is associated with the mind; and is a counterpart of the mind. You may even call it an extension of mind in the visible form. Every change in thought makes a vibration in the mental body and this, when transmitted to the physical body, causes activity in the nervous matter of the brains. This activity in the nervous cells causes many electrical and chemical changes. It is the thought activity which causes these changes. When the mind is turned to a particular thought and remains there, a definite vibration of matter is set up and often, if this vibration repeats itself due to someone's effort then it tends to repeat itself and thus this becomes the system and becomes automatic. The body imitates the changes of the mind.

In this electronic age you can get a biofeed back monitor at affordable prices. According to a leading psychologist "Biofeedback is one of the more recent and significant advances in medicine. It is being used to learn how to control an array of disorders such as headaches, high blood pressure and poor circulation. Through the use of instruments which record the body's minute electrical signals and feed them back in amplified form through a tone or some visual indicator on the machine, it's possible to be aware of certain changes in the internal body processes, to act on them and change the signal...high tones indicate considerable tension, lower tones, more relaxation. The aim is to reduce the tones by be relaxing. As you listen to signals and try to relax by giving yourself positive suggestion, you learn to connect the feelings of being relaxed to the corresponding tone. Feeling internal changes as they occur is the key to biofeedback."

WHAT IS BIOFEEDBACK?

As we know that normal life functions are carried on without the individual's conscious control or knowledge. Biofeedback is a process by which those automatic inner activities are brought to conscious awareness. One of the earliest devices, long before they were used for meditation, was the polygraph, better known as the lie detector. The polygraph has been used for years, not only in psychology but also in the area of physiological research. To use this machine, various receivers are attached to specific areas of the body. As the body responds emotionally and physically to certain stimuli, the sensors pick up these changes and record them on the machine, where they are transformed into a more readily identifiable form, such as lines drawn on a sheet of graph paper.

The EEG, (Electroencephalograph) measures the electrical output of the brain by means of electrodes placed on the skin around the region of the scalp. The sensors do not deliver any electrical charge but are receivers only. Every brain emits waves of energy, much like radio waves, of which the length and amplitude can be measured. A wavelength in excess of 13 cycles per second (cps) corresponds to the normal waking state, and is called the beta state. 7.5 cps-13 cps is the alpha state, indicating the mind is extremely relaxed or contemplative. The theta state, 3.3-.5 cps, is a much deeper state than alpha. It is a state at which much creative thought takes place. There is still a good deal to be learnt about this state, as well as about the theta state. At 0.5-3.5 cps, it is the state of deep sleep, where there is no consciousness. In a recent TV show on. "Guinnes Book Of Records" a person demonstrating his capability of mind could remember 50 objects in perfect serial numbers when passed one after another before him while he was blind folded. His great feat was attributed by him to the calmness of mind at below 7 cps close to alpha state.

While these various states are based on cycles per second, or length of brain wave, the magnitude of the energy output can also be measured. A reading of 30-40 micro volts is common for experienced persons practicing meditation and some yogis have recorded mental output in excess of 100 micro-volts at will in the alpha state. Brain waves will have amplitude no matter what the wavelength, or brain state is.

CALMNESS OF MIND

A person trained in yogic practices is fully aware of the various subconscious processes which take place in his mind and body, and is able to control his nervous system through the power of concentration. The average person cannot do this because he lacks the necessary physical and mental training and discipline. Disciplined trained yogis who have done great penance and have taught and practiced to control the involuntary functions of the body through concentration and meditation and on the other hand the general science did not pay attention to these things. Now, with the revelations of biofeedback research, many are convinced that the yogic theory is not only true but is also possible for anyone with only a minimal amount of training and effort. As the entire working of rudraksha is revolving around its effects on mind the above description opens up the approach to find out a suitable device like a lie detector or EEG to measure quantitatively effects before and after wearing rudraksha.

Chemical composition of rudraksha:

The gaseous composition as determined by C-H-N analyzer and by gas chromatography shows rudraksha consisting of : Carbon 50%, Nitrogen 0.95%, Hydrogen 17.89%, and Oxygen 30.53%. The radiographic analysis of rudraksha indicates following composition of metals in it two readings were reported 1/.2:

Copper	0.034 ppm/4.205 ppm
Iron	1.014/5.938 ppm
Silver	0.212 ppm
Manganese	1.158/1.276 ppm
Gold	0.013ppm/1.078 ppm
Barium	present/present

It is interesting to note that barium and gold are considered good for heart ailments. The physiochemical properties are as below:

Moisture	12.85
Oil	0.88%
Specific Gravity	1.6481(As sp.gr. is higher than 1, all rudraksha sink in water)
I.V.	68.2
A.V.	32.06
Saponification value	180.07
Saponification Equivalent	322.72
Unsaponification Matter	2.41
Refractive Index	1.501

Our recent analysis of rudraksha outer shell (MNC), inner

seed (MNS) has given following analysis done by spectro-photometry:

Mark	Copper (as Cu)ppm	Manganese (as Mn)ppm	Barium (as Ba)ppm	Iron (as Fe)ppm	Gold (as Au)ppm	Silver (as Ag)ppm
4MNS	17.51	37.42	8.76	78.22	1.10	4.71
4MNC	6.17	5.98	1.68	24.50	0.65	0.86
5MNS	17.36	36.31	9.47	72.42	1.15	3.89
5MNC	5.93	6.67	Not Detected	55.94	0.51	0.72
6MNS	17.66	34.33	9.72	82.35	0.98	4.05
6MNC	6.36	12.72	0.73	45.25	0.42	0.82
5MOS	16.95	38.82	8.67	74.69	1.08	4.46
5MOC	5.90	7.42	0.76	85.60	0.54	0.71

Tests by : CERA Laboratory, Mumbai

Magnetic Properties

One report states **(Ref. 13)** that rudraksha are diamagnetic, paramagnetic and ferromagnetic in their characteristics depending on type and source of rudraksha. Diamagnetism is due to organic compounds with non-polar bonds in which the molecules or radicals have no magnetic moment or the paramagnetic effect is suppressed by the diamagnetic effect...The Para magnetic properties are due to conduction electrons in alkaline metals. Ferromagnetism may be due to presence of Iron or their compounds.

Whatever results have been presented above may vary significantly due to change of source of rudraksha. Bigger Nepal beads may have different composition than say rudraksha from plains. Similarly, Indonesian beads are different in structure and hence it is necessary to specify the source.

Simply put how one should utilise effectively all these powers of Rudraksha?

Just wear them. In correct numbers and proper procedure.

Results come. Slowly and subtedly but in a natural and permanent way. We should not expect miracles to occur. By having Rudraksha, you come closure to nature and you get inclined to believe in Vadic systems of prayer, devotion and love.

IDENTIFICATION OF RUDRAKSHA 4

In Chapter 2, details have been given for of several types of *rudraksha* that are available from different sources. The main issue now is how to ascertain the genuineness of the bead and how to do the classification – Haridwar, Nepal, South India, Indonesia – as mentioned. As you will notice after going through this chapter, the whole issue of identifying genuine *rudraksha* is not so complicated yet as in the case of an Ayurvedic medicine or an agro-based product, it requires some expertise. There is no need for any expensive instrument or testing procedure for general checkup. However, some basic points need to be kept in mind while carrying out the tests.

Unfortunately, traditional sellers of *rudraksha* do not share the information on proper methods of identifying genuine beads for reasons best known to them. Most of the details given hereafter are known to these people. There are dozens of books on *rudraksha*, giving details of the *mantras*, prayers offered to Lord Shiva and stories glorifying *rudraksha*, but there is so far no book worth mentioning, which lists procedures that are to be adopted while identifying genuine *rudraksha* and making sure that one is procuring the right bead.

In spite of this, I must say that in certain typical cases some expertise is called for to ascertain the genuineness of the bead. For example, rare beads like *Trijuti* and 14 or higher *mukhi rudrakshas* are often available as fakes and complications arise because of the higher levels of skill used by unscrupulous elements in creating the fake beads like joining a section inside the bead. In some cases, even the genuine bead may have inherent aberrations in structure.

There is no equipment developed so far, which can be readily used, to check the genuineness or otherwise of a *rudraksha*. And it is quite unlikely that such equipment will be invented as the product to be tested is a seed of a fruit with varied structures depending on the sources of its origin. The electro-magnetic power flow is so subtle that even after setting up some standards for flow of energy, it is not likely to give results due to variations in parameters.

It is, therefore, necessary to adopt an indirect route to check for fake beads so that the chances of getting a spurious one are minimized.

If we study the fake *rudraksha* market closely, we may find following percentage of fake varieties against each:

		Out of total fake beads
1.	One *mukhi*	70%
2.	*Gaurishankar*	10%
3.	Higher than 7 *mukhi* and up to 21 *mukhi*	12%
4.	*Trijuti*	2%
5.	*Mala* beads 10 mm and below	3%
6.	Others (2 *mukhi* Nepal, 1 *mukhi Chandrakar, Sawar* etc.)	5%

This assessment is based on our experience of this market, but there can be large variations. It is therefore noticed that if we can identify one *mukhi* and *Gaurishankar* properly in about 80% of the cases, we can save ourselves from getting a fake *rudraksha*.

One *mukhi rudraksha* from Nepal

For all practical purposes, the one *mukhi* round variety *rudraksha* from Nepal is a rare bead. Almost all traders who have been in this business for several decades, are not confident of seeing a round variety of one *mukhi rudraksha*. Though, it finds mention in all the old texts, it has remained an enigma. Even the old collections from *ashrams* and *sadhus* or princely families do not seem to have such a *rudraksha*. If we go by the old *shastras*, then one *mukhi* Nepal variety remains as one of the biggest mysteries of our times.

There are several assumptions, myths and stories relating to the Nepal one *mukhi rudraksha*, some of which are:

- that only one tree bears this seed once in five or ten years (some say even each year).
- out of three seeds are created every year in one specific tree, one seed vanishes inside earth after falling, another goes to the King of Nepal, while the third is distributed randomly by hiding it inside *prasad* (of round ladoo sweets) on *Mahashivaratri* day, when lakhs of people assemble at the temple premises and the luckiest one gets it. (As there is no king now in Nepal, the saying is not relevant)
- trading of one *mukhi rudraksha* is banned in Nepal and any one found selling it can be imprisoned.
- Former Prime Minister Mrs Indira Gandhi or other

important politicians or some influential people had
one *mukhi rudraksha*

- it automatically comes on to the top if immersed in a
  bag containing rice overnight. If it is kept below *Bel
  Patra* leaves overnight, it comes on the top of the
  leaves.
- it has miraculous powers and makes the owner rich and
  famous.
- it is the cause of fame and prosperity for several film
  stars and business tycoons.

Let us evaluate some of the possibilities while studying a
one *mukhi rudraksha* in terms of references in the epics:

First possibility

There are cases where all the lines in a *rudraksha* do not
naturally get completed from one end to other and only one
line remains open and clear. Many people accept such a
rudraksha as a one *mukhi*. Such a judgment is disputable and it
is a matter of conviction to assume this bead as one *mukhi*.
This happens more often in a four *mukhi rudraksha* and some
times in five *mukhi rudrakshas*. A genuine *rudraksha* is devoid
of any tampering and each bead must have a natural hole. If
such a bead is cut horizontally, it shall show 5, 4 or 3
compartments depending on the *mukhis* it possesses.
Therefore, scientifically such a bead cannot be a one *mukhi*;
however the rarity of round one *mukhi rudraksha* compels
people to settle for any available alternative.

In some two *mukhi* Nepal variety *rudraksha*, the second line
either does not get completed fully or it is mechanically
suppressed (by putting a vice over the fruit mouth on the tree
itself before it ripens). Such a bead is also accepted as one

mukhi by many. The shape of such beads is not round as that of a genuine one *mukhi*. A genuine one *mukhi rudraksha* is one on which there is no tampering and there is only one clear line.

Second possibility

Rudraksha mentioned in *ancient scriptures* may be from regions other than Nepal. For example, the one *mukhi* bead from Indonesia. There are several *rudraksha* species and beads from these trees must have come to the notice of our wise saints. We now know that one *mukhi* from Indonesia is a genuine bead in this category. Though rare, these are available.

Third possibility

It is quite likely that the trees must have stopped producing this variety because of environmental changes resulting from pollution and the felling of old and rare trees. As the quantity of such beads is low, beads from the past are not visible now. The *rudraksha* kept at the Pashupatinath temple in Kathmandu appears as one among the rarest of beads. It has been noticed that even Indonesian one *mukhi* is not produced on a regular basis every year. It is also possible that nature has some unknown cycle or method to produce these rare beads. It might be interesting to note that as per one supplier of one mukhi of underdeveloped variety these are produced on a single tree in Nepal. This specific tree produces 1 and 2 mukhi or without any mukh only in round variety. These are accepted only on the basis of faith.

Fourth possibility

The *Sawar* is two beads naturally joined into one. Similarly, a Gaurishankar has two beads, one of which is essentially a one *mukhi*. This one *mukhi* bead is considered as a genuine one *mukhi* bead by some and they prefer to cut it out from the whole and wear it separately. Usually, there will be a hole in this bead and the shape is half moon. In many instances, the *Sawar* is used directly as a one *mukhi* bead without cutting the one *mukhi* from the twin bead.

As regards one *mukhi rudraksha* of Nepal, the following points must be borne in mind:

1. The bead shall be very expensive even if it is a *Sawar*.
2. Its shape may not be round but similar to two *mukhi Rudraksha* but in smaller size.
3. There will be a natural hole in the bead.
4. One mukhi *rudraksha* in the shape of half moon (also known as *Chandramukhi* or *Ardhchandrakar* or simply *Chandrakar*) is actually a substitute of the original and it can be procured on the basis of one's faith. The bead is from the species of *Elaeocarpus Tuberculatus* grown in South India and Sri Lanka, as already mentioned earlier.

In many instances, a *rudraksha* offered by a known saint, guru or any influential source gives excessive confidence to the recipient (because of the faith) and it is often impossible to convince him or her that the bead could be a fake one.

However, if some religious institutions are selling fake one *mukhi rudrakshas* (Nepal variety) for material gains, it is unethical and despicable.

Indonesian one *mukhi*

A genuine one *mukhi rudraksha* from Indonesia can be obtained if one has the right source. It is a small bead (max.

12 mm long and upto 6 mm in central width) having an oblong shape **(Fig. 6)**. It resembles the two *mukhi* of Indonesia but the exception is that the one line is complete on one side and on the other side it partially exists as the closing loop of the bead. In two *mukhi rudraksha*, both the lines clearly exist.

Indonesian beads of all *mukhs* have been disected and noticed that the number of inner clefts equal the number of *mukhs* outside. One *mukhi rudraksha* has one cleft inside, while a two *mukhi rudraksha* has two clefts and so on. In the case of *Chandrakar* one *mukhi*, it has one wide opening (not a hole). Such is the case with two or three *mukhi Chandrakar* too. Even Haridwar two, three and four *mukhi rudrakshas* have only one opening inside **(Fig. 10)**. This is a valid test to verify the *mukhs* in a *rudraksha* and it is fully relevant for Nepal or Indonesian beads, which also follow other characteristics as given in our ancient epics.

Indonesian one *mukhi rudraksha*, if available, is the best choice as on date for those aspiring to get one *mukhi* genuine *rudraksha*.

One *mukhi rudraksha* from other areas

Sometimes, we come across nearly round *rudraksha*-like seeds having sharp protrusions and thorns. And many a times, these beads would be having one *mukh*. However, these could be light in weight and would not be having a natural hole. Such beads are not accepted as *rudraksha*.

It is common on the streets of pilgrim centres and in large shops in places like Rishikesh, Haridwar and Banaras to see fake one *mukhi rudrakshas* openly being sold using marketing gimmicks. In several shops in Rishikesh, it is common to see such fake beads to be reverentially kept on a red cloth with a rich spread of vermilion. The salesmen will tell you that the sacred *rudraksha* will not be shown until morning, which will usually convince a naïve person of the genuineness of the bead. In most cases, such beads could be made from two or three *mukhi* Hardwar/Dehradun variety by removing one or two lines using some sharp tools. A large number of fake one *mukhi rudrakshas* is also made from five *mukhi* Nepal beads by removing four lines. **(Fig. 37)**

An artisan creating a fake one *mukhi rudraksha* will do the work only on such beads on which the lines are not deep, thus retaining the round shape even after removing four of the five lines. Such *rudraksha* beads are available from Assam area. One of the gimmicks is to stick the pieces on the bead over the lines so that a gullible person will not be able to look at the lines closely.

There are also people working on *Sheesham* or some other wood to carve *rudraksha*-shaped beads depicting *trishul*, snake, Om or *Shivling* and with one line with a deep groove. It is learnt that there are full-fledged workshops where such spurious beads are produced.

Bhadraksha beads found in Uttar Pradesh and Western Bihar areas of India are often used to make fake one *mukhi rudraksha* beads. *Bhadraksha* is a flat bead having texture and grooves resembling *rudraksha* but it can be easily identifiable. Mostly, *bhadrakshas* have two faces (3 *mukhi bhadraksha* is also found) and these are used to make one *mukhi rudraksha* by removing the line on one side and carving forms of a *Shivaling/yoni* or snake on the other.

One mukhi Chandrakar (half moon) variety of *rudraksha* has become popular in the last 15 to 20 years as a substitute to one *mukhi rudraksha*. It belongs to the **Elaeocarpus tuberculatus** species.

One *mukhi Chandrakar* is often considered as an alternative to one *mukhi* round Nepal variety. However, it is a matter of faith as it cannot be having the properties – like the natural hole, texture, density and shape of the original one *mukhi rudraksha*. In terms of internal structure, it has just one wide compartment. Even the two, three or four *mukhi Chandrakars* too have only one compartment inside which is contrary to the accepted norm of recognizing the *mukh* in a typical *rudraksha*. For wearing, it is clamped using a specially designed cage and hole is never drilled.

This *chandrakar* is, therefore, not a *rudraksha*, as per the definition given in our great ethics.

It is found that there is lot of publicity for one *mukhi Chandrakar* variety on TV channels. There is an exaggeration of the properties of this variety. All the claimed benefits are of the one *mukhi rudraksha* of Nepalese or Indonesian variety only and users must bear in mind that the half moon-shaped bead cannot match the characteristics of the genuine one *mukhi rudraksha*. These days most *chandrakar* variety is also being made manually by injection moulding and if some people are to be believed, some beads manufactured are coming from China?

Some fake *rudrakshas* are made from ordinary wood, betel nuts or seeds of wild berries with the figures of *Shivling*, snakes, moon, or *Om*, however, this practice is followed to make fake round one *mukhi* variety of Nepal.

Gaurishankar

Gaurashankar is one of the *rudraksha* varieties whose fakes are available in large numbers. It is estimated that about 10% of the entire fake *rudraksha* market consists of this variety. Usually two beads (five or six *mukhi*) are taken and cut flat on the edges and these are then glued together using superior adhesives so that the joined pieces do not come off even when these are treated with boiling water. Even ordinary wood is used to carve the *rudraksha*. In some cases, the individual pieces are joined in sections to outsmart the experts. An effective examination of a *Gaurishankar* is as follows:

1. The beads should not join close to each other in a flat way and the joint should emanate from inside the bead and not merely peripherally.

2. Use the boiling test as under:
   Boil the bead in water for about two hours. If it is a fake one joined together using common adhesives, the beads will come off. Even when quality adhesives are used, there will be discoloration at the joints indicating different colour at the joint than the beads. If it is a genuine *Gaurishankar*, the colour will be uniform throughout. This test is also useful in identifying fake beads of higher *mukhis* like *Trijuti*.

When a *Gaurishankar rudraksha* is cut horizontally, it will give the impression of a defined single bead with twin-space arrangement of beads. This may be seen in **Fig. 9**.

Sometimes, makers of fake *Gaurishankar rudrakshas* use sectional insertions so intricately that the lines are matched precisely and only sharp critical eyes can make out the joint. However, when the beads are boiled in water, there will be discoloration at these insertions.

Fake *rudrakshas* of higher *mukhis*

Rudrakshas of eight *mukhis* and above are often made out of lower *mukhi* beads. The most common method is to carve additional lines. For example, a 13 *mukhi rudraksha* can be easily made from an 11 *mukhi rudraksha*, a 14 *mukhi rudraksha* from 12 *mukhi rudraksha* and so on. This gives higher margin for the seller. For example, a 10 *mukhi rudraksha* may sell for Rs1,500, but if two additional lines are created to make it a 12 *mukhi rudraksha*, it can easily fetch him Rs 3,000. The profit is often distributed among the artisans, the trader and the retailer. If only one additional line is carved, the margin could be around Rs 800. Again, it depends on the *mukhs*. For example, if a 14 *mukhi rudraksha* is made from a 13 *mukhi rudraksha* by adding one line, the effort can get as much as Rs 5,000 per bead. It will require very close and expert examination to identity the additional line as the line tends to look nearly same as natural lines.

Often the additional line is made after heating the tool, which will normally be very sharp so that a clear line is created without any blurring. However, hot tool darkens the line.

The artisans, who create fake beads, are experts in their own way. It is for them to decide where to create the additional lines to avoid suspicion. Usually, the additional lines are created at the end of the longitudinal portion as there is more availability of space here. The artisan has also to be careful so that the lines do not look straight as created by a sharp instrument and they have to be serrated and the depth of the lines should match that of original lines.

It is unfortunate that unscrupulous elements are using this divine bead to exploit the gullibility of people. Even educated people are fooled by these elements, who pass on spurious seeds like betel nuts and berries as genuine *rudrakshas*. People should take extreme care and look for any minute differences in the size, shape and depth of the lines and reject such beads outright.

How to identify the created lines through a scientific procedure?

One way is to follow the X-ray technique **(Fig. 13)** whereby one can see the internal structure without damaging the beads. This test can work without much complication for *rudrakshas* up to nine *mukhis* but for higher *mukhi* beads, it may not give 100% accurate results due to the overlapping of the internal seeds. This technique needs to be further refined and developed as this is the only non-destructive procedure to verify the number of *mukhis*. For 10 *mukhis* and above, taking X-rays from different angles may help to count the inner seeds. CT scanning is the other way to help, but it is more expensive.

Another procedure, which is under development, is to create a standard of magneto frequency for five *mukhi* *rudrakshas* and then from the extent of frequency one can fix up the number of lines. However, the source and type of varieties, variation in the size of the beads and quality of the inner seeds are factors which can severely influence the results while using such a method. Infra-red reflection and other methods are being evaluable to identify the created lines.

In the absence of any direct scientific method as of now it

is advisable to follow the simple procedures given above for checking the originality of the beads. In simple words following can be said about checking:

1. A good and perfectly matured *rudraksha* should sink in water but this does not mean that all *rudrakshas* that do not sink in water are fake. Minute check for the lines or the joints before coming to a conclusion is required.

    A genuine *rudraksha* can also float in water if there is a hole in it and when air is trapped or if the bead has got dehydrated due to aging. There are some varieties of genuine *rudraksha* whose density is not enough to make it sink or which have been plucked from tree before maturity.

    Therefore, this test has limitations and should not lead to your final word but it can ensure that the seed was fully ripe and it belonged to a heavy variety.

2. Rotating the bead between two copper coins is also not a correct procedure as any bead having surface like that of *rudraksha* and having grooves and ups and downs can rotate in this condition.

3. Other tests like seeing whether the milk in which a bead is immersed does not ferment or the bead comes to the top automatically when kept in bag full of grains are not correct.

4. Proper examination of the bead with one's own eye is the best method available for which one does not have to be an expert. Do not buy a round one *mukhi*, even if it is available covered with a skin or with leaves or accept it if given free. Do not buy a *Gaurishankar* having flat end-to-end joint. The groove in a

Gaurishankar should join from inside as depicted in several figures shown. Higher *mukhi* beads (8 *mukhi* and above) should be examined carefully for additional artificially-created lines. Lines should be on mountains and not on ridges with certain exceptions.

5. In case of doubt, a destructive test by cutting the seed horizontally and counting the seeds inside will offer a conclusive proof. The number of seeds should be equal to the number of lines. Here again, it is absolutely necessary to understand that if the seed inside is not fully developed, then you shall see only a point or even an empty compartment instead of a seed. Normally, the inner seed is located just opposite the line. In some cases the inner seed is too large resulting from fusion of two seeds. This type of test can be useful for seeds up to 10 *mukhis*. Beads of higher *mukhis* should be examined and tested using special skills and counterchecking using CT scan techniques.

    Some of the non-destructive tests like X-ray or CT scan can be indicative but the methods are not perfected as of now and hence cannot be accepted as foolproof. These tests can be done correctly for beads up to eight *mukhis* but beyond that it may require patience and skill to count the internal seeds or additional checking using detailed visual inspection. One needs to engage an expert for this purpose, whose visual check might be correct.

6. Boiling in water for a minimum of two hours shall bring out whether the bead is created using an artificial joint. A perfect bead should remain uniform in color

even after the boiling process.

7. Always follow the guidelines to procure perfect beads, which are not damaged, have hard body, have thorny yet smooth surface and have natural hole (for highest quality beads). The color of the bead may be any, but it should be uniform throughout.

8. Predominant etching of *Om, Shivling or Trishul* should indicate that it is spurious although in some genuine beads such etching occurs, but in a very natural and merging manner.

MEDICINAL PROPERTIES 5

Rudraksha has been in use as an Ayurvedic medicine and finds mention in several books for herbal preparations both as a preventive and as a curative medicine. The residents of the area where *rudraksha* trees grow use the bark of the tree, its leaves and also the outer shell of the beads for various ailments, particularly mind-related disorders, headache, fever and skin diseases and to heal wounds. It is listed as a medicinal product in Indian *Materia Medica*. **(Ref. 41)**

As is widely known, a man's health can be properly maintained by balancing *vaat* (wind), *pitta* (bile) and *kaf* (phlegm) and without having to resort to allopathic medicines and thus protecting from their side effects. As *rudraksha* influences the mind through its subtle electro-magnetic properties, many diseases can be cured using it.

Vaat, pitta and *kaf* get regulated when a person's thought process is streamlined. This is possible as one becomes fearless and calms down and maintains a stable mind. A stable mind makes the body strong, which in turn wards off diseases.

Rudraksha may be having its effect in the following manner:

1. The subtle acupressure exerted on the body through the beads. The most advanced electro acupressure techniques

developed in China, Western Europe or the USA too adopt similar techniques. The modern gadgetry of acupressure can hardly match the natural characteristics of *rudraksha* because wherever the beads touch the body, continuously for several hours a day, which make both the mind and body to function properly.

2. Faith. Medicines cure illnesses more effectively when the patient has confidence in the doctor or on the medicine. Faith healing can take place only when one develops an inner confidence. *Rudraksha* is superior to any other form of natural healing as it is without any side effects. One does not require any special regulator or special training to wear or use *rudraksha*. Most importantly, this is the only healing technique, which uses spirituality in its most flexible form.

3. Research: There are a few published and unpublished research works on *rudraksha* showing its effectiveness as a medicine. For example, tests carried out at the University of Mumbai have established its positive impact on intelligence and memory and on cardio vascular disorders. There is ample scope for the bead to be used as an ingredient in making several herbal medicines. Experiences of local residents of the areas where *rudraksha* trees are found, have indicated that the most profound usage of this tree and the bead has been on mind-related disorders and in the control of blood pressure. Unfortunately, these beneficial aspects have never got noticed because the bead became a symbol of spirituality and its uses remained limited.

4. *Pauranic* Reference: Our ancient scriptures mention the bead as useful for several ailments.

Raj Nighantu: Rudraksha is acidic and warm and controls *vaat* and *kaf*. It removes headache, cures mental diseases.

Nepali Nighantu / Chandra Nighantu: Rudraksha belongs to Lord Neelkantha (Shiva); it is pure and destroys ghosts (all evil things). It is also known as *Sharvaksha, Shivaksha, Shivarpriya* and *Haraksha*.

Shaligram Nighantu: Properties described are similar to *Raj Nighantu*. **(Ref. 42)**

Swasth Vritta: Rudraksha is a good antidote for fever, *vaat* and *pitta*, for stomach disorders, mental imbalance, blood pressure, liver and breathing related disorders.

Dravya Gun Vigyan: Rudraksha is good for curing body swellings, infection, mental disorders, insomnia, headache, stress and for mental peace. It regulates blood flow and cures liver disorders. It is also extremely good for controlling blood pressure, breathing problems and problems of the heart. **(Ref. 43)**

Ras Yog Sagar: The beads are good for blood pressure, heart diseases and mental disorders. **(Ref. 44)**

Abhinava Nighantu: Rudraksha has heat-generating quality and is good as a remedy for poison and for diseases of children.

Vana Aushadhi Chandrodaya: Rudraksha is effective in the treatment of cancer, skin problems and tuberculosis; epilepsy, *vaat, pitta,* vomiting of blood, typhoid (the bead should be boiled in water and the concentrated form of this water should be consumed) and cough (taken in powdered form along with honey or a paste which can be made by rubbing the bead against a hard and clean surface, which can then be consumed by the patient).

Bhav Prakash: It explains various uses of shell (skin) of the bead for mental illness.

Rudraksha beads can be put in water that is meant for regular drinking purposes. Preferably, a mud pot can be used to soak the beads overnight and this is recommended for use in summer. When this water is consumed regularly in the morning on an empty stomach, it is found to control blood pressure and heart problems.

Wearing of five *mukhi rudraksha* is considered good for heart diseases and the beads are recommended to be worn in red thread and should touch the skin over the heart. The beads are also found to be very effective in treating insomnia, liver diseases, migraine and mental disorders.

In many of the references, it is recommended to take *rudraksha* in powder form twice a day and one time quantity is about 300 milligrams. The recent study done at University of Mumbai too, the recommended dosage was almost the same. (Please see page 309.)

Recent studies show that wearing *rudraksha* changes the *aura* of a person and this may lead to some changes in his or her physical condition. The results of Kirlian photography or Aura Imaging confirm this observation. While the effects of wearing *rudraksha* come to be felt rather slowly, these are always of permanent nature. It has been observed that wearing the beads helps to maintain the energy fields of a living organism properly. Although aura imaging has several flaws and inconsistencies yet there are noticeable changes in aura of persons after wearing rudraksha.

To summarize, wearing *rudraksha* is beneficial to the nervous system bringing in calmness and peace of mind. It controls blood pressure and consequently paves the way for mental stability, removal of stress and helps one to retain a healthy body.

Given below is a summary of the properties of *rudraksha* in curing various diseases. (These examples and results should be used as guidelines to understand the scope and benefit of using the beads and its potential as a medicine.)

It can be seen from the above classification that *rudraksha* is an age-old traditional medicinal herb used in various ailments. Now, whether it has to be used orally as powder or in the form of an extract or to be simply worn over the body is a matter to be seriously investigated. The benefits if any in oral administration is an interesting subject of study and several scientists are attempting to correlate the results. The emanating energy from *rudraksha mukhis* (mouth) is known to possess great remedial powers.

Rudraksha Type	Deity	Planet	Uses in illnesses
1 *mukhi*	Shiva	Sun	Thrombosis, urinary stones, respiratory diseases, heart diseases, diseases of the eyes and skin, fistula, dyspepsia, night blindness
2 *mukhi*	Ardha Nareeshwar	Moon	Heart and lung diseases, disorders of the left eye, leukaemia, liver, breast problem, loss of memory, infections and diseases of the urinary bladder.
3 *mukhi*	Agni (fire)	Mars	Infection of the blood, blood pressure, cholera, ulcer, swellings, weakness, eye protection, cleansing arteries, disorders of the sex glands and adrenal glands and cold (practically used in all health problems)

Rudraksha Type	Deity	Planet	Uses in illnesses
4 *mukhi*	Brahma	Mercury	Diseases of ear, throat and nose, paralysis, sexual problems, gall bladder diseases, memory loss, all mental ailments, diseases affecting hands, arms, lungs and thyroid gland.
5 *mukhi*	Kalagni Rudra	Jupiter	Diseases of the liver, fistula, acidity, blood pressure, breast ailments, problems of thighs, vertebral column and for memory, inflammability and cardiac problems.
6 *mukhi*	Kartikeya and Ganesh	Venus	Problems of throat, neck, kidney, sex organs, thyroid, sexuality, dropsy, urinary and eye diseases, conceiving problem, indigestion, arthritis and for all obstruction in veins/nerves
7 *mukhi*	Lakshmi, Saptarshi, Saptamatrikas, Anang (Kamdev), Anant (Snake Lord), Mahasen (Kartikeya)	Saturn	Weakness, stomach ache, paralysis, epilepsy, dumbness, impotence, abortion, problems in women, arthritis, purification of sperms and flow of ojas (divine energy)
8 *mukhi*	Mahasen (Kartikeya), Ganesh, Ashtamartrika (8 mother goddesses), Vasu, Ganesh, Batuk Bhairav	Rahu	Diseases of nervous system, prostrate, gall bladder and lungs, fear of snakes, cataract, hydrosil and breathing problems

Rudraksha Type	Deity	Planet	Uses in illnesses
9 *mukhi*	Bhairav, Nav Durga, Yamdev	Ketu	Diseases of brain, lungs, breasts, sexual organs, abortions, conceiving problems, epilepsy, eye problems
10 *mukhi*	Vishnu, Dashdigpal (Guardian of 10 directions), Yamraj, Mahasen (Kartikeya), Dash-Maha-Vidya	N.A.	Fear of someone standing behind, insomnia, conceiving problems, hear diseases
11 *mukhi*	Ekadashi Rudra (Hanuman), Indra	N.A.	Heart problems, blood pressures, diabetes
12 *mukhi*	Sun (12 Adityas), Vishnu	N.A.	All diseases of the skin, heart, eyes and nose and blood pressure, base disorders and for jyotishmati (seventh charka)
13 *mukhi*	Indra, Kamdev (along with Rati)	N.A.	Problems of throat, neck, kidney, sex organs, thyroid, sexuality, dropsy, urinary and eye diseases, conceiving problem, indigestion, arthritis, all obstruction in veins/nerves and psychiatric disorders
14 *mukhi*	Hanuman, Shreekanth Swaroop	N.A.	Weakness, stomach ache, paralysis, epilepsy, dumbness, impotence, abortion, problems in women, arthritis, purification of sperms, flow of ojas (divine energy), increase in secretions of eight charka (Vishnu)

Rudraksha Type	Deity	Planet	Uses in illnesses
15 *mukhi*	Pashupati (Shiva)	N.A.	Diseases of the heart, eyes, all general diseases, disorders of the lymph and throat area
16 *mukhi*	Lord Ram, Maha-kaleshwar	N.A.	Mental disorders, epilepsy
17 *mukhi*	Lord Vishwakarma, Katyayani Devi	N.A.	Stomach ache, skin diseases, ulcer
18 *mukhi*	Bhumi (Prithvi or earth), Avani	N.A.	Abortions, healthy child upbringing
19 *mukhi*	Narayan (Vishnu)	N.A.	For sexual disorders and various incurable diseases
20 *mukhi*	Brahma (Supreme Divinity)	N.A.	Diabetes, deafness and diseases as a result of planetary positions and to get power of eye
21 *mukhi* Gaurishankar, Shiv-Parvati	Kuber, Shiva	N.A.	To retain male power To maintain even flow of 108 frequencies in human body, fertility

Note: Consult your doctor before starting any of the above treatments oral administration of rudraksha powder has no side effects, yet prior consultation with doctor is advised.

Here are details of the effects of *Rudraksha* of various *mukhis* on different parts of the body: (This requires only wearing of *rudraksha* over the body in the form of a necklace or braclet)

1	*mukhi*	pineal, pituitary, optic chiasma, hypothalamus
2	*mukhi*	heart
3	*mukhi*	throat, celiac plexus
4	*mukhi*	adrenal, heart
5	*mukhi*	all major *chakra* points
6	*mukhi*	prostrate and reproductive organs, root *chakras*
7	*mukhi*	optic chiasma, pancreas
8	*mukhi*	medulla oblongata
9	*mukhi*	pineal, pituitary
10	*mukhi*	heart power
11	*mukhi*	abstract nerve energy
12	*mukhi*	cerebral hemisphere, hiatus of stomach, esophagus
13	*mukhi*	celiac plexus, prostrate
14	*mukhi*	heart
15	*mukhi*	ileocecal valve, lymphatic throat area system
16	*mukhi*	thyroid thymus, spleen, pancreas
17	*mukhi*	small intestine, lungs and bronchial tree
18	*mukhi*	liver, womb
19	*mukhi*	lungs, bronchial
20	*mukhi*	adrenal
21	*mukhi*	reproductive organs

For best results, *rudraksha* should be worn over the chest in proper numbers. Rare and expensive *rudraksha* can be worn along with cheaper and easily available *rudrakshas* – 12 *mukhi* with several of 5 *mukhi* or 6 *mukhi* beads – so that there are at least three beads. The beads should be bigger like *Amla* (12 mm and above) and in case only smaller beads are available (for example, Indonesian variety), use them in numbers like

27, 54 or 108. The number of beads to be worn is mentioned in Chapter 7.

Rudraksha can be worn either vertically (in the direction of its mouth) or horizontally, but in both the cases, the beads should touch the skin. How long the beads can retain their energy is difficult to say yet, because no material on earth can last for ever – be it the energy giver like a *rudraksha* or a flower that gives out its smell or a fruit that exhibits its colour. The energy packed inside *rudraksha* (the seed within the bead) normally may not decay even after 10 or 100 years, yet their effective lifespan is a matter of further study. The heavier *rudraksha* has wet seeds inside and the lighter beads have dried seeds. Nature has provided a protective and insulated outer shell so well made that the seeds do not get dried quickly and the energy gets dissipated through the *mukhi* (lines or facets) so subtly that the *rudraksha* remain effective for a very long time.

Experience gained by using the beads can answer this question to some extent. However, to be on the safer side, if *rudraksha* is being used for medicinal purposes, then the beads should be replaced after a maximum of five years.

In case the bead is being used for water therapy (whereby 3 beads of 5 *mukhis* are dipped in water at night), the effectiveness remains for one year and thereafter the beads should be replaced. The old beads can be used for worshipping as they will otherwise remain intact, except that they will turn almost black due to touch with water.

Arrangement of beads in a *mala* or combination

The epics mention that the beads should be strung in such a way that the mouth of one bead faces the mouth of another bead and the tail of one faces the tail of the other. In this way, the distances between the beads are automatically maintained. The *mala* thus made also looks balanced. However, the primary reason for such an instruction is to make the energy levels balanced. If all the beads are laid in one direction – for example all the mouths of the beads are positioned to face only one direction, say the south, then the energy flowing from each bead in the *mala* will get into the southerly direction. Hence, if the beads face each other – mouth to mouth and tail to tail – the positive and negative energies will get balanced. It is, therefore, very important to follow this principle. Even in case of small-sized beads, if one wants to have the best effects, the mouth and tail of these should be identified and strung accordingly.

Also, remember that the knot between the beads is a symbol of union of two forces. Hence it should be sanctified by chanting *Om* after each knot is placed by the artisan himself/herself. It is for this reason that *mala* making is always entrusted to a learned person having pious feelings and who follows these rituals properly. In this way, for all the 108 knots, the artisan must utter *Om* slowly and correctly. A *mala* made this way becomes a truly blessed item. In many ashrams in olden days, the Guru used to make *malas* under his own supervision choosing each bead carefully, checking the direction of the beads and placing knots in the silk/cotton thread (2½ times knot known as *Nagpash granthi*) properly, chant *Om* on completion of each knot and thus make a powerful *mala* for wearing or for *Jap*. Only the *meru mani* is placed with its mouth upwards in order to give support to the energies of all other beads.

For medical usage, it will be better if the beads are strung using a metal wire (copper, *panch-dhatu*, silver or gold). *Panch-dhatu* is an alloy of copper, bronze, gold, lead and silver. It is believed that the cumulative energies of all the beads will act all over the body, though there are differences of opinion on the beneficial uses of this method.

Rudraksha can also be worn on the wrist, arm or other parts of the body. It can be worn around waist (17 *mukhi*, 21 *mukhi*) to open *chakras* and to control internal energies. An expert's advice is recommended for such uses.

The oral administration of *rudraksha* is also done in any of the following ways:

1. Make a fine powder of the *rudraksha* after cleaning it. This powder can be orally taken in quantities of about 350 milligrams per day. (Average weight of *rudraksha* of 20 mm diameter is around three grams or 3,000 milligrams, which will mean that one *rudraksha* will be required per week.

2. Methanolic extract: Grind the beads and extract using medical grade methanol (or n-hexane). The solvent is evaporated in a distillation apparatus and then the extract obtained is orally administered to the patient in recommended dosages. Some *vaidyas*, who are unable to use extraction process, boil the crushed *rudraksha* in any edible oil (mostly *til* oil) and the oil of *rudraksha* gets mixed with *til* oil. This oil is administered as a drug. The oil may be filled in gelatin capsules and this may become one of the many ways of administrating *rudraksha* as a drug in times to come.

3. Using *rudraksha* as a paste: *Rudraksha* is rubbed over a hard and rough surface along with milk or water and a paste is prepared. This paste is orally given to the patient with additional water or milk. The efficacy of this treatment

cannot be vouched as the internal seeds are not used until the outer lignin shell is exhausted while making the paste.

4. Boiling in milk: Four or six *mukhi rudraksha* beads are boiled in milk for about 10 to 15 minutes and the milk is given to people suffering from any mental disorders, epilepsy, loss of memory and serious depression. It is also used for improving memory power and intelligence. This is a useful procedure to obtain benefits from four and six *mukhi rudrakshas*. Care should be taken to keep cleanliness of the bead after boiling. The beads should be replaced with a new set of beads after every month to get the best results. Sometimes the beads may break due to heat, but the broken pieces may continue to be used.

5. Treatment by wearing *rudraksha* over the head: A crown having 550 beads of four, five and six *mukhi rudrakshas*, if kept over the head of a person suffering from acute mental problems, may result in calmness and help the user. Some experts also make a pyramid or hut-shaped crown using *rudraksha* and make a person sit beneath it for meditation.

6. *Rudraksha* Ash (*Bhasm*): There are instances where *rudraksha* is burnt slowly and converted into ash, which is taken with milk or honey. This process needs to be scientifically investigated as *rudraksha* contains gold, barium and other metals, which can be medically effective if taken this way. In *ayurveda, bhasm* is usually made by putting the material in clay pots, which are sealed and then burnt using dry cow dung cakes. Some experts feel the properties of the seeds may get diluted or destroyed if burnt like this. Besides, the *bhasm* route of treatment needs to be examined for its usefulness.

7. *Rudraksha* Fruit's outer pulp is also a remedy for several ailments, particularly mind related diseases.

All these modalities are described in order to indicate the diversity of *rudraksha* and the manifold benefits out of its use. However, a thorough study is required to understand the best procedure to be followed and its advantage over wearing the beads over the body.

Ayurveda originated from Lord Shiva. He wears the crescent-shaped moon over his head. The moon (soma) is the preserver of all medicinal plants. Therefore *rudraksha,* being the blessed medicinal plant and its beads worn by Shiva, have special properties.

Following are some of the typical beliefs associated with the use of *rudraksha.* Some of these are known to and practiced by traditional doctors or *vaidyas.* All these need to be clinically evaluated but many of these are interesting.

Treatment by wearing:

1. It is believed that those who wear rudraksha on their right or left arm do not get paralytic strike.
2. Wearing three or five rudrakshas on the waist will give relief from back pain. The beads should invariably touch the back portion of the body.
3. Wearing mala made of five mukhi or large Nepali variety rudraksha along with 12 mukhi rudraksha can control blood pressure as well as prevent heart diseases.
4. Wearing rudraksha in the neck can give relief from ailments of the throat like tonsillitis and hoarse voice.
5. Wearing 11 mukhi rudraksha on the tuft over the head can cure headache, migraine, vertigo, *weak memory and continual cold.*

In addition to the above, I have mentioned several other treatments in the book while describing the properties of beads of different *mukhis*.

Treatment as medicine in different forms:

(These are some oral applications of rudraksha. Readers are requested to consult a vaidya, an expert or a doctor before they resort to these methods. Rudraksha is a very hard seed and making a fine powder of it is not an easy task and requires good grinding facility and sieving. If the powder is not made fine and there are hard particles of rudraksha shell, it may cause some harm.)

1. Crush *rudraksha* and put it in boiling water (the quantity of water should be six times the quantity of *rudraksha* by weight and the beads should be fresh). When it becomes one-fourth in volume, remove it from fire and use it as *quath*. When taken regularly along with honey, it is found to be useful as a blood purifier and a general tonic for energy.

2. Boil *rudraksha* along with *harad, adusa's bark* and raisin in equal quantities in water three times the weight of the herbs to make a *quath*. This *quath* can be taken along with honey as a cure for breathing problems, cough and general weakness.

3. Use the pulp of the *rudraksha* fruit or the bark of the tree or the bead itself and make powder. Use this to control epilepsy.

4. Use *rudraksha* and *apamarg* seeds four times the weight of *rudraksha* and make a *quath* as described earlier. 10 to 12 drops of the decanted *quath* should be consumed daily to cure piles. Piles can also be treated using powder made from *rudraksha, triphala* and *guggul* in the ratio of 1:4:4.

5. Make a *quath* of *rudraksha, devdaru, chitrak, harad,*

daruhaldi, giloy, saunth, punarṇava and *dharangi* in equal quantities and consume regularly to treat jaundice, stomach ache and liver problems.

6. Use *rudraksha* and the root of *kakoda* in the ratio of 1:4 and make a *quath* using one litre of water. Ninety per cent of the water should be allowed to evaporate and consume one spoon of the *quath* with twice the quantity of ghee made of cow's milk to treat poisonous effects due to bites, etc. of insects.

7. Boil four or six *mukhi rudraksha* in milk and take this milk regularly for a month to improve memory power.

8. To improve sexual power, make a paste of *rudraksha* by rubbing it on any hard and rough surface and apply the paste over the forehead. Wearing 13 *mukhi rudraksha* (for best results three beads) around neck along with six *mukhi rudraksha mala* has also been found to be very useful for this purpose.

Rudraksha as a beauty aid:

1. For wrinkles and black circles under the eye: Apply *rudraksha* paste made in water along with some drops of fresh lime and *tulsi* on the affected parts.

2. For skin diseases: Apply paste made out of five *mukhi* beads mixed with cow dung in water, preferably from Ganges, over the affected areas. This is helpful in treating ring worm infection, eczema etc.

3. For a glowing face: Mix *rudraksha* and *majeetha* powder with honey and ghee made out of cow's milk and rub the paste on the face to add a glow.

4. Clear skin: Prepare a paste of *rudraksha*, red sandalwood, leaves of *vat-vraksha* and *chameli* and apply it on the face. Wash it off with lukewarm water after 10 to 15 minutes. It will make the skin clear.

5. Removing wrinkles: Prepare a paste of eight *mukhi rudraksha* and almond seed powder in rose water, apply it on the face and leave it for about one hour. Wash the face in clean water not using soap. In a few days, it will add charm to the face and remove wrinkles. Wrinkles can also be treated in the following way: prepare a mixture out of fine powder of *rudraksha* and bark of *Arjun* tree and make a paste using honey. Apply it on face and leave it for an hour before washing with clean water.

Rudraksha to treat burns

1. Mix *rudraksha* powder in coconut oil and apply it on the affected part.

2. Mix powdered form of white sandalwood, *giloy* and *rudraksha* in limestone water (made out of adding limestone in water and decanting it) and add equal quantity of coconut oil. Apply this on the burnt part of the body.

Rudraksha to treat piles

1. Prepare a paste out of *rudraksha*, bark of *karanj* and *saur tumbi* leaves using goat's urine and add the juice of *aakada* (a type of fruit) to this. Apply this preparation locally.

2. Prepare a paste out of root of *kaner* and *rudraksha* (in a 4:1 combination) and apply it locally.

3. Take *rudraksha* and *triphala in* 1:4 ratio and prepare a paste. Mix this with honey and apply locally.

Rudraksha for hair

For premature graying of hair: Prepare a paste of *rudraksha*, iron powder, black soil and *bhringraj* and add sugarcane juice. Bury this preparation in a pot in the soil for about one month and then take it out and apply it on the hair three to four times a day. In three to four months, it will give back the natural colour of the hair and help in its growth.

Rudraksha water

Immerse three to five beads of *rudraksha* in one litre of water in earthen or copper pot for about 20 hours. Decant the water, allow the beads to dry for two to three hours and again put them back in the water for another 20 hours. Remove the beads thereafter. Drinking this water on a daily basis will help control blood pressure and is good for heart ailments. The same beads can be used upto one year.

This water can also be used in:

- headache or migraine (put a few drops in the ears)
- any external infection or wound (apply this water locally and also drink it regularly)
- cold and cough (put a few drops in the nose)
- eye diseases (put a few drops of this clear water in the eyes)

Detailed experimentation and studies were carried out at Mumbai University in the Department of Pharmacology under Professor Dr. A.V. Juvekar during the years 2005-2007. Following are the summarised finding of the same:

1. Evaluation of Anti-inflammatory activity of *Rudraksha* in experimental rats

(In all studies healthy Wistar rats sourced from Haffkine Biopharmaceuticals Corporation, Mumbai were used. Protocol as per approved practices was followed for maintaining, feeding and trials on the rats.)

Discussion and Conclusion

Herbal medicines derived from plant extracts are being increasingly utilized to treat a wide variety of clinical diseases, though relatively little knowledge about their mode of action is available. There is a growing interest in the pharmacological evaluation of various therapies used in Indian traditional systems of medicine.

Elaeocarpus ganitrus popularly known as *Rudraksha*, holds a very special place in Hinduism, and is credited to possess mystical and divine properties. *Rudraksha* beads are considered auspicious as well as powerful, and are supposed to have profound astrological and health benefits. According to the Ayurvedic medical system, wearing *Rudrkasha* can have a positive effect on the heart and nerves, and relieve you from stress, anxiety, depression, palpitations and lack of concentration. It is also known for its anti ageing effect, and electromagnetic and inductive properties. People with high blood pressure have benefited from the use of *Rudraksha* seeds. According to Ayurveda, fruits are sour, appetizer, sedative and useful in treatment of cough, bronchitis, nerve pain, epilepsy, migraine etc.

There are scanty reports that *Rudraksha* is effective in treatment and management of inflammation and related disorders. Hence the present work was undertaken to scientifically evaluate and validate the said claim.

The methanolic extract of *Rudraksha* was evaluated for its anti-inflammatory activity in acute model. Significant anti-inflammatory activity was observed for methanolic extract of *Rudraksha* in carrageenan induced oedema model. The extract showed inhibition in inflammation at the doses 200 mg/kg and 400 mg/kg. However, the extract showed maximum inhibition of 36.6% at the dose of 400 mg/kg after 3 h of drug administration. Carrageenan induced oedema is commonly used as an experimental animal model for acute inflammation and is believed to be biphasic, of which the first phase is mediated by the release of histamine and 5HT followed by kinin release and then prostaglandin in the later phase.

The overall results of the present sudy indicate that, under the given experimental conditions, methanolic extract of *Rudraksha* has anti-inflammatory activity.

2. Antidiabetic activity evaluation of *Rudraksha* powder

Introduction

Diabetes mellitus is a chronic disease in which blood glucose (sugar) levels are too high. Cells in the body break down glucose in order to provide energy for movement, growth, and repair. The hormone **insulin** is responsible for regulating glucose levels in the blood. Abnormally high levels of glucose can damage the small and large blood vessels, leading to diabetic blindness, kidney disease, amputations of limbs, stroke, and heart disease.

There are three common types of diabetes. **Type 1 diabetes** is usually (but not always) diagnosed in children and young adults. Persons with type 1 diabetes make no insulin and must take insulin every day. **Type 2 diabetes** is usually (but not always) diagnosed in adults over the age of 45. In type 2 diabetes, either the person is not making enough insulin, or the body is resistant to insulin and cannot use it properly. **Gestational diabetes** occurs during pregnancy: 2-4 percent of all pregnant women have gestational diabetes. If a woman has gestational diabetes, she has about a 40 per cent chance of having type 2 diabetes later in her life.

About 17 million persons in America have Diabetes mellitus, but five million of them don't even know it. Nearly 1 million new cases are diagnosed each year. The disease affects men and women of all ages and ethnic groups. African Americans, Latinos, American Indians, Alaskan Natives, Asian Americans, and Pacific Islanders are more affected than other groups.

Diabetes mellitus is a major endocrine disorder affecting nearly 10% of the population all over the World. In spite of the introduction of hypoglycemic agents, diabetes and the related complications continue to be a major medical problem. Since time immemorial, patients with non-insulin dependent diabetes mellitus have been treated orally by folklore with a variety of plant extracts. In the indigenous Indian system of medicine (Ayurveda), a mention was made on good number of plants for the cure of diabetes or 'madhumeha' and some of them have been experimentally evaluated and the active principles were isolated. However, search for new antidiabetic drugs continues.

Discussion

Diabetes mellitus is possibly the world's largest growing metabolic disease, and as the knowledge on the heterogeneity of this disorder is advanced, the need for more appropriate therapy increases. Traditional plant medicines are used throughout the world for a range of diabetic complications. The study of such medicines might offer a natural key to unlock a diabetologist's pharmacy for the future.

Rudraksha powder (Batch No. 013CS) at the dose levels 250,500 and 1000 mg/kg of body weight in normal non-diabetic rats shows significant decrease in blood glucose levels at 2 hr after treatment, but do not show significant decrease thereafter as compared to control group.

Streptozotocin induced diabetic rats after treatment with *Rudraksha* powder (Batch No. 013CS) for 30 days at dose levels 250,500 and 1000 mg/kg of body weight show decrease in blood sugar level as compared a baseline values (day 0 of the treatment). *Rudraksha* powder at dose 250 mg/kg does not show significant decrease in blood glucose level as compared to diabetic control group even after 30 days treatment. *Rudraksha* powder at dose levels 500 and 1000 mg/kg showed significant decrease in blood glucose level after 30 days treatment. Fifteen days after stopping the treatment there was increase in blood glucose levels of all treatment group animals. *Rudraksha* powder treated groups showed no significant decrease in blood sugar levels as compared to diabetic treated group but Glibenclamide (10mg/kg) treated group showed significant decrease in blood glucose levels of rats as compared to diabetic control group.

The *Rudraksha* powder (Batch No. 013CS) treated rats at

dose level 250mg/kg do not show significant changes in HDL-cholesterol and triglycerides levels but shows significant decrease in LDL and total cholesterol levels as compared to diabetic control group. *Rudraksha* powder at dose levels 500 and 100mg/kg (Batch No. 013CS) treated rats showed significant increase in levels of HDL-cholesterol (good cholesterol) and decrease in levels of triglycerides, LDL-cholesterol, VLDL-cholesterol and total cholesterol levels.

Conclusions

Current study indicated a significant lowering of blood sugar level with treatment of *Rudraksha* powder (Batch No. 013CS) at dose levels 500 and 1000 mg/kg of body weight in streptozotocin induced diabetes in Wistar rats. Hence *Rudraksha* might help preventing diabetic complications and serve as a good adjuvant in the present armamentarium of anti-diabetic drugs.

3. Evaluation of Cardioprotective Activity of *Rudraksha*

Introduction

Cardiovascular disorders account for 12 million deaths, annually worldwide and are known to be number one group of killer diseases. Ischemic heart disease (IHD) has emerged as a major health problem and is predicted that by the year 2020 this disease will persist as the major and the most common threat to human life.

Myocardial infarction or myocardial ischemia, commonly known as heart attack is the most dreaded among ischemic heart diseases and one of the major causes of mortality worldwide. It is associated with ischemic necrosis of cardiac muscle due to compromised supply of blood to a portion of myocardium for proper physiological function. The pathogenic mechanism of myocardial ischemic damage is still no completely understood, but the role of oxygen-derived free radicals (OFR's) in myocardial ischemia has been established although not completely characterized.

Oxidative stress is implicated in the etiopathogenesis of a variety of human diseases, including cardiovascular diseases. The antioxidant status has a major influence on the development of coronary artery diseases. Myocardial ischemia is invariably followed by several biochemical alterations, such as lipid peroxidation, free radical damage. Hyperlipidemia etc., leading to qualitative and quantitative alterations of the myocardium. Hence, screening natural compounds with antioxidant potential for their cardioprotective activity is a valid and viable approach.

Rationale & Objective of the study

There are scanty reports that *Rudraksha* is effective in treatment and management of cardiovascular and related disorders. Hence the present work was undertaken to scientifically evaluate and validate the said claim.

Discussion

Isoproterenol-induced myocardial infarction in rats has been shown to be accompanied by hyperlipidemia, increased activity of serum creatine kinase, lactate dehydrogenase and aminotransferases. Damage to the myocardium could be owing to the induction of free-radical-mediated lipid peroxidation by isoproterenol. The free radicals generated by isoproterenol administration initiate lipid peroxidation of membrane bound polyunsaturated fatty acids, leading to an impairment of structural and functional integrity of myocardial membrane.

The need for assessing the size of experimental infarction arises while evaluating the drugs for the beneficial effect against myocardial infarction. The serum enzymes serve as sensitive indices to assess the severity of myocardial infarction.

Pharmacological augmentation of endogenous myocardial antioxidants has been identified as a promising therapeutic approach in diseases associated with increased oxidative stress. During myocardial infarction these enzumes are structurally and functionally impaired by free radicals, resulting in myocardial damage. GSH has a direct antioxidant function by reacting with superoxide radicals, peroxy radicals and singlet oxygen, followed by formatting of oxidized GSH and other disulfides. The levels of endogenous antioxidant enzymes SOD, catalase and reduced glutathione were found to be significantly decreased in the heart tissue of isoproterenol treated rats. In EGM pretreated rats, there was augmentation of these endogenous antioxidant enzymes. These findings insinuate that the antioxidant enzyme systems may be directly related to the pathogenic mechanism of isoproterenol-induced myocardial infarction suggesting the protective effect of EGM on the myocardium.

Histopathological observations of the heart tissue of rats challenged with isoproterenol showed confluent necrosis, separation of muscle fibres and inflammatory infiltrations. EGM pretreatment protected these morphological changes, thus supporting the cardioprotective activity of EGM. The protection might have been mediated through EGM induced increase in basal myocardial antioxidant enzyme activities.

These results are comparable with the standard drug Captopril, which was used as a positive control in the study.

Conclusion

The present study showed that pretreatment of rats with methanolic extract of *Elaeocarpus ganitrus* (EGM) offers significant protection against myocardial oxidative stress-induced injury. (Similar results were obtained when *Rudraksha* power was used – in later studies.)

4. Evaluation of Nootropic Activity of *Rudraksha* extract

The test evaluates the drug's potential in improving learning and memory (Nootropic potential). The control cholinergic pathways play a prominent role in learning and memory.

Conclusion

Rudraksha extract significantly improved the acquisition and retention of memory in spatial memory test. It also significant improved basal and seopolamine-impared performance in all four quadrants showing.

How to Choose 6
Rudraksha and Power Combinations?

The most common and traditional way of wearing *rudraksha* is to buy a *mala* of five *mukhi* beads from a good source, ensuring that the beads are of uniform size and color, perform a normal *pooja* and prayers at home and then wear the *mala* around the neck. No specialised or expert knowledge is needed for this and thousands of people across the country have been wearing *rudraksha* in this manner for generations. (The *sadhus* and *sanyasis* wear larger beads.) In such cases, the wearer do not know anything about the beads or *rudraksha* per se, except their belief that the beads are divine, they help in spirituality and are good for health. It has also been the experience that people wearing *rudraksha*, say from the early age of 24 years, usually do not suffer from blood pressure-related problems or diabetes even though they have no knowledge about the medicinal properties of the beads. However, if we wish to adopt a rational approach to understand about the divine nature of the beads, it is necessary to know that these beads are capable of changing you from within so that you can lead a better life full of confidence and fearlessness. There are several people who wear one single *rudraksha* of five *mukhi* and claim that they have been immensely benefited. However, without disputing their claim, it must be pointed out that this type of wearing is not in accordance with the scriptures or as per the generally accepted procedures. There are different ways to follow in selecting and wearing different *rudrakshas* in multiple numbers or *rudrakshas* of various *mukhis*.

Some of the recommended practices are given below:

1. As per one's expectations: Here, the properties of different *mukhi rudraksha*s are taken as the basis and depending on the problems or expectations, the suitable *rudraksha* is chosen. For example, if you need to flourish in business and get wealth, then a combination of seven *mukhi* (Goddess Lakshmi), eight *mukhi* (Lord Ganesh) and 12 *mukhi* (Sun) beads may be selected. The basis of this suggestion is:

Seven *mukhi rudraksha* is assigned to Goddess Mahalakshmi, the goddess of wealth.

Eight *mukhi rudraksha*, assigned to Lord Ganesh, is intended to remove obstacles. Usually Mahalakshmi is worshipped along with Ganeshji. Twelve *mukhi rudraksha*, assigned to Sun, is chosen to develop administrative skills and authority, which are necessary to run a business. Also, this *rudraksha* helps the wearer to maintain good health.

In addition to this combination, if the person is suffering from high blood pressure, then three *mukhi rudraksha* (Agni) and five *mukhi rudraksha* (Kalagni) may be added or a full *mala* of 54 or 108 smaller beads may be made for wearing in order to increase the contact area over the body and to get better acupressure effects.

In case the person is suffering from blood pressure and/or diabetes, without any other expectations or problems, then five larger Nepali beads (two beads of three *mukhi* and three beads of five *mukhi*) can be strung in a *mala* along with smaller beads.

2. As per horoscope: Usually, this method is followed by priests or astrologers, whereby *rudraksha* representing a specific planet (or zodiac sign) is recommended for wearing. In such case, there is no stipulation of wearing a minimum of three beads or other combinations. *Rudraksha* is to be considered like a precious gem and has to be worn exactly like a gem. More information on this, including aspects of *rashi*, *lagna* and *nakshatra* and their correlations in choosing *rudraksha*, is given in Chapter 8.

3. Numerology: In this method, the selection of beads is done in terms of numbers associated with a person's psyche and his or her destiny. These numbers are then correlated to planets and then the most appropriate *rudraksha* is recommended. Numbers associated with names are used rarely for choosing a *rudraksha*. For many, this method gives very good results as horoscope, astrology and numerology are all combined to get the results.

4. *Guru prasad*: When a Guru or any saintly person offers any *rudraksha*, it becomes *guru prasad* and the same should be worn with extreme reverence. However, one can add other bead(s) along with this to fulfill any objective. If, for any reason the bead given by a guru or saintly person is not found to be genuine, never ever mention this to the giver, instead, the bead should be discarded with due respect in a river or sea as fake articles should not be kept at home.

Now, the first three methods of wearing is explained in details herebelow:

Wearing as per expectations

As per our ancient epics, *rudraksha* showers the blessings of gods/goddesses. These beads are much superior to gems as they have no side effects and they work with the help of spiritual effects and bio-energy. Selecting *rudraksha* according to one's problems and objectives is easy, the only pre-requisite being an ability to understand the properties of beads of various *mukhis*. You may wear several numbers of the same *mukhi rudraksha* or a combination of different *mukhis*. For example, if you have a problem of concentration and are not able to focus – in other words, if you have a wavering mind – then you can wear a complete *mala* of four *mukhi rudraksha* (27 beads of Nepali origin or 108 beads of Indonesian small-sized beads). Similarly, you may combine seven, eight and 12 *mukhi rudraksha* to gain wealth through any business activity or through a career in a senior position. (seven *mukhi* is assigned to Goddess Lakshmi, eight *mukhi* to Lord Ganesh to remove obstacles and 12 *mukhi* to Sun to give you immense energy/power to perform)

Some details in this regard are:

Objective	Recommended *Rudraksha*
Relationship problems within or outside the family	Two *mukhi* (preferably from Nepal) and/or a *Gaurishankar*
Life full of obstacles	Eight *mukhi*, or 11 *mukhi*, or 19 *mukhi*
Wavering mind, mental weakness	Four, six, eight or 11 *mukhi*
If the profession requires oratory skills, artistic presentation, charm (for marketing professionals, leaders, film stars, HRD persons)	13 *mukhi* (an alternative is six *mukhi*)

Objective	Recommended *Rudraksha*
Anxiety, sleep disorders	10 *mukhi*
Power for administration, authority, physical stamina	12 *mukhi*
Protection from jealousy, evil eye, black magic	10 *mukhi*, (for extra power, add nine, 11 *mukhis*)
Total protection from fear of physical nature, threats, loneliness.	Nine, 10 and 11 *mukhis* together
For marriage as well as for marital life	Two mukhi (Nepal preferably) good along with *Gaurishankar*
Victory over adversaries	16 *mukhi*
Winning in lottery, horse racing speculative businesses, etc.	17 *mukhi*, 14 *mukhi*
Education, memory, concentration General health, specifically hypertension, diabetes	Four *mukhi* and six *mukhi*
Stomach disorders with three and five *mukhis*	12 *mukhi* in combination
New projects, launch of public issues, large stakes in any large venture	18 *mukhi*
To solve problems related to sicknesses of children	18 *mukhi* or 12 *mukhi*
Wealth along with better visualization power	15 *mukhi*
Siddha meditation, one stop family protection and success in any type of profession	One *mukhi* to 14 *mukhi*, *Gaurishankar*, Ganesh (*siddha mala*)

Objective	Recommended *Rudraksha*
Meditation (high level)	One, three, five, nine and 11 *mukhi* and *Gaurishankar*
Meditation standard	Five *mukhi mala*, one *mukhi* or *Gaurishankar*
Living abroad, needing protection/Progress	One to 14 *mukhi siddha mala* or 11 *mukhi* or a *Trijuti*
For excellence in any field	14, 17, 19, 20 *mukhi* or a *Trijuti*
To get materialistic as well as spiritual bliss and total protection of high order	*Indra mala* (one to 21 *mukhi*) with *Trijuti*

This can at best be a guideline. Depending on one's budget and the analysis of problems and on the basis of priority, one may wear *rudraksha* initially in small numbers and use lower *mukhi* less expensive beads before gradually opting for rare and expensive beads.

The details are only illustrative and not exhaustive to cover the entire range of expectations as it is not possible to do so. However, it is strongly advised to understand that the price or rarity of beads has nothing to do with their powers. A cheaper and easily available six *mukhi rudraksha* may be more valuable and useful to you than higher *mukhi rudraksha* in terms of your specific needs. It is more so if the usage is for medicinal application. For example, to control blood pressure, a five *mukhi rudraksha* can be more effective than a 13 *mukhi* expensive *rudraksha*.

To help you to understand the logic behind selecting a particular combination, we give herebelow some examples:

a. Recommendation of individual beads

You may read individual bead properties carefully and try to correlate them to your own self so as to fill the lack of a particular aspect, which a particular *rudraksha* can do for you. For example, if your life is full of obstacles and nothing gets done easily or everything comes to a standstill at the last moment when actually you should have got success, then go for an eight *mukhi* (*Ganesh*) and add some additional beads to gain increased self confidence (like nine *mukhi* or 11 *mukhi*).

Individual beads can be chosen based on bead properties given in Chapter 2. Typical examples are given as under:

ONE *MUKHI RUDRAKSHA*

Personal Information and Concern

Spiritual Growth, higher state of consciousness and peaceful life, materialistic detachment.

Reference Information

One *Mukhi Rudraksha* is the symbol of Godhood, supreme truth and attainment of eternity. This *rudraksha* enlightens the super consciousness. One *Mukhi Rudraksha* is the symbol of the Supreme God. It brings the power to concentrate on an object. The wearer of one *Mukhi Rudraksha* experiences a change in the mental structure and brings beings to concentrate on the Supreme element.

Recommendation

Minimum of 1 Bead of the one *Mukhi Rudraksha* capped in gold or silver and strung on red thread or metal of choice also the wearing of as many of the one *Mukhi* as a person chooses to wear on a mala.

Now depending on your budget and availability, choose half moon shape or a genuine Indonesian one *Mukhi*.

TWO *MUKHI RUDRAKSHA*

Personal Information and Concern

Better family life and relationships with friends. Need peaceful relationship with family relatives and need to have more friends and maintain friendship.

Reference Information

The two *Mukhi Rudraksha* is the symbol of ArdhaNareeshwara, a joint image of Lord Shiva and Goddess Parvati as Shakti. It brings unity like the family unity in form, speech and meaning. The wearer's family finds the reverence and faith continuously increasing among themselves. The two *Mukhi Rudraksha* removes the differences of opinions and establishes unity between the teacher and pupil, the father and son, the husband and wife and friends. The wearer becomes capable of leading peaceful and sacred family life. Choose a Nepal two *Mukhi* Indonesian two *Mukhi* of Haridwar/Dehradun two *Mukhi* in order of purity & preferences.

THREE *MUKHI RUDRAKSHA*

Personal Information and Concerns

Daily unexplained problems which has destroyed quality of life and happiness causing intense anger, depression, anxiety, mental confusion, subjective fear and guilt, laziness.

Reference Information

Ruling planet Mars

Three *Mukhi Rudraksha* is the symbol of the God Agni and it purifies everything in the same way. The wearer gets rid of the sins done in past life and returns to a pure life.

It is the best for those who have fallen prey to inferiority complex or fear stricken and suffer from self hatred and mental strain.

FOUR *MUKHI RUDRAKSHA*

Personal Information and Concerns

Concentration and success in studies and research projects.

Reference Information

Ruling planet Mercury

The four *Mukhi Rudraksha* Bead is influenced by the creative wisdom of the four headed Lord Brahma. This *Rudraksha* gives the Wearer creative power and provides him learning and knowledge. All students must wear it. This *Rudraksha* is beneficial to teacher, scientist, intellectual, artist, writer and journalist. It increases wit and intelligence.

FIVE MUKHI RUDRAKSHA

Personal Information and concerns

High blood pressure, hypertension caused by high emotional tenstion, memory loss and difficulties remembering, depression, anxiety and diabetes.

Reference Information

Ruling planet Jupiter

The five *Mukhi Rudraksha* is the form of Lord Rudra named Kaalagni. We can recover our memory and recollect or remember the lost learning only after wearing the five *Mukhi Rudraksha*. Five *Mukhi Rudraksha* rectifies all the vices and faults of Jeeva and makes the wearer pure and Jeeva gains the form of pashupati the Lord of all creatures after becoming free from animal instincts. By wearing its Mala the mind of the wearer remains peaceful and as per Shiva Puran the wearer of five *Mukhi Rudraksha* never gets untimely physical death.

SIX MUKHI RUDRAKSHA

Personal Information and Concerns

Need recognition for supervisory and management skills and success in research, investigation and discovery work. Legal problems, personal relationships.

Reference Information

Ruling Planet Venus

The six *Mukhi Rudraksha* is the center of the power of Lord Kartikeya, second son Lord Shiva. This *Rudraksha* gives us learning, wisdom and knowledge and saves us from worldly sorrows. Lord Kartikeya influences the acquisition of leadership qualities and increased energy and courage.

SEVEN *MUKHI RUDRAKSHA*

Personal Information and Concerns

Business and investment income loss, financial difficulties, delay in achievements affecting physical health and feeling of hopelessness.

Reference Information

Ruling planet Saturn

Good health is blessed to the wearer of the seven *Mukhi Rudraksha*. This *rudraksha* needs to be worn by those suffering from miseries pertaining to body, finance and mental set up. By wearing the seven *Mukhi Rudraksha* the wearer can progress in business and service and spends life happily. This can be kept in safe, lockers or cash box.

EIGHT *MUKHI RUDRAKSHA*

Personal Information and Concerns

Difficulty in completing planned organized projects, interruptions in life limiting progress, losing business in contract negotiations, losing debates, feelings of frustration and anger due to lack of progress and problems with obstacles in life that limit freedom of action.

Reference Information

Ruling planet Rahu

The eight *Mukho Rudraksha* is Lord Ganesha who is worshipped prior to any other God. The wearer becomes unaffected by miseries that are physical, divine or mental. It gives the wearer all kinds of Riddhies and Siddies and leads to Shivloka. The Lord Ganesha Rudraksha also supports and influences clear intellect, gaining knowledge, improving finances and success in action.

NINE *MUKHI RUDRAKSHA*

Personal Information and Concerns

Persons experiencing unexplained fear, physical, weakness, lack of concentration and depression. Also people willing to increase their spiritual strength and for their protection peace of mind and self-confidence.

Reference Information

Ruling planet Ketu

The nine *Mukhi Rudraksha* is the form of Goddess Durga. The worshippers of the supreme power Shakti must wear this *Rudraksha*. This Rudraksha is the shield of Durga that protects against anything and everything that might harm the wearer. This is one of the most important Rudraksha for Women as nothing can destroy the shield of Goddess Durga.

The Goddess Durga nine *Mukhi Rudraksha* increases self power and makes the wearer fearless. By wearing the nine *Mukhi Rudjraksha* the wearer get the Blessings of Shakti the supreme mother and also gets endurance, bravery courage and name and fame spreads all around. Devotion to God increases and will power is strenghened.

TEN *MUKHI RUDRAKSHA*

Personal Information and Concerns

Need to pacify planetary influences from all nine planets. To nullify effects of jealousy, legal problems evil eye and insomnia.

Reference Information

Held to control all planets

The ten *Mukhi Rudraksha* contains the influence all planets and ten directions. Lord Vishnu becomes happy with the person who wears it. It is useful in pacifying nine planets. All sins done by the human organs are destroyed by wearing it.

ELEVEN *MUKHI RUDRAKSHA*

Personal Information and Concerns

Lack of self confidence, instability in business, fear of unknown, poor in diplomacy.

Reference Information

The Lord Human elevan *Mukhi Rudraksha* helps the people by removing the obstacles in yogic practices. It is an effective and successful *Rudraksha*. It makes the wearer strong and without disease. It also help in practicing meditation and religious rituals wearer gets stability in business or profession.

TWELVE *MUKHI RUDRAKSHA*

Personal Information and Concerns

Specific problem in life resulting in lack of recognition and respect in the work place, lack of personal relationship and friends, limited prospects for the future, lack of exciting and fulfilling life, lack of financial advancement and boredom.

Reference Information

The twelve *Mukhi Rudraksha* blessed by Lord Sun is the center of brilliancy, luster, radiance and strength. By wearing it there will be no worry, fear or suspicion. It gives the wearer money, knowledge, riches and all the earthly pleasures. The wearer gets administrative capacity limitlessly with the quality of the sun to move continuously with brilliant radiance and strength.

THIRTEEN *MUKHI RUDRAKSHA*

Personal Information and Concerns

Leadership power, name and fame, attraction. Excellence in fine arts, writing and oratory.

Reference Information

The thirteen *Mukhi Rudraksha* is the from of Lord Indra and Kamdeva.

The *Rudraksha* fulfills all the earthly desires and gives eight accomplishments or Siddhies. The god cupid Kamdeva is pleased with the wearer and fulfills all the wordly desires. It improves oratory power, charm and convincing power. It also helps in improving sexual performance.

FOURTEEN *MUKHI RUDRAKSHA*

Personal Information and Concerns

Need *Rudraksha* to wear for future sight, improve visualization and also meditation.

Reference Information

The fourteen *Mukhi Rudraksha* pleases Lord Shiva and gives the wearer power to see the future. It is the most precious divine thing known as Deva Mani. It awakens the sixth sense by which the wearer foresees the future happenings. It's wearer never fails in decision and gets rid of all the calamities, miseries and worries. The fourteen *Mukhi*

Rudraksha provides the wearer with safety and riches.

GAURI SHANKAR

Personal Information and Concerns

Marriage, family problems meditation and emotional stress.

Reference Information

A Gauri Shankar is a two naturally joined *Rudraksha*. This *Rudraksha* is the unified form of Lord Shiva and the Goddess Uma. This form becomes the cause of expansion of the universe providing fertility. It makes the husband and wife identify each other. Therefore it is considered the best thing for peace and unity in the family. It is a powerful for meditation also.

GARBH GAURI SHANKAR

Personal Information and Concerns

Difficulties in conception and possibly full term delivery.

Reference Information

Garbh Gauri Rudraksha is a form of Gauri Shankar where one bead is smaller that the other and it is recommended for those women who suffer defects in their conception and are prone to abortion.

b. Power combinations

Some people believe that only one type of *rudraksha* should be worn and different *mukhis* should not be mixed. For example, you may wear 27+1 beads of six *mukhi* only and not a combination of different *mukhis*. One person, who is known for a lot of controversial commercial actions of a well known institution, has even called the combination a "cocktail". This is not correct as our epics say that various *mukhis* should be procured with efforts and worn. The experience of thousands of people is a testimony to the fact that any combination which suits individual requirements can be worn.

There are several combinations possible with 23 types of *rudraksha* (one to 21 *mukhis*, *Gaurishankar* and *Ganesh*) by taking into consideration various factors such as:

Personal problems

Family problems

Professional problems

Health related issues

Horoscope influence (for believers)

External factors like jealousy/evil eye etc

Inherited mental setup

Legal issues

It all depends on the individual trying to choose his/her combination or on the person who recommends a suitable combination for him/her as to what factors are getting the priority and what are their own experiences of different *rudrakshas*. For example, someone will say 11 *mukhi rudraksha* has been amazingly useful for him in life or a six *mukhi* has been continuously giving good results. This has led to a strong build-up of faith in favor of *rudraksha* with certain *mukhis* and there can never be a unanimous view in this diversified world and with so much variable factors.

Even then, based on the vast experiences and pool of information, certain defined power combinations have been in use since the last several years. **(Fig. 38)**

Some of the details and the related benefits are as follows:

1. UNITY COMBINATION

Two beads of two *mukhi* and one bead of *Gaurishankar*, when used in a three-bead combination, is called Unity Combination (*Ekta Bandh*).This combination helps in the removal of differences of opinion among people and bring them closer to each other emotionally and thought-wise. It is good for family life, to improve relationships between the wearer and others (especially for married couples) and to improve relationships in the outside world with friends and colleagues. Although it is recommended that both the parties should wear to improve relationships, even one person, who wears this combination, will get the benefits as he or she is able to influence others.

The two *mukhi* beads preferred in this combination are the Nepal varieties. Since these beads are rare and expensive, one can settle for Haridwar/Dehradun variety beads also. The *Gaurishankar* may be from Nepal or Indonesia.

2. MOON BRACELET

Nine beads of two *mukhi rudraksha* preferably with pearls and silver spacers) make this bracelet to be worn on right hand. It pacifies malefic effects of planet Moon and as such controls anger and emotional behaviour. Those desiring calmness, peace of mind and harmony in family should wear this.

3. DURGA BRACELET

This bracelet has a nine *mukhi* (Durga) *rudraksha* with *sphatik* beads and two or four five *mukhi* small-sized *rudraksha* beads. This is worn on the left hand. The wearer becomes free from tensions generated within the family due to health problems of the family members, education of children, worry about husband's or wife's welfare and stress due to insecurity within the family life. The wearer gets energy, dynamism, fearlessness and mental strength.

4. SARASWATI

Two beads of four *mukhi* (Brahma) and one bead of six *mukhi* (Kartikeya) makes a *Saraswati* combination. It is useful for children to get concentration in studies, enhancement of memory and for good expression skills in writing or oral presentation. This three-bead combination has helped thousands of students to make a bright career. If a child is seven years or lower in age, then he/she can be given only one bead of four *mukhi*. For those above this age, the full three-bead combination can be used.

5. SWASTHYA

This combination is for those who do not wish to wear a full *mala* of smaller beads and want to maintain good health and protect themselves from general diseases. Usually, minor blood pressure problems or diabetes of initial stages can be controlled by using this five-bead *Swasthya* combination. It consists of two beads of three *mukhi* and three beads of five *mukhi*. To improve performance of this five-bead combination, many people get it attached to a five *mukhi mala* of smaller beads so that they are able to get a good coverage over the chest. Usually the *Swasthya* combination is used along with water therapy described in this chapter for better results.

6. DOSH NIVARAN

This combination is highly effective to rectify any *Vaastu* defect in the residential or commercial premises, or to nullify the ill-effects of jealousy, black magic, evil eye or any planetary bad influence. It consists of one bead of 10 *mukhi* strung in *sphatik* beads with a mercury ball (optional) attached to it at the bottom. This can be hung on the ceiling at any place without any hindrance to it and free area around it. It also helps in keeping the temperaments of people living in the house cool and the atmosphere remains very peaceful. Sometimes, a 12 *mukhi rudraksha* is used in place of 10 *mukhi*. This can be a good alternative for neutralising planetary effects.

7. PROTECTION COMBINATION

A combination of nine, 10 and 11 *mukhi rudrakshas* is recommended to remove fear of any kind and to instill confidence to face all adverse situations bravely. This can be fear of ghosts or lack of confidence or threats of physical assault. The beads can be worn on the left hand or around the neck. Sometimes, a few mercury beads are added to this combination to ward off evil effects created by opponents.

8. AJNA CHAKRA

This is a 14 *mukhi rudraksha* to be worn on the head touching the middle portion between the eyebrows or worn around neck. The 14 *mukhi rudraksha* is a powerful bead, also known as *Dev Mani*. It neutralises the effects of *Sade Saati* and also improves visualization power.

9. NAVAGRAHA SHANTI

This is a combination of three, five, 10, 11 and 12 *mukhi rudrakshas* to be worn around the neck. 10 and 11 *mukhi rudrakshas* remove negative planetary effects, while three and five *mukhi rudrakshas* remove negative effects of bad karmas committed and 12 *mukhi rudraksha* gives the confidence to look forward in life using the untiring power of the Sun.

10. DHYAN YOG

These combinations are for meditation purposes. There are different *malas* and combinations popular among people:

a. A simple five *mukhi mala* of 108+1 or 54+1 or 27+1 beads (most common being 108+1).

b. A five *mukhi mala* having one *Gaurishankar* at the top and one *mukhi* at the *meru* (Total number of beads including *Gaurishankar* and one *mukhi* should be 108+1.

c. A five *mukhi rudraksha mala* having the following beads: three, five, nine, 11 *mukhis, Gaurishankar* and 1 *mukhi*. This is known as *Dhyan Yog mala* as it covers all the aspects required for better concentration and meditation like good health (three and five *mukhi*), fearlessness (nine and 11 *mukhi*), identification with God (*Gaurishankar*) and Shiva's blessings (one *mukhi*). All these beads are strung in a five *mukhi* smaller bead *mala*, the total number of beads being 108+1, including large and small beads.

d. A 32 or 32+1 bead *Kantha* of large-sized *Gaurishankar* beads is used by *sanyasis* or those fully dedicated to spiritual work. While meditating, these people wear this *kantha* and *manasik* (silent) *japa* is carried out while

counting is done with the small-sized beads strung in
another *mala*. This combination is not recommended
for family persons. At best it can be kept in a *pooja*
place.

e. Higher level of meditation is done by using 14 *mukhi*
    rudraksha tied on the head keeping it at the *Ajna Chakra*
    and counting of the *mantra* using a *mala* of either five
    mukhi or 2 *mukhi rudrakshas*. It is useful for *kundalini*
    awakening, by combining the meditation with
    Pranayams and going upwards with *chakras*.

11. MOHINI POWER

A combination of two beads of six *mukhi* and one bead of
13 *mukhi rudrakshas* is used to increase affability and to
become acceptable to the masses or to one's own near and
dear ones. It is known as Mohini combination. Indra and
Kaamdev (Cupid) are the ruling gods for 13 *mukhi* and
Kartikeya rules the six *mukhi*. It can be used either for
physical attraction or to increase likeability from within. This
combination is very popular with young couples or those who
are artists, actors, anchors or leaders. Professionals with
marketing responsibilities or in HR may also find it useful.

12. VICTORY COMBINATION

Those who are fighting legal cases or involved in property
or any type of disputes or those facing serious competition
while marketing their products, find this combination very
useful. It has one bead of 10 *mukhi*, one bead of 11 *mukhi*
and one bead of 16 *mukhi*. The *jai rudraksha* having 16 *mukhis*
can defeat the adversaries and bring in victory while offering
full protection through 10 *mukhi* (Vishnu) and 11 *mukhi*
(Hanuman).

13. BUSINESS COMBINATIONS

For achieving success in business, the combination of seven *mukhi* (Mahalakshmi) and 8 *mukhi* (Ganesh) *rudrakshas* are used. Some people wear only a Ganesh-Lakshmi combination consisting of two beads of seven *mukhi* and one bead of eight *mukhi*. In other cases, depending on the type and nature of businesses, one seven *mukhi* and one eight *mukhi* along with additional beads as given below are also used:

> ➤ nine *mukhi* for working women.
> ➤ 10 *mukhi* for those lacking in direction or wishing to change their line of business. 10 *mukhi rudraksha* also helps those facing lot of hurdles or are also susceptible to evil eye or feel they are haunted by black magic.
> ➤ 11 *mukhi* for stability in business and for traders.
> ➤ 12 *mukhi* for those having manufacturing activity or construction/property business. 12 *mukhi* is worn singly also as *Surya* pendant and is believed to protect the wearer from various diseases. It will also bring in success in business.
> ➤ 13 *mukhi* for those engaged in marketing/brokerage work/any business related to art. If someone is persuing a political career, then 13 *mukhi* is useful.
> ➤ 14 or 15 *mukhi* for those engaged in speculative business like share market, property market, import-export, recruitment or anyone in senior and responsible position.
> ➤ 17 *mukhi* for those awaiting for an opportunity to acquire properties or finance and those wanting success to occur immediately.
> ➤ 18 *mukhi* for those involved in large projects, or for safety of children.

> ➢ 19 *mukhi* for highest level of competitions, against
>   black magic and jealousy.

> ➢ 20 and 21 *mukhis* for achieving highest level of success
>   and fame.

There are three other combinations using multiple
rudrakshas, which are used to achieve all round success and
can be used by any one engaged in business or profession:

Mangal Mala

Rudraksha from one to 10 *mukhi*, *Gaurishankar* and *Ganesh*
are used in this combination. With 10 *mukhi* as the lead bead,
this *mala* offers protection against enmity, competition, black
magic etc. Seven and eight *mukhi rudrakshas* offer prosperity
and remove obstacles and nine *mukhi rudraksha* makes one
fearless. *Mangal mala* is used for general welfare of self.

Siddha Mala

All *rudrakshas* mentioned in our scriptures, from one to 14
mukhis, *Gaurishankar* and *Ganesh* are used to make this
extremely powerful and popular combination. A *siddha mala* is
considered as one-stop solution for most of the general
problems one encounters in day-to-day life like obstacles,
stress, fear, legal issues and family problems. The 14 *mukhi* in
this *mala* improves the visualisation power so that wrong
decisions are not taken and one can judge what type of
people one is dealing with. Safety of self and entire family is
provided by this powerful combination. In *Shiva Puran*, Lord
Shiva says that one who wears all the beads (from one to 14
mukhis) becomes full of *Shaivatva*.

There are several designs possible for this type of *mala*. The beads can be in ascending order, that is, from one *mukhi* to 14 *mukhi* and at the bottom a *Gaurishankar* can be used; or all even number beads (two, four, six, eight *mukhi* etc.) can be on one side and odd numbers (one, three, five, seven, nine, etc.) on the other side with *Gaurishankar* in the centre (**Fig. 39**).

Some of the designs use a *Ganesh rudraksha* after every *mukhi* bead. If there are 15 beads in the *mala* from one to 14 plus a *Gaurishankar*, then 14 *Ganesh rudraksha*s are used, one after each bead.

In a *siddha mala*, one can use small beads around neck and the bigger beads at the lower end, or use all bigger beads as illustrated in various designs of this *mala*.

A *siddha mala* should preferably be worn touching the body or it should be kept at the place of worship at the feet of Lord Shiva's statue or near the *Shivaling*. The *mala* can be worn by the worshipper during his/her meditation and as long as required and then kept back again at the *pooja* place.

Sidha mala can be made in wool or any metal like copper, silver, gold or *panch dhatu*. It is a very precious possession a family can have and should be regularly energized using the ritual of *abhishek* or by chanting of mantras dedicated to Lord Shiva or using the seed mantras and following the worshipping procedure given in Chapter 9.

Indra Mala

Indra or *Indrakshi mala* is the rarest of all *malas*, which can be made, acquiring all possible beads from nature. It has one to 21 *mukhi*, *Gaurishankar* and *Ganesh* beads. A *trijuti* is also added, if available, but is not compulsory **(Fig. 40)**. It is said that the wearer of *indra mala* can fulfill all of his/her desires – both materialistic and spiritual.

All negativities, as a result of jealousy, evil eye, ghosts or from the fear of unknown get removed by using this *mala*. It gives blessings of all Gods whether in incarnation form (*Sagun*) or in the *Brahma Swaroop* (*Nirgun*).

As per one unofficial survey done in the year 1989, there were only five such *malas* in the world, one of which was outside India. Another estimate is that up to the year 2006, there were 25 such *malas* in the whole world including India. The estimate is based on availability of 20 and 21 *mukhi rudrakshas* from Nepal, which were traded each year. There is no statistical data of traditionally-owned *malas* of this type, which surely existed in few well-off families. *Indra mala* made from Indonesian beads exist in larger numbers.

An ideal *indra mala* is made with total of 108 beads, out of which one to 21 *mukhis*, *Gaurishankar* and *Ganesh* make up for 23, while the rest should be five *mukhis*. It is believed that 108 types of *Gayatri* in different forms reside in this *mala* and is therefore divinely powerful. A *mala* of 27+1 beads is also popular, and here, other than 21 beads (1 to 21 *mukhis*), a *Gaurishankar* and *Ganesh*, five beads of any *mukhs* are added.

Indra mala can be worn or kept at the place of worship and due care should be taken to maintain it in view of the rarity of the beads. For example, all beads should be firmly fastened with wires or thread and preferably capped using silver or gold for protection of the beads at their mouth or tail. Monthly cleaning of the beads and application of oil as described for bead maintenance should be strictly followed, if the *mala* is being worn. If it is being kept at *pooja* place, then keep some camphor near the *mala* and make the place insect-free.

As people who can afford this type of *mala* are either from the rich class and/or are deeply devoted to Lord Shiva, it is difficult to get a clear opinion as to what this *mala* does after one wears it! Our experience is that only spiritually inclined and pious people or really rich people go for such investments and they get full return for this in terms of protection, name and fame. People attach several mystical stories to this *mala* but they may not be entirely correct. However, it is true that those who possess these beads and either wear them or keep them at *pooja* place with devotion, always retain their top positions in their business or profession.

Following set of seed *mantras* may be used to charge and worship this mala:

One mukhi	:	Om Hreem Namah
Two mukhi	:	Om Namah
Three mukhi	:	Om Kleem Namah
Four mukhi	:	Om Hreem Namah
Five mukhi	:	Om Hreem Namah
Six mukhi	:	Om Hreem Hum Namah
Seven mukhi	:	Om Hum Namah,
Eight mukhi	:	Om Hum Namah
Nine mukhi	:	Om Hreem Hum Namah
10 mukhi	:	Om Hreem Namah Namah
11 mukhi	:	Om Hreem Hum Namah

12 mukhi   :   Om Kroam Kshoam Roam Namah

13 mukhi   :   Om Hreem Namah

14 mukhi   :   Om Namah

Gaurishankar and Ganesh: Om Namah Shivaya

Higher *mukhi* and special *rudrakshas* can be worn using *Panchakshari* mantra or *Mahamrityunjaya mantra*. In some books, special *mantras* have been mentioned for these:

15 mukhi   :   Om Haim Sum Hreem Aim Om

16 mukhi   :   Om Vaam Kram Taam Hlaam Aim Shreem

17 mukhi   :   Om Hlaam Kraam Kshaum Swaha

18 mukhi   :   Om Hleem Shreem Kleem Saum Aim Hreem

19 mukhi   :   Om Hum Sum Aim Hreem Shreem

20 mukhi   :   Om Gyam Gyeem Lum Um aim

21 mukhi   :   Om Heem Heem Heem Shreem Shreem Shreem aim

INDRAKSHI STOTRA

Namo Devi Indrakshi srushti sthiti karini
Namah kamal patrakshi sarvadhare namostute
Savishwa taijas praagya viraat sutratnike namah
Namo vyakrat rupaye kootsthaye namo namah
Durge sargadi rahite dushta sanrodhanargale
nirargal prem gamye bharge devi namostute
Namah shree kalike matarnamo neel saraswati
Ugrataare mahogrey tai nityamaiva namo namah
Namah peetambare devi namastoipursundari
namo bhairavi maatangi ghoomavati namo namah
Chhinamaste namostute ksheersagar kanyake

Namah shaakambharee devi namaste rakta dantike
Nishumbha shumbha dalinee, raktabeej vinaashini
Dhoomralochan ninaarshe vritrasur nivarhini
Chandmund pramathini daanavaantkare shive
Namaste vijaye gange, sharade vikachaachane
Prithvi rupe daya rupe taijorupe namo namah
Praan rupe, maha rupe bhoot rupe namostute
Vishwa moorte daya moorte dharma moorte namo namah
Dev moorte, jyoti moorte, gnan moorte, namostute
Gayatri varde devi saavitri cha saraswati
Namah swahe swadhe matardakshine te namo namah
Naitnaiteeti vakyerya boadhate sakalaagamaih
Sarvapratyak swaroopam taam bhajaamah pardevataam
Bhramarair vashtikaa yasmaad bhraamari ya tatah smrahta
Tasyai devayai namo nityam nityamaiva namo namah
Namaste parshvayoh prushthe namaste puratombike
Namah urdhav namashchadhah sarvatraiva namo nahah
Kripaam kuru mahaadevi manidwipaadhi vaasini
Anant koti brahmaand nayakai jagadambikai
Jaya devi jaganmatarjay devi paraatparai
Jay shri bhuvaneshaani jay sarvottmoottame
Kalyaan gun ratnaamaakarai bhuvaneshwari
Praseed parmeshaani praseed jagtoranai
Dinakar poonamaanandam parmaanand maarateem
Namaste maatararidrakshi nityamaiva namo namah

NUMBER OF *RUDRAKSHA* 7
TO BE WORN

There are two approaches to determine how many *rudrakshas* one should wear. In the first approach, one can follow what the epics say about the number of beads to be worn on specific body parts like the neck, the wrist, the arm and so on. The second approach is to follow the traditions practised in the society in which one lives or the family to which one belongs, as these have also got evolved based on beads' availability and experiences.

The number of *rudrakshas* to be worn on different parts of the body as recommended in our epics is summarized as follows:

Body parts/organs	No of beads	Epic sources
Shikha (crown hair)	1	*Shrimad Devibhagavata*
Wrists (both right & left)	12/12	*Shrimad Devibhagavata*
Neck	32	*Shrimad Devibhagavata*
Forehead	40	*Shrimad Devibhagavata*
Ears (both right & left)	6/6	*Shrimad Devibhagavata*
Chest	108	*Shrimad Devibhagavata*
Shoulders	500	*Shrimad Devibhagavata*
Yajnopaveet (sacred thread)	108	*Shrimad Devibhagavata*

Body parts/organs	No of beads	Epic sources
Neck	2 rows	*Shrimad Devibhagavata*
Other parts of the body e.g. as earrings, crown, waist belt, in abdomen, etc.	3 rows	*Shrimad Devibhagavata*
Crown	550	*Shiva Puran*
Crown	1,100	*Shiva Puran*
Yajnopaveet (sacred threat)	360 (3 rows) & 120 each	*Shiva Puran*
I (crown hair)	1 & 3	*Shiva Puran*
Ears (both right & left)	6/6	*Shiva Puran*
Neck	101, 50, 32	*Shiva Puran*
Forearm (both righ & left)	11, 16, 24	*Shiva Puran*
Karpoordvara	11	*Shiva Puran*
Wrists (both right & left)	11, 12	*Shiva Puran*
Yajnopaveet (sacred thread)	3 strings each of 108	*Shiva Puran*
Waist region	5	*Shiva Puran*
Forehead	30, 40	*Shiva Puran*
Shoulders	500	*Shiva Puran*
Heart (chest)	108	*Shiva Puran*
Forehead	30	*Shiva Puran*
Neck region	36	*Shiva Puran*
Forearms (both right & left)	16/16	*Shiva Puran*

Body parts/organs	No of beads	Epic sources
Wrist (both right & left)	12/12	*Rudrakshajabalopanishad*
Shoulders	15	*Rudrakshajabalopanishad*
Yajnopaveet (sacred thread)	108	*Rudrakshajabalopanishad*
Neck region	2, 3, 5 & 7 rows	*Rudrakshajabalopanishad*
Crown	–	*Rudrakshajabalopanishad*
Kundal (as earring)	–	*Rudrakshajabalopanishad*
Ear ornament	–	*Rudrakshajabalopanishad*
Wrists	–	*Rudrakshajabalopanishad*
Waist	300 (mean) 500 (medium) 1,000 (best)	*Rudrakshajabalopanishad*
Eyes (both right & left)	4/4	*Nirunayasindhu*
Neck region	32	*Nirunayasindhu*
Forehead	40	*Nirunayasindhu*
Ears (both right & left)	6/6	*Nirunayasindhu*
Wrists (both right & left)	12/12	*Nirunayasindhu*
Forearms (both right & left)	16/16	*Nirunayasindhu*
Sikha (crown hair)	1	*Nirunayasindhu*
Heart (chest)	108	*Nirunayasindhu*

The total number of *rudrakshas* to be worn over the body also varies in different epics. For example, it can be 108, 249, 1,000, 1,008 or 1,111 *rudrakshas*. The picture **(Fig. 41)** shows our house priest wearing a *rudraksha* meditation dress with 1,111 beads. We have made a meditation dress with 2,780 *rudrakshas* (after consulting different epics and with the highest number mentioned in them for a particular part of the body) for wearing over head, arms and wrists, heart, neck, waist, ears and eyes. Wearing such a divine and powerful dress and performing meditation will lead to calm and serene feeling from within. However, it is not practical for all to use such large number of beads on a regular basis. My suggestion is to use as many *rudrakshas* as possible and make it a point to choose larger beads for wearing over chest to get better acupressure effect. The *malas* on the neck must go up to the level of the heart at the minimum and it should be two inches above the navel as maximum length.

It is necessary to understand the difference between a *mala* and a combination of beads. The main differences are:

1. A *mala*, whether for wearing or for *jap*, is continuously strung with beads with gaps for knots only. Generally, a *mala* has only one type of bead; for example, a *rudraksha mala* will have only *rudrakshas* and a *tulsi mala* will have only *tulsi* beads.

2. A combination can be in the form of a thread or silver/ gold chain around neck and beads at the bottom. Different materials can be used in a combination, e.g. gems can be used along with *rudraksha*. *Sphatik* beads can also be used in some regularity for adjusting length or for good looks.

Wearing of different materials (which are accepted as useful and may have some curative or divine properties) is perfectly right for spiritual purposes. One can wear **tulsi, sphatik, sandalwood, *keharwa* (amber)** and ***rudraksha* malas** separately, if one has faith in a particular God (Shiva,

Durga, Vishnu, Ram, Krishna, etc.). However, if these materials are being used for health purposes, it is advisable to consult an expert. For example, those suffering from asthma are not advised to wear *sphatik* along with *rudraksha*.

Some people get *taabeej* (talisman) made from some source, which they consider very powerful while others choose tiger nails (though these are banned, some get them from old stocks or through inheritance). Many are found choosing metal pendants of *Shree Yantra*, Ganesh, Hanuman, Krishna or any God or Goddess and become confused whether to wear these with *rudraksha*. Our opinion is that as *rudraksha* is a natural and holy product having no specific branding, it can be used with devotion for worshipping any God or Goddess.

People wearing fake *rudraksha* beads are advised that they should remove such beads after it is confirmed as fake or spurious by any expert or by oneself as anything, which is not genuine, is likely to give negative influence.

Further, in accordance with family traditions or due to mindset, many do not use *tulsi* and *rudraksha* beads together. There is nothing wrong in wearing these holy materials together. We find that in Hindu culture a lot of effort has been made in the past to bring *Shaivaites* and *Vaishnavaites* together. There are temples in which *Hari* (Vishnu) and *Har* (Shiva) are worshipped in a unified form. Goswami Tulsidas had composed *Harishankari* verse to offer unified prayers of Lord Shiva and Lord Ram. It is included in *Vinayapatrika,* which is one of the finest works of poetry in Hindi literature. In *Ramcharitmanas,* which is the greatest work of this poet, Lord Ram says "anyone calling himself my devotee and by conviction is an opponent of Lord Shiva will be condemned and he is destined to get punishment within this life and also in the next life" *Shaligram shilas*, which are revered by *Vaishnavaities*, have been used to make *Shivalinga* and several efforts have been made to bring these two sects into one fold. Lord Krishna has worshipped Lord Shiva and vice versa. Lord Vishnu had offered one of his eyes when He fell short of one lotus flower while worshipping Lord Shiva and Lord Shiva has worshiped Lord Vishnu. Therefore, *rudraksha* is not confined to only *Shaivites*. I feel a majority of people in our country accept this view.

A *mala* is a continuous arrangement of the beads without a break, while a combination can be made of few beads threaded or capped using metal and tied to a thread or chain around neck, wrist and/or on arms. In case of combination also, one should use a minimum of three beads. There are divergent views on this as wearing of one bead is also recommended. Experience, however, suggests use of a minimum of three beads and preferably a full *mala* of 108+1 beads even if the size of the beads is smaller. One should get more coverage from *rudraksha* as suggested by most of the epics. In case you wish to wear an expensive or rare bead, which you have only one, then it can be used along with two other cheaper and easily available beads like four, five or six *mukhis* of bigger size or get it attached to a *mala* made of smaller-sized beads making a total of 54+1 or 108+1.

Shiva Puran defines a meditation dress as:

Three strands of 120 *rudrakshas*, each to be worn across the chest as *Yagnopaveet*, one strand of 108 *rudraksha* for chest, 11 *rudraksha* each on both wrists and arms (total 44), six *rudrakshas* on each ear, five *rudrakshas* on naval, 32 *rudrakshas* on throat, and 550 *rudrakshas* on head. This way, a total of 1,111 *rudrakshas* make a meditation dress and is considered auspicious for attaining *rudrahood*.

Shrimad Devibhagwat **(Ref. 2)** recommends:

One on the tuft, 30 on the head, 36 on the neck, 16 on each arm (total 32), 12 on each wrist (total 24), 50 on the shoulders, and 108 as *Yagnopaveet*. In addition, some *rudrakshas* should be worn around the neck to make the total number to 300. As per this epic, 300 numbers of *rudrakshas* is the minimum, 500 is recommended and 1,000 is the best.

Rudrakshajabalopanishad, **(Ref. 15)** suggests:

One on tuft of hair (*shikha*) 30 on head, 36 on neck,16 each on arms,12 each on each wrists,15 on shoulders, 108 as *Yajnopaveet* and 2x108 or 3x108 or 5x108 or 7x108 around neck.

In general, it can be said that epics recommend the use of as many *rudrakshas* as possible.

In case of a *mala* for *jap*, use 27+1, 54+1 or 108+1 beads. Those believing in numerology should consider the following numbers as auspicious for different objectives (for *jap* only):

> ➢ 32 or 30 for wealth
> ➢ 100 for thousands of *mahapurashcharans*
> ➢ 102 for merits and knowledge
> ➢ 104 for health and strength
> ➢ 107 for final liberation (*nirvan* or *moksha*)
> ➢ 108 for righteousness (*dharma*), wealth, desire and the final liberation.

For *Gayatri jap*, some people make special *mala* having 24 beads and a *meru* separately.

For **wearing,** use any odd number, say 3, 5, 7 etc., in case of a combination. Avoid wearing a single *rudraksha* with following exceptions:

Fourteen *mukhi* can be used singly, preferably wearing over forehead (on the *ajna chakra* between the eyebrows). It can be used around neck also.

Eleven *mukhi* has to be knotted on the tuft of crown hair (*shikha*). (This is not practical in today's context and hence it is better to wear around the neck.)

One *mukhi* around neck

Nine *mukhi* on the left hand wrist

Six, thirteen *mukhi* on the right arm

Five *mukhi* as a *mala* around neck.

Shrimad Devibhagawat has given importance to following *rudrakshas*:

One *mukhi*, five *mukhi*, eleven *mukhi* and fourteen *mukhi*.

These can be worn as mentioned above.

Gaurishankar rudraksha should be worn around neck only and avoid using it on arms or wrist.

Fifteen and higher *mukhis* should be worn around neck

The total number of beads in a *mala* for wearing around neck or over the chest near the heart can be any of the following: 27, 54, 108, 32, 36, 50, 101; however, out of this, 108 is the most auspicious. There is no need to put an extra bead as '*meru*' in such a *mala* as it is not being used for *jap*. Smaller Indonesian beads are comfortable to wear in more numbers, but one should try to wear as many bigger Nepal beads as possible. Please note that while counting the number of *rudraksha* beads, no other bead of *sphatik*, gold, silver, sandalwood, etc. should be included; count only the *rudraksha* beads to arrive at the auspicious number mentioned above as desired. Also keep a clear distinction between a *mala* and a combination.

Normally, it is recommended that the *mala* or *rudraksha* you are wearing around the neck or over the heart is not visible to others. It is therefore necessary to select the length of the *mala* carefully. Exceptional cases can only be the oversized beads, which cannot be covered and hidden under the collar of the shirt or you wish to wear around neck strictly as per yogic practices for meditation. If you are wearing a bracelet over the wrist or on the forehead or on the tuft as laid down in the epics, it shall be visible and it is graceful. There are some people who say that cosmic energies from the skies get absorbed by *rudraksha* if it is exposed. But, this is not true. The most important requirement is that *rudraksha* should touch the skin. Except for *sadhus* and *gurus* who may not be wearing shirts, it is better not to make the beads visible to others. But, since it is a beautiful spiritual symbol there is no harm as such in wearing it outside, if the situation so demands.

Significance of 108 numbers

1. There are 108 *upanishads*
2. The four segments *(charans)* of each of the 27 lunar asterisms *(Nakshatras)*, that is, 27x4 makes 108. Hence, it is a cosmic number.
3. The bead symbolizes the 108 sensate foci in our body.
4. In Sanskrit language, there are 50 alphabets and seven vowels. The alphabets, if written in opposite direction *(anulom)*, give another 50 numbers. The letter '*ksh*' is a central extra letter having a unique place. Total becomes $50+7+50+1=108$. In *mala sanskars*

(purification) ritual, each bead is sanctified using one letter as given in this description.

5. The names of Vishnu and Shiva as given in the *Mahabharat* are also 108 each.

6. Major psychiatric illnesses, according to the Ayurvedic system, are 108

7. *Shatpath Brahman* states in its tenth part that one *sanvatsar* has 10800 auspicious moments (*muhurts*). *Rigved, Yajurved* and *Samved* have 10800 couplets (These numbers if shared by each one year of theoretical life span of a human being, which is 100 years, we get a figure of 108 for *muhurts* and also couplets.).

Jap mala in other sects

In **Jainism** a *japmala* has 108 beads. Usually, the *mala* is made using sandalwood, thread, gold, silver, marble, *gomed* (precious stone) or vegetable seeds.

In **Buddhism** the *mala* is called '*rudra*' and has 108 beads. It is a symbol of *Avlokiteshwar*, a king who killed 108 bandits who attacked the Buddhist monastery. The beads are made from sandalwood, pure wood, gold, silver, pearls, diamond, ruby, glass, bone etc.

Sikhs call it '*simarni*' and it has 108 beads. It is based on the fact that there are 108 quotes of the guru in '*Guru Granth Sahib*'. The *mala* is made of *rudraksha*, sandalwood etc.

In **Christianity**, it is called '*rosary*' and has 58 beads strung with a cross. The numbers are based on the following belief:

a. The cross indicates faith in God and in the memory of Jesus, who underwent suffering on the cross.

b. The first bead adjacent to the cross is God

  c.   The next three beads are the three forms of energy –
       energy of will, energy of knowledge and energy of
       action.
  d.   The fifth bead is in memory of the mission of the
       Lord
  e.   The three triangular beads symbolize happiness,
       unhappiness and bliss
  f.   10×5 = 50 beads represent the following five secrets of
       Jesus – Creation, Sustenance, Dissolution, The
       covering of great illusion and the Initiation.

These *malas* are made from the stem of the rose plant.
Mother Mary was fond of roses and hence the name rosary.

Among **Muslims** the *mala* is called *Tasabi*. It has 33 or 99
beads. Allah has 99 names. *Tasabi* is made from marble,
opium, ivory, camel bones, seashells, date seeds, cannabis
seeds, horn and pearls. Beads made of clay from Mecca are
the most sacred.

In **Zoroastrian,** the *mala* is called *Tasabi*. It has
101+1=102 beads. This represents 101 names of the Lord.

Acccording to many astrologers, *rudraksha* is the ultimate solution for removing the bad effects of the planets. While gems are commonly used for this purpose, many astrologers recommend the use of *rudraksha,* if the wearer is not satisfied. Not only do the planets get pacified, but the wearer gains comfort and happiness. One should only know which *rudrakshas* will be useful for this objective. Although the ancient epics do not mention any correlation between planets, *nakshatra* and *rudraksha,* the information below is being given for those who strongly believe in wearing *rudraksha* in accordance with horoscope and planetary positions. One must be beware of those astrologers who, for commercial gains recommend rare *rudraksha* like 1 *mukhi,* 14 *mukhi* etc. and try to supply these beads themselves, exploiting their customers.

One *mukhi* and Twelve *mukhi rudrakshas*

Both these *rudrakshas* are blessed by Sun (*Surya*), the center of the solar system, around which all planets revolve. They effectively control the malefic effects of Sun, such as diseases of the right eye, headache, ear ailments, bowel problems, bone weakness, etc. These *rudrakshas* also help at the emotional level like overcoming lack of confidence, increasing charisma and personal power, inculcating leadership qualities and bringing in prosperity.

Two *mukhi rudraksha*

The ruling planet of this *rudraksha* is Moon. It effectively controls the malefic effects of Moon such as diseases of the left eye, kidney and intestines. It also solves problems like lack of harmony in relationship, etc.

Three *mukhi rudraksha*

Mars is the ruling planet of this *rudraksha*, which is astrologically represented by *Agni* or fire. Malefic effects are diseases of the blood, blood pressure, weakness, disturbed menstrual cycle, kidney ailments, etc. The bead is helpful in curing these diseases and disorders and problems such as depression, negative feelings, guilt feelings, inferiority complex, etc.

Four *mukhi rudraksha*

The ruling planet of this *rudraksha* is Mercury. In mythology, this represents Goddess Saraswati and Brahma. Malefic effects of Mercury include dullness of mind, lack of grasping and understanding power and difficulty in effective communication. Four *mukhi rudraksha* nullifies these malefic effects and pleases Goddess Saraswati. This *rudraksha* governs logical and structural thinking.

Five *mukhi rudraksha*

The ruling planet of this *rudraksha* is Jupiter. Malefic effect of Jupiter are considered to cause lack of peace of mind, utter poverty, lack of harmony, diseases caused by fat, of kidney, thigh and ear, diabetes, etc. This *rudraksha* is known to sublimate their effects.

Six *mukhi rudrakha*

Its ruling planet is Venus, which governs genital organs, throat, valour, sexual pleasure, love, musical talent, etc. Its malefic effects can cause diseases and problems involving the above organs or aspects.

Seven *mukhi rudraksha*

Its ruling planet is Saturn (*Shani*). This *rudraksha* sublimates the malefic effects of *Shani* such as diseases occurring suddenly without any apparent cause, impotency, cold, obstruction, hopelessness, despair, delay in achievements, long lasting diseases, scarcity, worry, etc.

Eight *mukhi rudraksha*

The ruling planet being *Rahu*, this *rudraksha* is helpful in neutralising its malefic effects, which are similar to that of *Shani*. There could be sudden fall in status, diseases of the lungs, feet and skin, cataract, hydrocele and snake bites.

Nine *mukhi rudraksha*

The ruling planet is *Ketu,* which is a shadow planet like *Rahu* and it resembles Mars. This *rudraksha* is beneficial to sublimate the ill effects of *Ketu* like diseases of the lungs, fever, eye pain, bowel pain, skin disease, body pain, etc.

Ten *mukhi rudraksha*

10 *mukhi rudraksha* has no ruling planet and is used to nullify malefic effects of all the planets. The wearer gets a sense of security.

Eleven *mukhi rudraksha*

It has no ruling planet. It induces courage and confidence in the wearer to lead an adventurous life. It is also helpful in meditation and removes problems in completing yogic practices.

Twelve *mukhi rudraksha*

Its ruling deity is Sun. Effects are as mentioned for one *mukhi rudraksha*.

Thirteen *mukhi rudraksha*

The effects are similar to that of six *mukhi rudraksha*. It is helpful for meditation and spiritual attainments.

Fourteen *mukhi rudraksha*

It improves intuitive thinking. It is worn to sublimate the malefic effects of Saturn. This rudraksha is also known as *Maha-shani*.

Fifteen *mukhi rudraksha*

The impact of this *rudraksha* is similar to that of 14 *mukhi rudraksha* like improving intuitive, abstract and lateral thinking. The wearer finds high energy levels to put into action his thoughts and ideas.

Astrologically, the following correlations exist among different *nakshatras*, planets and *rudraksha*.

	Nakshatra	Planet	*Rudraksha*
1.	Ashwini	Ketu	Nine *mukhi*
2.	Bharani	Venus	Six *mukhi*
3.	Krittika	Sun	One, 12 or 11 *mukhi*
4.	Rohini	Moon	Two *mukhi*
5.	Mrigashira	Mars	Three *mukhi*
6.	Ardra	Rahu	Eight *mukhi*
7.	Punarvasu	Jupiter	Five *mukhi*
8.	Pushya	Saturn	Seven *mukhi*

	Nakshatra	Planet	Rudraksha
9.	Ashlesha	Mercury	Four *mukhi*
10.	Magha	Ketu	Nine *mukhi*
11.	Purvaphalguni	Venus	Six *mukhi*
12.	Uttaraphalguni	Sun	One, 12 or 11 *mukhi*
13.	Hasta	Moon	Two *mukhi*
14.	Chitra	Mars	Three *mukhi*
15.	Swati	Rahu	Eight *mukhi*
16.	Vishakha	Jupiter	Five *mukhi*
17.	Anuradha	Saturn	Seven *mukhi*
18.	Jyeshtha	Mercury	Four *mukhi*
19.	Mula	Ketu	Nine *mukhi*
20.	Purvashadha	Venus	Six *mukhi*
21.	Uttarashadha	Sun	One, 12 or 11 *mukhi*
22.	Shravana	Moon	Two *mukhi*
23.	Dhanishtha	Mars	Three *mukhi*
24.	Shatabhisha	Rahu	Eight *mukhi*
25.	Purvabhadrapada	Jupiter	Five *mukhi*
26.	Uttarabhadrapada	Saturn	Seven *mukhi*
27.	Revati	Mercury	Four *mukhi*

Some correlations relating to birth *rashi*, money, controlling auspicious planets and *rudraksha* are given in the following table:

	Birth *Rashi* lagna	Auspicious planets	Rudraksha
1.	Mesha (Aries)	Mars, Jupiter	Three & Five *mukhi*
2.	Vrishabha	Mercury, Saturn (Taurus)	Four & Seven *mukhi*

	Birth *Rashi* lagna	Auspicious planets	*Rudraksha*
3.	Mithun (Gemini)	Mercury, Venus	Four & Six *mukhi*
4.	Karka (Cancer)	Moon, Mars	Three & Two *mukhi*
5.	Sinh (Leo)	Sun, Mars	Three & Twelve *mukhi*
6.	Kanya (Virgo)	Mercury	Four & Six *mukhi*
7.	Tula (Libra)	Venus, Saturn	Six & Seven *mukhi*
8.	Vrishicika (Scorpio)	Jupiter, Moon	Two *mukhi*
9.	Dhanu (Sagattarius)	Jupiter, Sun	Five & Twelve *mukhi*
10.	Makar (Capricorn)	Saturn, Venus	Six & Seven *mukhi*
11.	Kumbha (Aquarius)	Saturn, Venus	Six & Seven *mukhi*
12.	Meena (Pisces)	Jupiter, Mars	Three & five *mukhi*

RUDRAKSHA WEARING AND WORSHIPPING

9

Following check-list may be reviewed before starting the wearing procedure:

1. Ensure that the *mala* or combination has the correct number of beads. Check that the beads are not used earlier by anyone and are without any damage.

2. Ensure that the *mala* is made with beads having the correct directions (face to face and tail to tail).

3. Remember that it has to be taken off the body while drinking alcohol, eating non-vegetarian food, while having physical intimacy with women and going to a funeral (additionally for females during menstrual period). Do not feel guilty if this is not followed unintentionally. In that case, just re-purify the beads by washing in pure water and chanting *Om Namah Shivaya* five times.

4. Ensure that you have paid fully for the beads or *mala* to the seller. It is observed that unless the commercial deals are completed in full, (except in cases where it is received as a gift), *rudraksha* does not offer its full effects and gives negative feelings. This leads to suspicions about its worth. Stolen *rudraksha* should not be used at all.

5. *Rudraksha* is not confined to any specific religion. It is for the entire mankind. The rituals are incidental and are to be followed willingly and with respect.

6. *Rudraksha* does not cause any side effects hence undue suspicion about its effects may be misplaced. Do not over-expect changes or magical effects to happen. Its wearing is also not a short term activity. It has to be worn for the entire life span.

7. Always use new *rudraksha* and never use *rudraksha* worn by someone else. If you have received these as legacy or legitimately from near and dear ones, then first perform the purification ritual or *abhishek* and then wear them. Old *rudraksha* should be specially checked for any damage or holes or cracks and if found these should not be used.

It has been emphasized in all the epics which have highlighted the merits of *rudraksha* that at the time of wearing *rudraksha* and even while regularly wearing it, it should be worshipped as per prescribed procedures and particularly by chanting the recommended mantras. *Shrimad Devibhagawat* says that *rudraksha* should be worn without any expectations and with total devotion and happiness. In doing so, one tends to obtain the knowledge of Shiva. It says that the power of *rudraksha* is such that even if worn without reciting the *mantras,* it will be beneficial. However, for *brahmins* (including those who have converted themselves to *brahminism* by taking second birth, or twice-born called *Dwij,* by sticking to strict disciplined life style) it is necessary to use *mantras. Shiva Puran,* while giving the *beej mantras,* says that blessed are those who wear *rudraksha* chanting these mantras. Even listening to these mantras gives good results.

Rudraksha needs to be blessed, purified and energized before they are worn. This is done by performing *Rudrabhishek* and chanting of *pranpratishtha mantras* and seed *mantras.*

Seed *mantras* for all *mukhis* are given below once again for easy reference (as per *Shiva Puran*):

One *mukhi*	*Om Hreem Namah*
Two *mukhi*	*Om Namah*
Three *mukhi*	*Om Kleem Namah*
Four *mukhi*	*Om Hreem Namah*
Five *mukhi*	*Om Hreem Namah*
Six *mukhi*	*Om Hreem Hoom Namah*
Seven *mukhi*	*Om Hoom Namah*
Eight *mukhi*	*Om Hoom Namah*
Nine *mukhi*	*Om Hreem Hoom Namaa*
Ten *mukhi*	*Om Hreem Namah Namah*
Eleven *mukhi*	*Om Hreem Hoom Namah*
Twelve *mukhi*	*Om Krom Kshom Rowm Namah*
Thirteen *mukhi*	*Om Hreem Namah*
Fourteen *mukhi*	*Om Namah*

For other beads, please refer to Chapter 2. It has been mentioned that the common *mantra* for all *rudraksha*s irrespective of their *mukhi* or type is *Om Namah Shivaya* or *mahamrityunjaya mantra* given in the following pages.

Pooja or blessings of *rudraksha*

Choose an auspicious day or any Monday for blessings

Follow this simple ritual prior to wearing a *rudraksha*:

1. Wash or sprinkle *rudraksha/mala* with Ganges water or pure water
2. Apply sandalwood paste.
3. Offer incense/*dhoop*.

4. Offer any white flower
5. Touch the *rudraksha* on a *Shivaling* or Lord Shiva's photo and chant *Om Namah Shivaya* for a minimum of 11 times. Thereafter, the *rudraksha* can be worn or put at *pooja* place.

Rudraksha Abhishek

For an elaborate *rudraksha pooja* or blessing, the following procedure may be adopted. Blessing may be done by the wearer, his *guru* or a priest:

Arrange the following items:

Panchgavya, a mix of cow's dung, urine, milk, ghee and curd. In its absence, use *panchamrit* which is mix of unboiled milk, honey, sugar, ghee and curd.

Ganges water in an *achamani* pot with *kusha* grass for sprinkling. Use spoon if *kusha* grass is not available and in the absence of Ganges water, use clean pure water.

- nine leaves of *peepal* tree arranged on a plate. (ignore this step if *peepal* leaves are not available)
- dhoop, incense sticks, camphor, sandal paste, aromatic oil, rice grains, preferably mixed with *asthagandha*, ghee lamp with one wick, offerings like cloth, flower, fruit, betel nut, betel leaves, coconut.

After taking bath and with a calm and composed mind and a clear body, sit on an *asan* (mat or clean carpet) facing the east.

Wash the *rudraksha* with *punchagavya* or *panchamrit*
Then wash it with water/Ganges water.
Place the *rudraksha* along with nine leaves of *peepal* tree.
Place an empty plate in front to make offerings.

Chant the *mantra* **Om Namah shivaya** three times

Sprinkle water over yourself and all the items of *pooja*

Chant:

*Om Apavitrah Pavitro va sarva Vastan Gatopi Va Yah smaret
Pundari Kaksham Sa Bahya Bhyantarah Shuchih
Om gurubhyo namaha, Om Ganeshaya namaha, Om kula
devatabhya namaha, Om ishta devatabhya namaha, Om mata
pitribhyam namaha*

three times

Take water in right hand with a spoon or *achamani* and sip
it after each of the three chantings.

Chant:

*Om Keshavaya namaha, Om Narayana namaha, Om Madhavaya
namaha*

Take water or right hand and pour on ground.

Chant:

Om Govindaya namaha

Do three short rounds of *pranayama* breaths.

Chant:

*Om pranavasya parabrahma rishihi paramatma devata
daivi Gayatri chandaha
pranayamae viniyogaga*

Sprinkle water on *rudraksha* with *kusha* grass or a spoon or
achamani

Chant:

*Om Sadyojatam prapadyaami sadyajataajava namo namaha
Bhave bhavenaati bhave bhaavasvamaan bhavodbhavay namaha*

Take a flower and dip in sandal paste and aromatic oils and
touch on the beads.

Chant:

Om Vamdevaya namaha, jyeshthaay namaha shreshthay namaha, Rudraay namah, kaalay namah, Kala vikarannaay namah, Bal vikaranaay namah, Balaay namah, Bala pramathanaay namah, Sarva bhoot damanaay namah, Manomanaay namah.

Offer *dhoop* to the *rudraksha* beads.

Chant:

Om Aghorebhyo ghorebhyo ghor ghor tarebhayaha
Sarvebhya sarva sharvvebhyo namaste astu Rudra roopebhyaha

Again, take a flower and dip in sandal paste and touch on beads.

Chant:

Om Tatpurushaaya vidmahe Mahadevaay dheemahi tanno Rudraha prachodayaat

Chant *Eeeshan mantra*

Om Eeeshan sarvavidyaanam eeshwar sarvabhootaanaam
Brahnaadipati brahmanaadhipati Brahma Shivome astu sadaa Shivom

Chant *Pranpratishtha mantra* (Life giving mantra). Offer rice into plate placed in front of *rudraksha* while chanting this.

Chant:

Om aas hreem krom yum rum lum vum shum sum sum haum hum sah asya malaya prana eha prana.
Om aas hreem krom yum rum lum vum shum shum sum haum hum sah asya malaya jeeva eha sthitha
Om aam hreem krom yum rum lum vum shum shum sum haum hum sah asya malaya sarveindrayani vagmansyachakshu shodragranapadani ihevagatya sukham chiram thithantu swaha.

Chant these next mantras and give the offerings or give rice to the plate in front of *rudraksha*:

(offering to the lotus feet of Shiva Maha Devaya, I bow)

(Invocation) *avahanam samarpayami Shri Shiva Maha Devaya charana kamalebhyo namaha*

Offer:

(Seat) *Asanam samarpayami Shri Shiva Maha Devaya kharana kamalebhyo namaha*

(Cloth) *Vastram samaroayami Shri Shiva Maha charana kamalebhyo namaha*

(Sandalwood or scent) *Chandanam samarpayami Shri Shiva Maha Devaya charana kamalebhyo namaha*

(Rice) *Akshatan samarpayami Shri Shiva Maha Devaya charana kamalebhyo namaha*

(Flower) *Pushpam samarpayami Shri Shiva Maha Devaya charana kamalebhyo namaha*

(Ghee lamp) *Deepam samarpyami Shri Shiva Maha Devaya charana kamalebhyo namaha*

(Water) *Achamaniyam samarpayami Sri Shiva Maha Devaya charana kamalebhyo namaha*

(Fruit) *Naivedyam samarpayami Sri Shiva Maha Devaya charana kamalebhyo Namaha*

(Water Drink) *Achamaniyam samarpayami Shri Shiva Maha Devaya charana kamalebhyo namaha*

(Betal nut-paan) *Tambulam samarpayami Shri Shiva Maha Devaya charana kamalebhyo namaha*

(Coconut) *Shriphalam samarpayami Shri Shiva Maha Devaya charana kamalebhyo namaha*

Burn camphor and circle it clockwise three times in front of the plate and chant:

Karpura Shivam karuna vataram samsara saram bhujagendra haram
Sada vasantam hridaya ravinde bhavam bhavani sahitam namami

Chant *Gayatri mantra* three times

Om bhur bhuvesh swaha
Om tat saviturva renyum bhargo devasya dheemahi dhiya yonaha prachodayat

Chant *Surya mantra* three times

Om bhu bhuvaha, om swaha,om maha, om janaha, om tapaha, om satyam

Repeat and after each mantra each touch right eye, left eye and forehead

Om apo jyothi
Raso amtritam
Brahma bhu bhuvaha swarom

Chant *Mahamrityunjaya mantra* five times and offer rice to the plate in front of the *rudraksha* after each round:

Om Haum Joom Sah, Om Bhur Bhuvaha Swaha, Om Tryambakam Yajamahey Sungandhim Pushti Vardanam, Urvarukamiva Bandhanan, Mrityor Muksheeya Mamritat, Om Swaha Bhuvaha Bhu Om Sah Joom Haum Om

Chant *Beeja mantra* nine times each

Om Namah Shivaya, Om Hreem Namah, Om Namah, Om Kleem Kleem Namah
Om Hreem Namah, Om Hreem Hum namah, Om Hum Namah, Om Kraum Kshom Rom Namah

Bow or supplicate, then chant this last prayer:

Om Purnamadah Purnamidam Purnat Purnamudachyate,
Purnasya Purnamadaya Purna Mevavya Shishyate

Om Shantih Shantih Shantih!

Although several different procedures and worshipping details are followed in terms of various epics, the above-referred common *pooja vidhi* is complete. However, many would like to wear *rudraksha* using detailed worshipping for each *mukhi*. We are giving below the ritualistic *Vedic* procedure as given in *Shiva Rahasya*. **(Ref. 5)**

Facetwise wearing of rudraksha using Vedic rituals

Skand Says:

"O Lord *Mahadev!* Please remove my doubts and explain how *rudraksha* got produced and how to wear it? I have heard that in this planet and other *lokas, rudraksha* wearing is considered very auspicious."

Mahadevji says:

"Once upon a time, a demon king, Tripurasur, became so powerful that he defeated Brahma, Vishnu, Indra, Takshak and other *Devas* and thereupon all the *Devas* approached me with prayers to protect them. To liberate them from tyranny of this demon, I equipped myself with a weapon named as *Kalagni,* which was astoundingly bright, fierce and divine *Aghorastra.* I closed my three eyes for one thousand divine years and meditated. Thereafter, due to fatigue and sadness (because of the destruction done by the demon), some tears fell from my eyes. Wherever these tears fell on this Earth, where there are the birth and death cycles (*mrityulok*), *rudraksha* trees grew. From that time, *rudraksha* became famous in all the three *lokas* (earth, sky and *patal*). By touching *rudraksha*, one gets benefits one lakh times, by wearing one hundred lakh times and by using a *mala* and offering *jap* tens of lakh times.

"A person who wears *rudraksha* on his hand, ears, forehead and throat will be able to move on this Earth without fear.

"A person wearing *rudraksha* is like Shiva and is worshipped by *devas* and demons alike. A person full of sins, impurity and repulsive habits also becomes free from sins by just touching *rudraksha*.

"Even an animal like a donkey, if dies after wearing *rudraksha* becomes *rudraswaroop*, what to say for human beings."

Kartik asks:

"Lord Shiva! Please tell me the properties of one to fourteen *mukhi rudraksha*."

Lord Shiva replies:

"One *mukhi* is *Shiva swaroop* (Like Shiva) and purifies one of sins like *brahminicide*. Two *mukhi* is God of Gods (*Mahadev*) and purifies one from the sins of cow slaughter. Three *mukhi* is blessed by fire and purifies one from the sin of killing a woman. Four *mukhi* is Brahma and it purifies the wearer from the sin of committing manslaughter. Five *mukhi* is like Rudra Himself and purifies from the sins of adultery and consuming prohibited items like alcohol, meat etc. Six *mukhi* is Kartik himself and the one who wears it on the right arm purifies himself from sins like that of getting abortion done. Seven *mukhi* is Anant (Kamdev) and the wearer of this gets freedom from the sin of committing theft of gold and also of cow slaughter. Eight *mukhi* is Ganesh Himself and the wearer gets freed from physical relations with women other

than one's own wife. Nine *mukhi* is *Bhairava* and should be
worn on left hand. It cleanses one from the sins of several
million kinds. Ten *mukhi* is Lord Vishnu (Janardan) and
removes fear of planets, ghosts, evil spirits and snakes. Eleven
mukhi is *Ekadash Rudra* (Hanuman). One who wears it on the
tuft (*Choti/Shikha*) gets the benefit of conducting thousands
of *Ashwamedha Yajnas* and hundred *Vajpeya Yajnas* and
donation at the time of lunar eclipse. Twelve *mukhi* is like
Sun. One who wears it around the neck gets freed from sins
of cow slaughter, manslaughter and gold theft. He will not be
afraid of thieves, fire, elephant, horse, deer, ox, pig, Lion,
jackal, etc. Thirteen *mukhi* is Indra. The wearer fulfils all the
desires and gets blessed by good fortune and wealth. They get
gold, diamond, silver and mercury and get freed from all
kinds of sins. Fourteen *mukhi* is blessed by Hanuman and
those who wear it on the forehead continuously get eternal
bliss and *Nirvan*."

Skand expressed his desire to learn *mantras* of different
mukhis to which Lord Shiva replied as under:

"Wearing of *rudraksha* is very auspicious and the wearer
reaches *rudralok* (*Kailash*) after his death.

"Any person wearing *rudraksha* without *mantras* shall be
punished with a life in hell.

"The worshipping details are: *(Note: The mantras detailed are
different from those given along with the bead description in Chapter 2.
Even in some cases, the Gods to which the rudraksha is assigned are
different. This diversity is typical of our culture, but all the mantras
given here are Siddha mantras and the method is fully Vedic and hence
can be followed. If any one wants to use those mantras mentioned
earlier, it can be done without any confusion.)*

One *mukhi rudraksha*

Mantra

Om Aim Hum Aaum Aim Om
Viniyogah

Take water in hand and chant the following after which throw the water on the floor.

Asya shreeshiva mantrasya prasad rishih, panktih chandhah, shivo devata, hankaro beejam, aaum shaktih, mama chaturvarg siddhyarthe rudraksha dharanarthe jape viniyogah.

Angnyasah

These mantras are for your whole body.

Vaamdev rishiye namah, shirasi, panktishchhandase namo mukhe, rim aim aim namah hradi, ham beejaye namo guhye, aaum shaktaye namah padayoh.

Karanyasah

These mantras are for the five fingers and the palm.

Om Ham Angushthbhyam namah, Om Aim hreem tarjaneebhyam swaha, Om hreem hoom madhyamabhyam vashat, Om Aam hreem Anamikabhyam hum, Om aim Haaum kanishthikabhyam vaushat, Om Om Hrah kartalkarprashthabhyam phat.

Hridayadinyasah

Touch heart, head, place of tuft, arms, eyes and chant:

Om Hraum hridayay namah, Om aim hreem shirase swaha, Om ham hoom shikhaye vashat, Om aum Hreim kawachaye hoom, Om aim hreem netra trayaya vaushat, Om Om hah astraye phat.

Dhyanam

This prayer is offered during meditation of the particular God, who has blessed the *rudraksha*. Concentrate on Him/ Her and say these prayers.

Muktapeen payod mauktikaj pavarnermukheh panchbhih
Ruyksherajit meeshamindu mukutam poornendu kotiprabham
Shoolam tank- kripan-vajradahan nagendra ghanta shukam
Jastabjeshvabhayam varashch dadhtam tejojjwalam chintaye.

Afterwards, place a copper pot over a vessel full of water. Keep the *rudraksha* on the empty pot and take the water pot in left hand and pour water over *rudraksha*. Keep chanting *Om Namah Shivaya*.

Take out the *rudraksha* and then wear it.

Two *mukhi rudraksha*

(Please follow the different karmas as mentioned in one mukhi)

Mantra

Om Khseem Hreem Kshaum Vreem Om

Viniyogah

Asya shree davdevesh mantrasya atririshih Gayatri chhandah, dev devesho devata. ksheem beejam, kshaum shaktih, mam chaturvarg siddhayerthe rudraksha dharanarthe jape viniyogah

Angnyasah

Atri rishiye namah, shirasi, gayatri chhandase namo mukhe, devdeveshshaye namo hradi. ksheem beejaye namo guhye, ksheem shaktaye namah, padayoh.

Karanyasah

Om Angushthbbhyam namahm, Om kshaum tarjaneebhyam swaha, Om Hreem madhyamabhyam vashat, Om ksham anamikabhyam hum, Om ksheem kanishthikabhyam vaushat, Om kartalkar prashthbhyam phat.

Hridayadinyasah

Om Om Hradayay namah, Om ksheem shirase swaha, Om hreem shikhaye phat, Om khaum kawachye hum, Om vreem netre trayaya vraushat, Om astraya phat.

Dhyanam

Tapan   Somahu   taashanlochanam   dhansamangalam shashisuprabham
Abhaya-chakra pinakvaraan karerdhat mindudharam girisham bhajet

Three mukhi rudraksha

Mantra

Om Rum Iim Hreem Hoom Om

Viniyogah

Asya Shree agni mantrasya vashishthaj rishih,Gayatri chhandhah, Agni devata, Hreem beejam, Hum shaktih, chaturvargsiddhayarthe jape rudraksha dharanarhte viniyogah

Angnyasah

Vashishthaaj rishiye namah shirasi, gayatrichhandase namo mukhe, agni devataye namo hradi, Hreem beejaye namo guhye, hoom shaktaye namah paadayoh

Karanyasah

Om Angushthabhyam namah, Om rum tarjaneebhyam swaha, Om iim madhyamadhyaam vashat, Om hreem anamikabhyam hoom. Om Hoom kanishthikabhyam vaushat, Om Om kartalkarprashthabhyam phat

Hridayadinyasah

Om Om Hridayay namah, Om rum shirase swaha, Om Iim shikhaye vashat, Om Hreem kawachaaye hum, Om hoom netra netrayaya vaushat, Om Om astraye phat

Dhyanam

Ashtashaktim swstikaamaati muchcherdeerghere Bhidharyantam japamam
Hemakalpam padmastham trinetram dhyayed vahi baddhamaulim jatabhih

Four *mukhi rudraksha*

Mantra

Om Vaam Kraam Taam Ham Eem

Viniyogah

Asya Shree Brahma mantrasya bhargava rishih anushtupchhandhah, Brahma Devata, Vaam Beejsam Kraam Shaktih, abhheshtsiddhayarthe rudraksha dharanarthe jape viniyogah

Angnyasah

Bhargavarishiye namah shirasi, anushapchhandse namo mukhe, Brahma Devataye namo hradi vaam Beejaye namo guhye, kraam shaktaye namah paadayoh

Karanyasah

Om Om angushthabhyam namah, Om vaam tarjaneebhyam swaha, Om kraam madhyamadhyam phat, Om taam anamikabhyam hum. Om ham kanishthikabhyam vaushat, Om Eem kartalkar prashabhyam phat

Hridayadinyasah

Om Om Hradyaye namah, Om vaam shirase swaha, Om kraam shikhaye vashat, Om taam kawachye hoom, Om ham netra netrayaya vaushat, Om Eem astraye phat

Dhyanam

Pramya shirsa shashva dashta vaktram chaturmukham Gayatri sahitam devam namami vidhimeeshwaram

Five mukhi rudraksha

Mantra

Om Hraam Aam kshamyoun swaha

Viniyogah

Asya Shree mantrasya Brahma rishih, Gayatri chhandah, Sadashiva Kalagni rudro devata, Om Beejamm, Swaha shaktih, abhhesht siddhayarthe jape viniyogah

Angnyasah

Braharishaye namah shirasi, Gayatri chhandase namo mukhe, here Sadashiva Kalagnirudra devataye namo hradi, Om Beejaye namo guhye, swaha shaktaye namah paadayoh

Karanyasah

Om Om angushthabhyam namah, Om hraam tarjaneebhyam swaha, Om Aam madhyamabhyam vashat, Om kshamyon anamikabhyam hum, Om sawaha kahishikabhyam vaushat, Om ham aam kshamyoum swaha, karatalkar prashthabhyam phat

Hridayadiyasah

Om Om hradyaye namah, Om Hraam shirase swaha, Om aam shikhaye vashat, Om kshamyoam kawachaya hoom, Om swah netra netrayaya vaushat, Om hraam aam kshamyoun swaha, karatalkar prashthabhyam phat

Dhyanam

Haav Bhaav vilasaardhnarikam bheeshanrdhamathawa maheshwaram
Daash sotpal kapaal shoollinam chintaye japvidhau vibhootaye

Six mukhi rudraksha

Mantra

Om Hreem Shreem Kleem Saum Aim

Angnyasah

Dakshinamurti rishaye namah shirasi. Panktich chandase namo mukhe. Kartikeydevataye namo hradi. Aim beejaye namo guhye. Saum shaktaye namah Paadayoh

Karanyasah

Om Om angushthabhyam namah, Om Hreem tarjaneebhyam swaha, Om Shree madhyamabhyam vashat, Om kleem anamikabhyam phat, Om Saum kanishikabhya vaushat, Om Aim kartalkar prashthabhyam phat

Hridayadinyasah

Om hridayaye namah Om hreem shirase swaha. Om shreem shikhaye vashat. Om kleem kawachye hum. Om Saum netranetraya vaushat. Om Aim astraye phat

Dhyanam

Mayoor Vaahanam Veeram Taarakaasoora Mardanam Vande Shadaananam Devam Kaartikeye Shivaatmajam

Seven *mukhi rudraksha*

Mantra

Om Hreem Kreem Gleem Hreem Sroan

Viniyogah

Asya Shree Anant mantrasya Bhagwan rishih, Gayatri chhandah, Ananto Devat. Kreem Beejam. Hreem shaktih, abbhesht siddhyarthe rudraksha dharanarthe jape viniyogah

Angnyasah

Bhagwan rishaye namah shirasi, Gayatri Chhandase namo mukhe. anant devataye namo hradi. Kreem Beejaye namo guhye. Hreem shaktaye namah paadayo.

Karanayasah

Om Om angishthabhyam namah, Om Hreem tarjaneebhyam swaha, Om Kreem madhyabhyamvashat, Om Glaum anamikabhyam hoom, Om Hreem kanishthikabhyam vaushat, Om Saum karatalkat prashthabhyam phat

Hridayadinyasah

Om Om hradyaye namah, Om Hreem shirase swaha, Om kreem shikhaye phat, Om Glaum kawachye hoom, Om Hreem Netra netrayaya vaushat, Om Sraum astraye phat

Dhyanam

Anantam pundareekaksham phanashat vibhooshitam
Vishwa bhandhook aakaram,koormaroodham prapoojayet

Eight *mukhi rudraksha*

Mantra

Om Hraam Greem Lam Aam Shreem

Viniyogah

Asya Shreeganesh mantrasya Bhargav rishih, anushtapchhandah,
vinayako devata, Greem beejam, Aam shaktih, chaturvarg sdhyarthe
rudraksha dharanarthe jape viniyogah

Angnyasah

Bhargav rishaye namah shirasi, anushtapchhandase namo mukhe,
vinayak devataye namo hradi, Greem beejaye namo guhye, Aam
shaktaye namah paadayo

Karanyasah

Om Om angushthabhyam namah, Om hraam tarjaneebhyam swaha,
Om Greem madhyamabhyam vashat, Om anamikabhyam hoom,
Om Aam kanishthikabhyam vaushat, Om shreem
kartalkarprashthabhyam phat

Hridayadinyasah

Om Om hradayaya namah, Om Hraam shirase swaha, Om Greem
shikhaye vashat, Om Lam Kawachye hoom, Om Aam netratraya
vaushat, Om shreem astraya phat

Dhyanam

Haratu kulganesho vaghna sanghan sheshan
Nayatu kulsaparyam poornataa saadhakanam

Pibatu batuknaathah shonitam nindakaanaam
Dishatu sakal kaamaan kaulikaanaam Ganeshah

Nine *mukhi rudraksha*

Mantra

Om Hreem Vam Yam Ram lam

Viniyogah

Asya shree Bhairav mantrasya Naarad rishih, Gayatri chhandah, Bhairavo devata, Vam beejam, Hreem shaktih, abhhwshtasiddhayarthe rudraksha dharanarthe jape viniyogah

Angnyasah

Narad rishaye namah shirasi, gayatri chhandse namo mukhe, Bhairav devataye namo hradi, Vam beejaye namo guhye, Hreem shaktaye namah paadayoh.

Karanyasah

Om Om angushthabhyam namah, Om Hreem tarjaneebhyam swaha, Om Vam madhyamabhyam vashat, Om Yam anamikabhyam hum, Om Ram kanishthiukabhyam vaushat, Om Lam kartalkar prashthabhyam phat

Hridayadinyasah

Om Om Hradyaya namah, Om Hreem shirase swaha, Om Vam shikhaye vashat, Om Yam kawachya hum, Om ram netre traya vaushat, Om Lam astraya phat

Dhyanam

Kapalhastam bhujgopveetam kushnachavim danddharam trinetram Achintya madyam madhupaanmattam hradi smared bhairav mishtadam nranaam

10 *mukhi rudraksha*

Mantra

Om Shreem Hreem Kleem Vreem Om

Viniyogah

Asya shree Janardan mantrasya narad rishih, anushtupchhandah, Janardano devata, Shjreem beejam,Hreem shaktih, abhhesht siddhyarthe rudraksha dharanarthe jape viniyogah

Angnyasah

Narad rishiye namah shirasi, anushtupchhandase namo mukhe, Janardan devataye namo hradi, Shreem beejaye namo guhye, Hreem shaktaye namah paadayoh.

Karanyasah

Om Om Angushthabhyam namah, Om Shreem tarjaneebhyam swaha, Om Hreem madhyamabhyam vashat, Om Kleem anamikabhyam hum, Om Vreem Kanishthikabhyam vaushat, Om kartalkar prashthabhyam phat

Hradayadinyasah

Om Om Hradaya namah, Om shreem shirase swaha, Om Hreem shikhaye vashat, Om hreem kawachye hum, Om vreem Netra tryaya vaushat, Om astraya phat

Dhyanam

Vishnum Sharadchandra-koti sadrasham shankham rathangada Mambhojam dadhatam sitabja nilayam kaantyam jaganmohanam Aabadhamad-haar kundal maha-mauli sphurtkankan Shreevatsank mudaar kaustubh dharma vande muneendreh stutam

11 *mukhi rudraksha*

Mantra

Om Room Kshoom Moom Yoom Aum

Viniyogah

Asya Shri rudramantrasya Kashyap rishih, anushtupchhandah, rudrao devata, Room beejam, Kshoom shaktih, abhheshsiddhayarthe rudraksha dharanarthe jape viniyogah

Angnyasah

Kashyap rishuye namah shirasi, anushtupchhandase namo mukhe, rudra devataye namo hradi, room beejaye namo guhye, Kshoom shaktaye namah paadayoh

Karanyasah

Om Om angushthanabhyam namah, Om room tarjaneebhyam sawha, Om Khsoom madhyamabhyam vashat, Om Moom anamikabhyam hoom, Om Yoom kanishthikabhyam vaushat, Om kartalkarprashthabhyam phat

Hridiyadinyasah

Om Om hradyaya namah, Om room shirase swaha, Om kshoom shikhaye vashat, Om moom kawachaye hoom, Om yoom netra traya vaushat, Om aum astraye phat

Dhyanam

Balkaaryut tejasam dhrat jataa jootendu khando jjwalam Naagentreih hrutsheram japvateem shoolam kapaalam kareih Khatvangam dadhtam trinetra vilastpanchhananm sundaram Vyaghratvakta paridhanamabjnilayam shree neelkantham bhajet

12 *mukhi rudraksha*

Mantra

Om Hreem Kshaum Ghrinih Shreem

Viniyogah

Asya Shree Surya-mantrasya Bhargave rishih, Gayatri chhandah, Vishweshwaro devata. Hreem beejam, Shreem shaktih, Ghranih keelakam, rudrakshadharanayarthe jape viniyogah

Angnyasah

Bhargava-rishaye namahshirasi,Gayatri chhandase namo mukhe. Vishweshwaro devataye namo hradi, Hremm beejaye namo guhye, Shreem shaktaye namah paadayo

Karanyasah

Om Om Shree angushthabhyam namah,Om Hreem Shreem tarjaneebhyam swaha, Om Kshaum shreem madhyamabhyam vashat, Om Gham Shreem anamikabhyam hum, Om Nih Shreem kanishthikabhyam vaushat, Om Hreem Kshaum Ghranih Shree kartsakkar prashthabhyam phat

Hridyadinyasah

Om Om Shreem hradyaya namah, Om Hreem Shreem shirase swaha, Om Kshaum Shreem shikhaye vashat, Om Hreem Shreem kawachaaya Hoom, Om Nim Shreem netra trayaya vaushat Om Hreem Kshaum Ghranih astraya phat

Dhyanam

*Shonambhoruh sansthitam trinayanam vedtrayee vighram
Daanaambhoj yugaabhayaani dadhatam hasteih pravaal prabham
Keyuraangad kankan dwayadharam karne satkundalam
Lokotpatti vinaasha paalan karam suryam gunaaghrim bhajait*

13 mukhi rudraksha

Mantra

Om Eem Yaam Aap Om Iti

Viniyogah

Asya Shree Indra mantrasya Brahma rishih panktih chhandah, Indro devata Eem beejam Aap iti shaktih, rudraksha dharanayarthe jape viniyogah

Angnyasah

Brahma rishaye namah shirasi.panktih chhandase namo mukhe, Indro devataye hradi. Eem beejaye namo guhye,Aap Iti shaktaye namah paadayoh

Karanyasah

Om Om angishthabhyam namah, Om Eem tarjaneebhyam swaha, Om Yaam madhyamabhyam vashat,Om Aap anamikabhyam Hoom, Om Om kanishthikabhyam vaushat, Om Eem Yaam Aap Om kartalkar prashthabhyam phat

Hridiyadinyasah

Om Om hradayaya namah, Om Eem shirase swaha, Yaam shikhaye vashat, Om Aap kawachaaya hoom, Om Om netra trayaya vaushat, Om Eem Yaam Aap Om astraya phat

Dhyanam

Peet varnam sahastraksham vajra padmadharam vibhum Sarva lankaar sanyuktam naumeendraadik meeshwaram

14 mukhi rudraksha

Mantra

Om Aum Hasphrein Khabphrein Hastraun Hasabphein

Viniyogah

Asya Shree Hanuman mantrasya Ramchandra rishih, Jagatee chhandah, Shreem Hanumaddevata, Om beejam, Hasphrein shaktaye namah paadayoh

Angnyasah

Ramchandra rishaye namah shirasi, Jagatee chhandse namao mukhe, Hanumaddevtaaye namah hradi, Aau beejaye namo guhye, Hasphrein shaktaye namah paadayoh,

Karanyasah

Om Om angishthabhyam namah, Om Aum tarjaneebhyam swaha, Om Hasphrein madhyamabhyam vashat, Om Khabhprein anamikabhyam hoom, Om Hastraun kanishthabhyam vaushat, Om Hasabphein kartalkar prashthabhyam phat

Hridiyadinyasah

Om Om hriyadaya namah, Om Aum shirase swaha, Om Hasphrein shikhaye vashat, Om Khabhprei kawachhaya hoom, Om Hasabphein astraya phat

Dhyanam

*Udyan martand-koti prsakat ruchyutam chaaru veeraasanstham
Maujjeeyagnopaveeta bharan ruchi shikha shaubhitam kundalaabhyam
Bhaktanbhish daan pravan manu dinam veedanaad pramodam
Dhyayeddevam vidheyam plavag kulpatim goshpadee bhoot vaardhim*

RUDRAKSHA MALA AND MEDITATION   10

A rudraksha mala is commonly made by using five mukhi rudraksha beads, which are available easily and in different sizes. Usually 7 mm to 10 mm sizes are good to be handled by fingers. A *mala* for chanting of *mantras*, known as *Jap Mala* has 108+1=109 beads, although 54+1 and 27+1 beads can also be used. The +1 bead in the continuous *mala* is known as *Meru Mani* (or *Meru* bead) and it functions like a stopper while counting the *mantras*.

The *jap* is usually done in the following manner:

As the *mantra* is chanted, the *mala* is made to rotate using middle finger and thumb. As soon the *meru* is reached, the *mala* is turned back without crossing the *meru*. The count is noted by different means – using a pen to write down or by keeping some loose beads on the ground.

Each bead of the *mala* is charged with a specific letter and this procedure is known as *Martrika Pratishtha*. In *Akshamalokaupnishad,* (**Ref. 12**) details have been given about this along with methods to purify and charge the *mala*. For a general user, a *rudraksha mala* can be used just by following the *rudraksha pooja* procedure given in Chapter 10.

Chanting of *mantras* on a *mala* is called *Jap Yog* and as Lord Krishna has enunciated it in *Bhagvadgita*, it is the best form of *yogic* practice. **(Ref. 5)** *Jap* can be done using any *mantra* on *rudraksha mala.*

For general information, different types of *malas* are used to propitiate *Dash Mahavidyas* (ten forms of Shakti):

Kali	:	*Dantmala* (of teeth)
Tara	:	*Asthimala* (of bones)
Chhinamastika	:	*Nar-asthimala* (of human bone)
Tripura	:	*Raktachandan* (of red sandalwood)
Bhairavi	:	*Swayambhumala*
Matangi	:	*Gunjamala* (of flower)
Dhumavati	:	*Khardantmala* (of donkey's teeth)
Baglamukhi	:	*Haridramala* (of tamarind seeds)
Kamala	:	*Kamal mala* (of Lotus flower)
Bhuvaneshwari	:	*Sphatikmala* (of crystal beads)

People who follow the rituals strictly use specific *malas* as mentioned below for different Gods:

Vishnu	:	*Shankhmala* (of conch shell)
Sharabhshalav	:	*Bhadraksha mala*
Ganesh	:	*Gajadant* (ivory from elephant tusk)
Govind (Krishna)	:	*Tulsimala*
Surya	:	*Pravalmala*
Shiva	:	*Rudraksha*

Different types of *malas* are recommended in epics for different objectives as mentioned below:

Complete success and fulfillment of desires	*Rudraksha mala*
For *nirvana* (to overcome cycle of birth and death)	*Muktafal mala*
For *kanti* (beauty)	*Chandan mala* (Sandalwood)
For attraction (*Vashikaran*)	*Praval mala*
To attain kingdom	*Rudraksha mala*
Maran (to harm some one)	*Ber mala* (Berry)
To face enemies (*Vidveshan*)	*Arishtakmala* (Reetha-soap nut)
To overcome fear	*Kalimirch mala* (Pepper)
Full destruction of enemies (*Sarvashatrunash*)	*Asthi mala* (Bone)
For oratorial skills	*Sphatik mala* (Crystal)
Destruction of ghosts	*Audumbar mala* (Fruit)
Sattvik and *Rajasi* accomplishments	Silver beads
Bhairavi Sadhana	Gold, silver or *mukta mala*

There is mention of special *malas*, for e.g., *rudraksha* with gold for Shiva and Vishnu (known as *Hariharatmika Mala*) and *rudraksha* and silver for Shiva and Brahma.

There are certain traditions and procedures, which are to be followed for ritualistic usage of *rudraksha malas* during *jap* and these are:

1. Nails should not touch the beads. Use only the

forepart of your fingers. Usually thumb and middle fingers are used for rotation.

2. Do not use left hand for *jap* and do not touch the *mala* with left hand.

3. Use right number of beads.

4. Do not cross the *Meru Mani* and reverse the *mala* after reaching this bead.

5. While doing jap, the mala beads should come toward you. (Devotion, grace of the Lord coming towards you.)

6. The index finger should point opposite to you. (Ego going out.)

7. Keep the mala in a bag (known as *Gomukhi*) while in use or afterwards.

8. The length of the *mala* should be up to the heart level during *jap*.

9. The positioning of your God whom you plan to meditate should be at level higher than the *mala* level.

10. Face East while doing *jap* and keep your backbone straight. Sit in normal *Sukhasan* (sitting normally by cross-folding of legs) or *Padmasan* **(Fig. 43)** which requires practive.

11. Always sit at a fixed place.

12. Always do *jap* at a fixed time.

13. Always do *jap* by heart.

14. Cover your head while doing the *jap*.

15. Focus on the *Ajna Chakra* located between two eyebrows.

Fig. 43: Padmasan

16. *Jap* can be silent, *upanshu* or by normal utterance
    (upanshu jap is the one in which the sound uttered can
    only be heard by you). Silent *jap* requires better
    focusing and concentration and is the best.
17. *Mantra* can be: given by *guru*, chosen by you, or *Om*
18. Do not share your *mala* with anyone.
19. Do not wear a *jap mala* and vice-versa.
20. After completing one round on *mala*, use balls (made
    of *raktachandan, sindoor*, lac or cow dung) to count the
    number of rounds of the *mala*.

Direction to face while doing *jap* depends on your
objective, although facing east is recommended as most
common practice. Other options are:

• Face West if objective is solely for wealth.
• Face North for mental peace, protection, health and
  knowledge.
• Face East to attract a person within the self, for *sadhana*
  and spirituality
• Face South for *tantric* practices

The *mala* can be made using cotton, silk, silver, copper or
gold. If it is thread, it can be red or black. The *rudraksha*
beads should be strung face to face and tail to tail. The
natural shape of *rudraksha* is such that when strung face to
face and tail to tail, the beads will maintain natural distance
and look balanced.

After each bead is strung, the maker should utter *Om* to
remember the supreme lord for ending and restarting the
effort. To ensure that two beads do not touch each other, use
a bigger knot (knot diameter should be twice the hole
diameter), in case a thread is being used. Alternatively, use

metal wire loops and caps to make the bead rigid so that it does not rotate. If *rudraksha* bead rotates using a metal wire then the bead will get damaged due to friction of *rudraksha* with the metal wire.

For higher *mukhi* beads, which are rare and expensive, always use wool thread inside the hole of rudraksha bead even if metal wires are being used so that these do not get spoiled over a long period of time – may be several years – due to friction in case the bead becomes free.

Beej Mantras:

1. Shreem: It is a *Mahalakshmi mantra*. *Sh* is Mahalakshmi, *r* represents wealth, *ee* is contentment. *ikar* is the mother of the universe, and *m* (bindu) is the dispeller of the sorrow.

2. Aim: It is a *Saraswati mantra*, *i* is for Saraswati and *m* (bindu) is the dispeller of the sorrow.

3. Kleem: *Ka* means Kamdev, the lord of desire or Cupid. It also means Lord Krishna. *La* means Indra, the ruler of skies and heaven and also the ruler of senses (Indriyan). *Ee* means contentment and m (bindu) means dispeller of sorrow.

4. Hreem: This is the *mantra* of Mahamaya or Bhuvaneshwari. *Ha* means Shiva, *ra* is *prakriti*, *ee* means *Mahamaya*, the Ikar *matra* is the mother of the universe and *m* (bindu) is the dispeller of sorrow.

5. Kreem: It is the *mantra* of Kalika. *Ka* is Kali, *ra* is Brahman and *ee* is *Mahamaya*, *ikar* is the mother of universe and *m* (bindu) is the dispeller of sorrow.

6. Dum: *Da* represents Goddess Durga, u means to protect, m (bindu) means action and dispeller of sorrow.

7. Haum: *Ha* is Shiva, *au* is Sada Shiva, *m* (bindu) means to dispel sorrow. This is the *mantra* of Lord shiva.

8. Gam: In this mantra, **ga** means Ganesh and **m** (bindu) is the dispeller of sorrow.

9. Glaum: This is also a *mantra* of Ganesh. **ga** means Ganesh, **la** means that which pervades, **au** means luster or brilliance and **m** (bindu) is the dispeller of sorrow.

10. Hoom: Here, **ha** is Shiva, **u** is Bhairav, **m** (bindu) is dispeller of sorrow.

11. **Kshraum**: This is the seed *mantra* of *Narasinha*, a fierce half-lion, half-man incarnation of Lord Vishnu, **ksha** is Narsinha, **ra** is Brahma, **au** means teeth pointing upwards and **m** (bindu) is the dispeller of sorrow.

With every mantra **Om** is added in the beginning and at the end to complete the cycle.

There are thousands and even more *mantras* for all types of *karmas* (specified as *Shat-Karma*) which are:

1. *Shanti karma* for peace
2. *Vasheekaran* to get control of someone
3. *Stambhan* to control the movement of any person
4. *Vidweshan* to create enmity amongst some targets
5. *Uchhatan* to create dissatisfaction and depression among targeted people
6. *Maran* to take away life of any person.

For doing *jap*, one can use *mantra* as given by a *guru* (your acknowledged and sanctified *guru*), or you can choose your own *mantra*, which you do not need to change later on, or just chant *Om,* the letter form of the supreme Lord. Some of the most popular and powerful *mantras* are:

1. **Gayatri Mantra**
   Om Bhoorbhavah swaha tatsviturvarenyam,
   Bhargodevasya dheemahi dhiyo yonah prachodayat

2. **Shiva Mantra (Shadakshri-six letters)**
   Om Namah Shivaya

3. **Pranav Mantra**
   Om

4. **Mahamrityunjaya Mantra**
   Om Haum Joom Saha, Bhoorbhvah Swaha
   Tryambakam Yajamahe Sugandhi Pushti Vardhanam
   Urva Rukmiv Bandhanan Mrityormukshiya Mamrataat
   Bhoorbhavah Swaroam Joom Saha Haum Om

   It can also be chanted this way:
   Om Tryambakam Yajamahe Sugandhim Pushti Vardhanam
   Urva Rukmiva Bandhnana Mrityormukshiya Mamrataat

5. **Devi Navarna-Mantra**
   Aim Hreem Kleem Chhamundaye Vichhe

6. **Ram Krishna Mantra**
   Hare Ram, Hare Ram, Ram Ram, Hare Hare
   Hare Krishna, Hare Krishna, Krishna Krishna, Hare Hare

7. **Ganapati Mantra**
   Om gum Ganapataye Namah

8. **Vishnu Mantra**
   Om Namo Narayan

9. **Krishn Mantra**
   Om Namo Bhagwate Vasudevaye

10. **Ram Mantra**
    Ram (or)
    Om Shri Ramaya Namah

11. **Laksmi Mantra**
    Om Shreem Hleem Kleem Mahalakshmaye Namah

Of all the *mantras*, the common ones are the deity *mantras* in which a specific form of a lord with attributes is visualized and the *mantras* repeated. *Shiva mantra* is used to remove negativities. Those believing in responsible and ideal family life should meditate on the name of Ram. Those who see God as infinite, all loving and even a little playful shall chant Krishna. It is, however, important to understand that visualization of the deities assist you in focusing the mind. Repeating the *mantras*, which are essentially the names of deities, take the power internally within yourself along with the vibrations, which are contained in the name.

Scientists have explained that when the energy breaks down, it forms patterns and it dances. This is true of Lord Shiva. Fritj Capra, author of *The Tao of Physics,* explains in one of his lectures: "Modern physics explains the matter not as passive or inert but as continuously dancing and vibrating.... They have actually used words 'dance of creation and destruction' or 'energy dance'. This naturally comes to mind when you see some of the pictures of particles taken by physicists in their bubble chambers. Of course, physicists are not the only one talking about the cosmic dance. They are the modern version of the dance of Shiva who is performing a cosmic dance."

A physical form of any God is therefore a cosmic reality, either explained through above example or through mind and body relationships and quantum theories. Word, sound and *mantra* are the integral parts of Hindu mythology and cosmology and cannot be separated from it. *Jap* (repetition of mantras) is a path from microcosm to macrocosm; it is the vehicle that carries the individual back to the source. The Vedas say *Soham* (I am He) and the *jap* assimilates you with the Supreme as salt mixes with water.

Mantra, sadhana and meditation are not within the scope of this book and the readers are advised to refer to some of the references given in bibliography.

Lakshmi *mantras*

The following are *mantras* dedicated to Goddess Mahalakshmi (Please choose any one of these):

Om Shreem Namah
Shreem Shriyei namah
Om Kamalyei namah
Om Hreem padme namah
Om Shreem Hreem Kleem shriye namah
Aim Shreem Hreem Kleem
Om Shreem Mahalakshmayei namah
Om namah Kamalvasanyei namah
Om Hreem Shreem namah
Om Hreem Shreem Kleem Shree Siddhi Lakshamayei namah
Om Mahalakshmayei cha vidmahe,Vishnupatneem cha dheemahi
Tanno Lakshmi prachodayat
Om Shreem hreem Kleem Mahalaksmayei namah
Om Hreem shreem Kleem Hrasaunha jagatprasootyayei namah

There are some *mantras,* known as *chetak mantras,* primarily for getting wealth and prosperity. These *mantras* are recommended to be used after worshipping the deity with the regular *mantras* for some time and getting familiar with *Lakshmi poojan.* These *mantras* have specified numbers for *jap* to give desired results.

1. *Ekakshar mantra* **Shreem**

    Most *Lakshmi mantras* begin with this word as this is the

main name of Mahalakshami.12 lakh (1.2 million) is the number of times this *mantra* is to be chanted for *siddhi* and success. Generally, devotees prefer to chant *Om Shreem namah* to give respect to the name and to complete the same as per standard ritual.

2. **Namah Kamal Vaasinyei Swaha**

Mahalakshmi sitting on a lotus flower is the form to be worshipped along with chanting of this *mantra* 10 lakh (1 million) times.

3. **Aim Hreem Shreem Jyeshtha Lakshmi Swayam Bhuve Hreem Jyeshthaya namah**

This *mantra* is to be recited only one lakh times (0.1 million) for getting results, mainly acquisition of wealth.

4. **Glaum Shreem anatam Mahayannam ma dehyannadhi pate**

Mamannam pradapaya   Swaha Shreem Glaum

To get wealth accompanied by fame and respect, one may recite this *mantra* one lakh (0.1 million) times.

Shreesukta is recited regularly by people to get blessings of Mahalakshmi.

Many of the successful Indians who have acquired global positioning among rich successful people, are devoted rudraksha users and offer regular prayers to Goddess Lakshmi. Apart from their own hard work, genius and opportunities, which came their way, these holostic approaches have also helped them.

Rudraksha is a gift of Lord Shiva to the mankind and it is a manifestation of the devotion to Shiva and Shiva *bhakti* so much so that *rudraksha* and Shiva are synonymous and integral to each other. In *Akshmalikopanishad*, it is said that even Rudra gets *Rudratva* (Rudrahood) by wearing *rudraksha*.

Rudraksha dharanadev Rudrau rudratvamapnuyaat
Munayah satyasankalpa Brahma brahmatvamaagatah

In *Shrimad Devibhagwat*, **(Ref. 2)** the following description is given with regard to seeding of *rudraksha* on Earth, as told by Lord Shiva Himself to his son Kartikeya:

"In olden times, a demon named Tripur won over all *Devatas* and killed many of them. Lord Brahma and Vishnu, along with others, approached me to get rid of him. I looked out for a weapon and identified *aghor*, which was powerful and full of fire and meant to overcome Tripur. In order to accomplish the task, I had meditated for 1000 divine years keeping my eyes open. From my tired eyes, tears rolled down on the Earth and took the form of *rudraksha* trees.

"As per classification, there are of 38 types of *rudrakshas*. From the eyes of Sun, came 12, from the eyes of Moon 16 (all bright varieties) and fire produced 10 (black in colour). In terms of tradition, white is for Brahmins, red for Kshatriyas, mixed for Vaishyas and black for Shudras"

Shiva Puran **(Ref. 1)** also gives a similar version as told by
Lord Shiva.

"Long back, I did penance (*tapa*), keeping control over the
heart (*man*) and body. I became distressed seeing the suffering
of the mankind and I closed my eyes to think of a solution.
Then, tears rolled down from my eyes and wherever these
fell, mighty trees sprang up. These trees got the name
rudraksha and assumed the role of saviours of mankind. For
the disciples of Vishnu, these trees grew in *Gaud Pradesh**.
They also grew in places identified with me like Mathura,
Ayodhya, Lanka, Malayachal (Mysore), Sharyaparvat
(Maharashtra), Kashi and other ten countries and helped
mankind in getting over sins. There are four types with color
variations — white, blood-red, yellow and black. *Shubhaksha*
(*bhadraksha*) also belong to these species."

It is not understood how Nepal and the Himalaya region
are not mentioned. Also *bhadraksha*, which does not fall into
the given definition of pure *rudraksha*, gets special mention
here. The only explanation could be that over the past several
thousand years, the trading community would have influenced
the copying of the original epics and no one for sure knows
which are the original ancient texts and which ones are added
later (called *kshepak* in traditional terms).

It is, however, established that Lord Shiva gave these beads
to overcome the sins of mankind and offer solace. It is up to
us now to make use of these divine beads in proper way.

Wearing *rudraksha* may have different objectives for people
but so far the opinion of most *rudraksha* users is that

---

* Gaud Pradesh: Part of Afghanistan and Punjab, including Kurukshetra,
  Gonda Basti Janpad, West Bengal

rudraksha got its divinity and its mystical powers due to the blessings of the great Lord Shiva, also known as Mahadeva (Greatest among gods). Blessings of Shiva are obtained prior to wearing *rudraksha* and regular spiritual charging of the beads is recommended by doing *abhisheks* similar to *Rudra Abhishek*. Whether these beads bring benefits without any prayers while used for medicinal purposes is yet to be confirmed, but they are known to behave strangely, according to observations made by researchers at reputed laboratories where research on these beads are being carried out. Therefore, it is useful and auspicious to know about the creator of these beads, that is, Lord Shiva. He can be understood marginally through devotion and blessings.

The word Shiva means auspiciousness and prosperity-bestowing principle. The reverse of Shiva is Vash meaning to enlighten; therefore the one who enlightens is Shiva. Shiva is absolute, self-radiant and illuminates the world. Following forms of Lord Shiva are known to us as having typical characteristics:

Rudra

During the Vedic period, Rudra was known as a destroyer and a fearful God. Rudra means the one who cries (ru) and the one who runs away while crying (dru). Rut also means sorrow of the materialistic world and the one who vanquishes and overcomes it is called Rudra.

'Rut' also means the truth, the base principle of the Upanishads. Therefore, one who has realized or expounded the truth is Rudra.

Rut is speech consisting of words or the knowledge of self-realization expounded through this medium. One who bestows this to the worshippers is Rudra.

Rudra's subordinates are many and known by different names. These subordinates reside in heaven, destroy evil doers, protect the righteous, observe the *pashupat* (vowed religious observance), vanquish obstacles of the *yogis* and serve Lord Shiva perpetually. The 11 Rudras as per *Shrimad Devibhagwat* are *Har, Bahuroop, Trayambak, Aoarajit, Shambhu, Vrishakapi, Kapardi, Raivat, Mrigvyadh, Sharva and Kapaali.*

Ardhanareeshwar

Creation and life cycle of this universe is not possible without the unification of male and female forms of humans. Lord Shiva took the *Ardhanareeshwar* form in order to represent this aspect to mankind. Every human body has bi-sexual characteristics built into itself and it procreates from within itself. *Agnishomatmakam jagat,* says *Shruti* (Vedas). Fire is the male principle and is present in the menstrual flow of females. The Moon (*Som*) is the feminine principle and is present in the sperm of the male. Desire (Kaama) is the force that brings the two together. The above two principles get attracted to each other due to Kaama. In *Adwait Shaivagam,* the divine energy is not to be renounced, but it has to be accepted as the energy of the Brahma, the supreme lord. The permanent union of Shiva and Shakti is considered as *adwait* or non-duality. The right half of Shiva is a female form, says Hemadri, the writer of *Chaturvargachintamani.* This *Ardhnareeshwar* form of Shiva has equal male and female powers (a unified form of Shiva and Shakti). **(Fig. 15)**

Kalbhairav

He is one of the eight Bhairavs and was created from Shiva's wrath. After Shiva had severed the fifth head of Brahma through Kalbhairav, He directed Kalbhairav to stay at Kashi (Banaras). Kalbahirav is thus the guardian of Kashi. On entering Kashi, one must pay obeisance to Him first.

Virbhadra

He has made Vetal his vehicle. It is believed that Virbhadra is the first to worship Shiva in the *linga* form.

Bhairav

Bhairav literally means the Earth and Bhairavnath is its Lord. Sixty-four types of *Bhairavs* have been described, of which *Kalbhairav* and *Batuk Bhairav* are more famous. It is said that the Bhairavs guard each seat of divine energy (*Shaktipeeth*). The *Shakti pooja* is not considered complete by some sects without the inclusion of Bhairav.

Vetal

Vetal literally means the one who can dance to his tune. When *ahat* and *anahat* sounds fuse, frequencies are generated. They correct the abnormalities. Vetal is also called *Agyavetal, Jwalavetal or Pralayvetal*. These Vetals are included among the attendants of Shiva. Idols of Vetal are made of wood and many villages He acts as a village deity.

Bhootnath

He is a deity similar to Vetal and if someone is possessed by a spirit, then it is driven off by summoning Bhootnath.

Nataraj

Body movements, which depict a particular event, are called *natan* or *natya*. The one who performs *natan* is a *nat*. Shiva as Natraj is a promoter of dance and He is a pioneer among actors (*nat*). The universe is His school of dance. Just as He is the dancer He is also the observer. Nataraj's dance is considered to represent five actions of God namely creation, sustenance, dissolution, the covering of the great illusion (*Maya*) and initiation (*Anugraha*). The Nataraj's dance form is to liberate a person from the great illusion. **(Fig. 44)**

The dance in which the sound (*naad*) in every cell of the body (*bhuvans*) is that of Shiva is called *tandav* dance. It is a dance performed by males and consists of postures (*madras*). For instance, the *dhyan mudra* is performed by touching the index finger to the thumb.

There are seven types of *tandav* dance: *anandtandav, sandhyatandav, kalikatandav, tripurtandav, gauritandav, sanhartandav and umatandav.*

Fig. 44: Nataraj

At Chidambaram in Tamil Nadu, Lord Shiva is doing *sandhyatandav*. In this form of dance, Shiva performs dance and Gauri (Parvati) sits on a throne studded with jewels. Saraswati (Goddess of Learning) plays the musical instrument veena, Indra plays the flute, Lakshmi sings, Vishnu plays the *mridang* and several other deities watch. In this dance, Shiva has two hands.

Of the seven types, the most fearsome is *gouritandav* and

umatandav, wherein Shiva dances in a crematorium assuming the form of Bhairav or Virbhadra and is accompanied by Gauri. In *anandtandav*, various postures illustrate different meanings as given below:

Different earrings in each ear	Ardhnareeshawar
The small hourglass-shaped hand drum in the right hand	Creation of Brahman in the form of sound and word (Sanskrit language evolved through these sounds
Fire in the left hand	Purification of Brahma by sound and word
The front right hand	Protection to devotees
The front left hand	Points to the foot raised for liberation of embodied souls
The demons *Apasmar* or *Muyalak* crushed under the right foot	Destruction of ignorance
The surrounding circle	Cycle of illusion (*Maya*)
The hand and foot touched to *Chakra*	Purifying great illusion (*Maya*)
Five *lingas* arising spontaneously from the flames of the *Chakra*	The subtle five cosmic elements

Kirat

This is the *Kapalik* form of Lord Shiva. He is engrossed in various sports of pleasure and Bhagwati Uma accompanies Him.

SHIVA'S FAMILY

Wife-Parvati (also known as Uma)

Known by several names like Shakti and as Sati (daughter of Daksha), she is worshipped along with Lord Shiva wherever He is worshipped in human form. In the *linga* form, Shakti is placed on the backside of the *linga* and is also worshipped.

Sons (two)

Kartikeya: He is known as Skand and in southern India known as Subramanya or Murugan. He had killed the powerful demon Tarakasur.

Ganesh: He is first among all the Gods to be worshipped due to his great mind and devotion to parents. He is great writer of the epics as told by Maharshi Vyas and is a lovable God eager to remove obstacles from one's life.

Nandi

Nandi in the form of a bull is Shiva's vehicle. He is paid obeisance before Shiva. In temples of Shiva, Nandi stands on one leg and the other three are bent at the knees. This signifies that in Kaliyug, righteousness exists only to the extent of one fourth.

Lord Shiva is known by several names because of his multifold qualities and attributes. A thousand names of Shiva are recited in *Shiva Sahasranam*. Some of the popular names are *Mahadev, Shankar, Mahakaleashwar, Bhalachandra, Karpurgaur, Neealkanth, Ashutosh, Sharva, Pashupati, Kamari, Mahesh, Ugra, Ishaan*, and *Umapati*.

It is interesting to learn about the physical features of Lord Shiva in some of the commonly known forms, which will also throw some light on the importance of *rudraksha*. In the physical form, He is associated with the following:

Ganga

The stream of consciousness of Ganga comes from the combined energy of Brahma, Vishnu and Shiva. The energy has its origin in the toe of Vishnu and then is collected by Brahma and given a charming divine form. She is cursed by Durvasa Rishi for her impertinence and is forced to descend from the higher *lokas* to Earth as a river. Before Ganga descends on Earth, she is held captive in the hair locks of Shiva and becomes charged with the energy of Shiva. She thus possesses the combined energy of Brahma, Vishnu and Shiva. In her journey to Rishi Kapil's hermitage, where she meets the ocean, she is swallowed by Rishi Janu and becomes purer than before.

It has been scientifically established that Ganga water does not decay even when stored for a very long time. It is kept in all Hindu homes and one wishes to have this water at the time of one's death. Even King Aurangzeb, a moghul king who ruled most parts of India in sixteenth century A.D., whose dislike for Hindu rituals and his barbaric deeds toward Hindus are well known, drank only Ganga water because of its healing qualities. Most of the immortal Hindu scriptures have been written on the banks of river Ganga.

Moon

Shiva adorns *Chandrama* (moon) on his forehead.
Chandrama has absorbed the frequencies of Prajapat, Brahma,
Vishnu, Minakshi and Shiva and imparts them to others along
with energies of Indra. 'The one which gives pleasure" is the
meaning of *Chandrama*. It gives affection, mercifulness and
motherly love. It is also known that Moon (*Som*) is
responsible for the growth and internal powers of all herbs.
It, therefore, plays an important role in the survival of the
humans and in keeping them happy. It is a powerful
ornament adorned by Lord Shiva.

The Third Eye

The Third Eye of Shiva is located above the middle point
of the eyebrows. It is also the greatest seat of extrasensory
energy and is endowed with names such as *Vyaspeeth,
Jyotirmath* etc. *Chandra, Arka and Vaishvanar* are the three eyes
of Lord Shiva. *Arka* is the sun from the *ajanaj* region (*lok*)
while *Vaishvanar* is the Sun from the *karmadev* region.
Therefore, Shiva can view everything in the universe. He can
perceive events in the past, present and future as well. In *yog*
science, it is called Cushman channel (NADI). The *ajna chakra*
gets activated by the Third Eye.

The serpent

Serpents are ladders in the *yog* science whereby the *Sadhak*
holds the tail of serpent and climbs up. Shiva adorns serpents
at nine sites on his body — one on the head, one around the
neck, one on each arm, one on each wrist, one around the
waist and one on each thigh. These nine serpents are referred
to as *Navanarayan* and also *Navanaths* (The nine saints of the
Nath sect have originated from these nine serpents.). The

path of activation of spiritual energy (*Kundalini yog*) indicates that five serpents wander in the body as five vital energies. Other four serpents are also needed to achieve success in the spiritual path.

Holy ash

All those who take birth blend with ash. *Bhasma* is the ash of the one who is born. In Shiva *pooja*, application of *bhasma* on the body after bath is a desired ritual. Ash contains the following types of memories from the time of taking birth:

a. *Yajanasmriti*: memories of sacrificial fires.
b. *Parthivsmriti*: memories of death, which are full of agony and sorrow, with reference to Earth.
c. *Tanmaysmriti*: memories of sacrifice in the context of the region from Earth to the northern region (Shiva direction) and the southern region.

The three horizontal stripes of ash on the forehead of Shiva represent these three memories.

Human ash is applied to *Jyotirlingas*. This gives the message that our physical body is not real, it is fake and it has to go. The holy ash derived from the fireplace of an *Agnihotra* is the purest one. *Agnihotra* people keep fire burning all the time during their lives. The ash obtained after the cremation of a corpse amidst chanting of *mantras* is called human ash (*Chitabhasm*). In Varanasi, the *Jyotirling Vishveshwar* is always smeared with human ash.

Vibhuti is a synonym for holy ash. It is used in *tantra, mantra*, black magic, etc., to guard the directions as self-protection. Ashes of gold, pearls, etc., are used in Ayurveda for medical applications to cure diseases.

Tiger skin as garment

Tiger skin represents *rajas* and *tamas* attitudes and Lord Shiva wears this skin after killing a tiger. It is to establish that the mind must follow the *satvik* mode with purity only to achieve peace and tranquility.

Flowers of *dhatura*

Dhatura is a wild flower having intoxicating properties but in appearance it is beautiful. Use of this flower only indicates the same feature of *rajas* and *tamas* and that Lord Shiva symbolises the power to capture all that is harmful to the ordinary people. He had swallowed the poison that came out of the churning of the ocean by the *Devas* and *Asuaras*, because He found that this poison would destroy ordinary people and for their survival, He drank it and kept it in His throat giving blue color to this part of his body. He is thus known as Neelkanth.

Damru

It is a musical instrument and resembles a hand drum with two strings and drubbing balls. Sounds from this drum had created the *Maheshwar sutras*, which are also known as the 14 *pratyahars* of Sanskrit language. (Sanskrit is based on sound form and is the only correct basic language in this universe. There are 49 types of *Marut* (wind) and with each wind form a special letter of Sanskrit language is formed. (Sixteen letters of *swar* (sounds), 33 letters of *vyanjan* (vowels) and one special vowel letter make up the 50 letters of this powerful language).

Sanskrit language has the power to express divine laws more rationally and even in the materialistic world it can be a unifying force to bring all conversations on one platform. It is

a very scientific and complete language, which did not get its
due place. While it is not likely that it will ever get its due
place in the future, it should not be allowed to become sick
further. If the origin and purpose of earth is to be
understood correctly, Sanskrit should not be allowed to
extinct.

As Pashupati, Shiva adorns *pinaka* (*ajagava*), *Parasu* (axe), *Pas*
(sling), *Yog Dand, trishul,* Fire and *khatwang* (skull stick). In all
His forms, He wears **Rudraksha Malas**. This is an essential
part of His ornaments. The *rudraksha malas* decorate his
wrists, neck, biceps and headgear.

He also wears *kapaals* or *nar-munds* (shrunken heads) strung
as beads and is known as Kapaleeshwar.

The above description is helpful in understanding one fact
that like all chosen ornaments of the Lord, *rudraksha* has a
meaningful application and it is from a power class.

Lord Shiva is ...

1. **Yogi:** He performs severe penances and is a great *yogi*.
   He is one God who chants the supreme lord's name
   continuously. He is always seated in a *bandha* or *mudra*.
   His temperature rises due to severe austerities, hence
   needs cooling effect, which He gets from the flow of
   Ganga, the moon on his crown and while living in the
   Himalayas.
2. **Short-tempered:** If someone disturbs His penance, he
   may get destroyed.
3. **Helpful:** He goes to any extent to help others. He
   drank the poison that came out of the churning of the
   oceans as he knew if it falls on the universe, it will be
   the end of the universe. This attitude has caused Him

inconveniences as He gives great boons to his
followers without knowing their antecedents and these
followers grow in strength and start harassing others,
forcing Him to step in again to save the situation. He
gave great boons to King *Ravan, Tarakasur, Tripurasur,
Banasur* and others, who later tried to defeat the Gods
and become all-powerful. Usually, Vishnu comes to His
rescue in such situations.

4. **Ashutosh:** The one who can be most easily pleased.
5. **Master of spirits:** Worshipper of Shiva is not
   possessed by the spirits.
6. **Resides as a deity in most serene but difficult
   locations:** The locations of all famous Shiva temples
   and *Jyotirlingas** are in the most difficult terrain and
   difficult to reach. Mount Kailash (Nepal), Amarnath

---

* **Jyotirlingas:** We believe that all the 12 *jyotirlingas* (Lord Shiva in *linga*
form having sourced from light) were established using the lighted
energies fallen from the space (meteorites). They got materialized in
the radiant form. Following are the 12 *jyotirlingas:*

Somnath	Near Veraval-Gujarat
Mallikarjuna	Shrisailam in Andhra Pradesh
Mahakal	Ujjain in Madhya Pradesh
Omkareshwar	Omkareshwar, near Khandwa in Madhya Pradesh
Kedarnath	Himalayas (North of Uttaranchal)
Bhimashankar	In Pune district, Maharashtra
Vishveshwar	Varanasi in Uttar Pradesh
Trambakeshwar	Nashik in Maharashtra
Vaidyanath	Parli, in Maharashtra, or Vaidyanathdham in Bengal
Nagesh	Darukavan in Maharashtra or Almoda in Uttar Pradesh
Rameshwar	Near Kanyakumari in Tamil Nadu
Ghushneshwar	Verul in Maharashtra

Cave (India), Mansarovar (China) and 12 *Jyotirlingas* are typical examples, though Shiva temples are common in practically all the villages, towns and cities of India. The erstwhile kings and royalties were disciples of Shiva (or Hanuman) and even now the most authentic *Sanatan Dharma* legacy is found among Shiva worshippers throughout India and more particularly in the south.

7. **Urdhvaretas:** *Urdhvaretas* are those whose semen is not ejaculated. The semen gets converted to *oja* (divine energy). Shiva, being a *Urdhvareta,* can procreate by merely making a resolve (*sankalp*). It is contended that if mercury is consumed in amounts which the body can tolerate, semen flows upwards gradually. Hence mercury is called Shankar's semen. (Phosphorous is considered to be Parvati's menstrual blood and mica her ova.)

8. **The Shaiva sect believes that Shiva is the creator of this universe.** The cycle of different segments of Earth consists of the following periods in human years: *Satyug*: 17,28,000; *Treta*: 12,96,00; *Dwapar*: 8,64,000 and *Kaliyug*: 4,32,000. (All figures are in no. of human years).

Since Lord Yama (Yamraj) **(Fig. 24)** is controlled by Shiva and Yama is the master of south, all *Jyotirlingas* face southwards. The *lingas* in such cases have more energies than those facing some other direction in exceptional cases.

Some special features of ritualistic worship (*pooja*) of Lord Shiva:

1. In the most ritualistic worships of Shiva, no conch

shell is used, neither its water offered over the *linga*. If a *banalinga* is part of the five-fold family of deities (Shiva Panchayat), then one may sprinkle the *banalinga* with water from the conch. However, a *banalinga* with a *pindi* of Lord Mahadev should not be sprinkled with this water. Blowing of the conch before the ritual of *aarti*, or worshipping with lamps, is allowed. Rather it is considered very auspicious to blow a conch during *aarti*. Banlinga is the one which gets linga shape from bones of human corpses thrown in rivers.

2. Tulsi leaves are not offered to Shiva. However, if these leaves are first offered to Lord Vishnu in the form of a *Shaligram*, then these leaves can be offered to Shiva.

3. It is said that on the eighth day of the dark fortnight of the Hindu lunar month of Jyeshtha, Lord Shankar (Shiva) is ritualistically worshipped and on the 14th day, Revati is worshipped using blue flowers. On that day, blue color has the ability to absorb the Shiva energy as much as the green of the *bel* leaves. On *Mahashivaratri*, *kevada* flower is used.

4. *Bel* leaves, white flowers and the food offered to the *pindi* of Lord Shiva are not accepted as *prasad* as they can induce detachment, which an average person would not want.

5. People belonging to different sects like *Shaiva, Kapalik, Gosavi, Virashaiva*, etc. use various *lingas* – earthen (*parthivlingas*), *lingas* in a silver box donned around the neck (*kanthasthalinga*), *lingas* of crystal glass (*sphatik linga*), *banalinga*, a five- stringed linga (*panchsutri*), stone *linga*, etc.

6. Circumambulations (*linga parikrama*) are offered to

Lord Shiva. The path is like half moon. The channel, which runs towards the Moon from the base of the *linga* till the boundary of the temple, is called the *som sutra*. When circumambulating, one should begin on the left hand side and continue till the channel of the *Yoni* from where the water is offered during the ritualistic bathing (*abhishek*) flows. Without crossing it, one should complete a circumambulation by moving in the reverse direction up to the other side of the channel. This applies only if the *Shivalinga* is installed or created by men; it does not apply to a *swayambhu linga* (like *jyotirlingas*) or the *Chal lingas* kept in the house. The flow of the *shalunka* (*yoni*) is not crossed over as it is the flow of the energy.

7. Lord Shiva loves being worshipped with liquids. Shiva is offered *abhishek* by reciting a hymn from Yajurved called *rudra*. It is of two types – *namakar* (*namak*) and *chamakar* (*chamak*). In *namakar*, the word *namah* appears frequently and in *chamakar* the word *chamah*. This *abhishek* is performed by reciting the *rudradhyaye* 11 times. Eleven rounds of (*avartans*) of the *rudradhyaye* constitute one *ekadashni*. Eleven *ekadashnis* make up one *laghurudra* and 11 *laghurudra*s make one *maharudra*. Finally 11 *maharudras* constitute one *atirudra*. It is said that the person who does *atirudra* with devotion gets *nirvan* and goes to *Shiva Lok*, never to follow the cycle of birth and death.

8. Chanting the name of Shiva *"Namah Shivaya"* is a *Panchakshari mantra*, which finds mention in *rudradhyaye*. **(Ref. 3),** which is a subdivision of Yajurved. When it is prefixed with sacred syllable *Om* (*Parma*), it becomes *Om Namah Shivaya*, the six letter *Shadakshari mantra*.

The spiritual meaning of this *mantra* is:

Na: The foremost deity of all the regions.

Ma: the bestower of supreme spiritual knowledge and destroyer of the greatest sins.

Shi: Benevolent, serene and responsible for the initiation by Lord Shiva.

Va: the representative of a bull as the vehicle and the *Vasuki* and *Vamangi* energies.

Ya: The auspicious abode of supreme bliss and Lord Shiva.

Usage of *Om* with the *Panchakshari mantra* is helpful in gaining energy to blend *Sagun* with *Nirgun* (manifest with unmanifest). *Om* chanting should be done with great devotion and patience. At many places, women are forbidden from pronouncing *Om*. Instead, it is recommended that they chant only *Namah Shivaya* or *Shri Namah Shivaya*. We however, do recommend women to prefix *Om* and recite it with full concentration.

9. *Shiva Gayatri*: *Tatpurushaye Vidmahe, Mahadevaye cha Dheetah, Tanno Rudraha Prachodayat*

It means: We are quite familiar with that Supreme Being Mahadev. We meditate on that Mahadev. May that *rudra* inspire our intellect benevolently!

Some of the humankind's most beautiful poems, *shlokas*, verses and *mantras* in Sanskrit as well as other languages in India have been composed in praise of this versatile, beautiful and mystical God whose appearance, deeds and charm is flexible, adoptable and absolutely fascinating. Intellectuals will realise how their creative minds can get boost and skills sharpened if they can meditate keeping Shiva in their focus.

RUDRAKSHA, PRANAYAM AND YOG 12

Rudraksha is helpful in achieving calmness of mind that can lead us to a super-conscious and divine state of thoughts and search for our own source and objective of life. All great souls in any period of history could achieve their pure objectives only because they were calm, fearless and self-confident.

This chapter aims primarily at discussing *Ashtang Yog*, the true path for any human being, but difficult to achieve. *Rudraksha* is a useful tool in traversing this path as it activates and motivates the mind to reach a state of calmness, necessary to take up this task.

An answer to the perennial question about the objective of our birth in this world and how to fulfill the tasks earmarked lies in understanding the four basic principles — **Dharm** (designated duties), **Arth** (wealth and materials), **Kaam** (pleasure and self- contentment) and **Moksh** (liberation from the cycle of birth and death). The great *Rishis* of the past have outlined these principles as the objectives for the human life. One can fulfill these objectives by having two basic factors — a healthy body and concentration of mind. Since ancient times, there are two types of spiritual path being followed by the great achievers — *Snaky* (the way of knowledge), propagated by Kapil Muni, and *Yog* (the path of unifying mind and body) established by Patanjali.

The path of knowledge is tedious and beyond normal perceptions and one life seems insufficient to follow this path. Still, this path has attracted many and the great philosophical approaches have been laid down to understand the meaning of life and ways to achieve the objectives of birth.

In the second path, one has to practise *Ashtang Yog* (eight types of controls and practices), as propagated by the great sage, Patanjali, thousands of years ago with astounding correctness and proven at all times and in trying situations. These practices have been mentioned stepwise in a progressive manner as: *yam* (abstentions), *niyams* (observances), *asanas* (postures), *pranayam* (control of breath dimensions), *pratyahar* (withdrawal of senses), *dharana* (concentration), *dhyan* (meditation) and *samadhi* (the highest level of consciousness or super-conscious state). We shall understand these steps in more detail.

1. Yam

These are essential deeds to purify body and to cleanse the thoughts (*man*). As per *Bhagwadgita* there are 12 *yams*:

Ahimsa

No cruelty should be shown to anyone, whether it is man or animal, physically, verbally or mentally.

Satya

Truthfulness in words, deeds and intentions is the credo. Not only should we speak truth, it must be ensured that it does not hurt anyone.

Asteya

One must abstain from stealing. Materials (wealth, land, properties, food or anything physical) that do not belong to one should not be grabbed by any means.

Brahmacharya

Practicing celibacy (married people having sex for purposes of procreation is considered as *brahmacharya*) is an important factor. To control sensual desires, one must abstain from food items that increase such desires (like alcohol, drugs and *tamasik* (non-vegetarian food) and should not see, read or think of obscenity in any form.

Aparigraha

Greed for things for self-consumption should not be there. There has to be a balance between necessity and stock and one should store only in terms of need.

Astikta

Cultivate spirituality and belief in the existence of God. This only can motivate you to engage yourself in doing good things in life.

Lajja

Have a sense of shame while doing things that are bad or undesired. In a state of shamelessness, it will be just routine to commit any indecent act.

Asang

Give up attachment and avoid bad company.

Maun

Silence is one of the greatest qualities. Speaking consumes

energy in an unorganized manner as thought and expression can never be fully synchronized. By observing silence, one can improve concentration and gain better wisdom.

Sthirta

This is cultivating stillness of thought and action. It improves self-confidence and brings in peace of mind.

Kshama

One must seek pardon from all people around and from God for any mistake committed. This will lead to a clear conscience and humility.

Abhaya

Be fearless. A fearless approach is required to have a stable mind, which in turn is needed in taking correct decisions. This will increase one's confidence in almighty.

2. Niyams

Niyam means a determination, which has to be followed at all times and it is like a *tapa* (penance). Following five *niyams* are important: *shauch, santosh, tapa, swadhyaya* and *ishwar pranidhan*

Shauch

Purity of the body, by keeping the surroundings clean and making the atmosphere favorable and pleasant, and purity of mind, by imbibing good thoughts, processes and believing in the good of others.

Santosh

An inner satisfaction in all situations. One should not become greedy and crave for certain things intently, losing peace of mind. *Brahmadilok paryanta dwiraktya yallbhetpriyan* means that even after getting the pleasure from abodes of Lord Brahma and other Devas, the one who remains unattached and happy from within is known to have *santosh* or satisfaction.

Tapa

Tapa means to get heated up for purifying body and mind. *Tapa* can be for body, speech and mind. The body *tapa*, as Maharshi Vyasa has defined, consists of bearing the inner consciousness to fight with hunger, thirst, heat, cold, place, seat, silence of movement or speech and various fasts. The body, after intense *tapa*, should become used to bear so much of pain and other negative aspects that no amount of further pain may ever have an impact. Such a *tapa* also wards off the fear of death. However, Vyasa also prescribes that it should be practiced in such a way as not to disturb the equilibrium of the three body systems of *Vaat*, *Pitt* and *Kaf*.

The *tapa* of speech should be for controlling words of anger, use of kind words, telling the truth and acquisition of knowledge.

The *tapa* of the mind is for getting trained to keep inner consciousness clean, thinking positive, doing good to others and praying to God.

Swadhyaya

To achieve liberation from the cycle of birth, it is necessary to study the knowledge already acquired and conveyed to us through Vedas, Darshan, Upanishads, etc. *Omkar-* and Gayatri-related epics should be studied along with doing *japa* with *mantras*. It is for self-realization that this self-study is being propagated and not for any worldly attainments.

Ishwar Pranidhan

God is the power that had been there from the beginning, is there now and will remain for ever. The entire movement of the universe, the *pran* and the atoms are getting the energy from God, in existence, but with no form. It is the total surrender to the God which has been termed as *Ishwar Pranidhan*.

Maharshi Vyasa also terms God as the *param guru* and says that all our actions should be surrendered to God who is our *param guru*. (teacher of teachers)

3. Asan

Sthirsukhmasanam, as Maharshi Patanjali says, is to sit comfortably with stability. It is called *asan*. *Yogasan* is one of the types of *asan*, but is highly specialized and very useful for health. For doing any *asan*, the floor should be flat, the mat should be cushioned and it may be of wool, *kusha* grass or cotton — a material not conductive to electricity. The area should have free flow of air but not noisy or infested with flies, mosquitoes, etc.

As *yog* is very useful and those wearing *rudraksha* will find that one gets better concentration and thus better results if *yog* is done with *rudraksha mala* over the body, except while doing some typical *yogasanas* like *Sarvangasan,* for purposes of convenience only. In choosing the various types of *yogasan*, one should look at the benefits for different parts of the body like waist, stomach, legs and shoulders. And a proper blend should be made under the guidance of a *yoga* teacher.

In **(Fig. 45)** the following *asanas* have been shown for information purposes only.

Padmasan, Halasan, Bhujangasan, Siddhasan, Matsyasan and Mandookasan

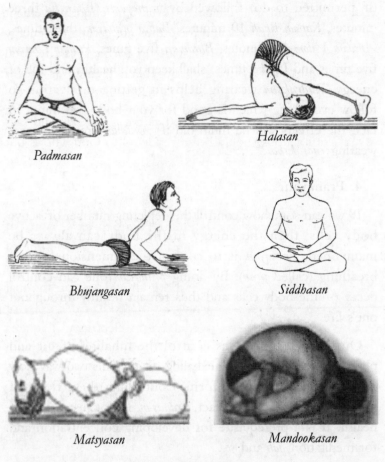

Padmasan

Halasan

Bhujangasan

Siddhasan

Matsyasan

Mandookasan

Fig. 45: Asanas

The choice of any *asan* depends on many factors but primarily it should be decided on the basis of your needs, schedule of your activities, type of work you do and opportunity of learning. A blend of exercises like running (jogging or treadmill), gym workouts like pushups, stretching, weight lifting etc., can be combined with *asans* for waist and back, shoulders, and stomach like *ushrashtasan* and *sarvangasan* (if permitted to do) followed by *pranayams* (*Bhasrika* three minutes, *Kapaal Bhati* 10 minutes, *Bahya pranayam* three times, *Anulom Vilom* 10 minutes, *Bhramari* five times, *Pranav Dhwani* five times and *Ujjai* 5 times) shall keep you healthy and full of energy. *Rudraksha* wearing helps in getting motivation to follow everything which is good for your body and mind. In fact, the effects will be multifold if *yogasanas* are performed, wearing *rudraksha*.

4. Pranayam

If we can somehow control the depleting number of active body cells, then the energy in the body can always be maintained. *Pranayam* is to control the dimensions of the breathing (called *pran*). By doing *pranayam* one can control decay of the body cells and thus remain healthy throughout one's life.

Our knowledge senses control the inhaling of air and physical senses control the exhaling of air. This two-way flow of *pran* controls the life form. Controlling these flows of breathing is *pranayam*. In fact, *pranayam* is not just for good health. It is a prerequisite for developing concentration and for meditation, *jap* and *yog*.

It is also important to know that for doing *pranayam* in a perfect way, purification and preparation of the body by doing any or all of the following six forms of *karma* are useful:

Dhauti (putting a cloth through the mouth and into the intestine and then taking it out)

Vasti (enema to clean the bowels)

Neti: (In thread *neti*, a thread is inserted through the nose and taken out from mouth. In *jal neti*, water is sucked in through the nose and thrown out from the mouth.)

Tratak (Looking at an object without blinking the eye until tears come in the eyes is known as *tratak*. One can look at a lighted flame of candle.)

Nauli (This is rolling the intestines from left to right and right to left and also in the middle. Recommended for people under 40, this is an excellent exercise to strengthen digestive powers and curing several diseases of liver, kidneys or stomach.)

Kapal bhati (It is done by exhaling air from the stomach in a rhythmic manner. The stroke is given from inside and air is exhaled. There are other variations like breathing in from left nostril and breathing out from right and vice versa. *Kapal bhati* is also done by sucking water from mouth and throwing it out from nostrils.

Pranayams are of eight types:

1. *Surya Bhedan*
2. *Ujjai*
3. *Seetkari*
4. *Sheetali*
5. *Bhasrika*
6. *Bhramari*
7. *Murchya*
8. *Plavini*

All these methods should be learned from an expert and should be done for specified times and with full precautions.

Good *pranayam* practices lead to awakening of *Kundilini*. This is a nerve, which normally lies in sleeping stage at the bottom of the spinal chord (at the *muladhar chakra*) with its mouth facing the bottom side. After *Kundilini* awakening, one gets the light of the cosmos within the body itself and enjoys the highest level of inner pleasure. However, it is a complicated subject and it should be attempted only under a successful *yogi*.

5. Pratyahar

It is control of the senses by focusing the mind inward. The following six habits are responsible for a shaky state of mind: desire, anger, greed, attachment, ego and laziness. If these six feelings are controlled, one can achieve *pratyahar* as one will then start focusing within oneself. Ultimately, it is the state of *vairagya* which is attained by looking inward and finding answer to the perennial questions as to why we have come to this world and what are our responsibilities. The senses can be controlled only if our objectives for life are well defined and are above the normal human perception.

6. Dharana

Dharana means capability to absorb and face self-realization. It is like making one worthy for the great objectives for which one has done rigorous practice through the above five types of *yog* — *yam, niyam, asan, pranayam* and *pratyahar*. It is reposing faith in the Almighty and total surrender to Him which make you worthy for *dharana*.

7. Dhyan

It is meditation and we have already discussed this in

Chapter 11. *Dhyan* is the control of the ever-fluctuating mind. There are two states of *chitta* – one having speed and the other static. In the state of speed, the mind is unstable and the static state is *dhyan*. It is focusing at one point and becoming one with what you meditate for.

8. Samadhi

It is the ultimate aim of *yog* and the highest level for it. Maharshi Patanjali says *tasya vachakah jajjpastadarth bhavanam*, meaning the spoken form of the Lord is *Om (pranav)*. By chanting it and going deep into it and understanding the meaning of it is *samadhi*. When the objective itself becomes less important and the desires from heart become almost none, then the stage of *samadhi* is reached. *Samadhi* can be of six types:

1. *Dhyanyog Samadhi*
2. *Nadyog Samadhi*
3. *Rasanandyog Samadhi*
4. *Laysiddhiyog Samadhi*
5. *Bhktiyog Samadhi*
6. *Rajyog Samadhi*

These stages are for those whose aim in life is to explore the outer boundaries and have different objectives of life, which these days are even difficult to express. *Samadhi* takes you to the level of Brahma and oneness exists then with the supreme Lord. *Rudraksha* shall be with you to achieve success in each stage of the above *Ashtang yog*.

FREQUENTLY ASKED QUESTIONS AND ANSWERS

13

The number of people wearing Rudraksha is growing. Some of these wearers are keen observers, and thoroughly analytical as they are educated and have noted down their experience which they have willingly shared with us. Based on their reports and our studies some new facts have emerged. Some of these may prove to be beneficial for the mind, body or consciousness. Therefore it was considered fit to share these with the readers of this book. As regards to our own studies we have used the following procedures in addition to taking general feedback from a large section of wearers:

1. Used Aura measuring devices like RFI (Resonant Frquency Imaging) system, PIP (Polycontrast Interference Photography), both supplied by The Centre for Biofield Sciences, Pune (India), Biofeedback Energy Testing Unit supplied by (Technical & Scientific Research Centre, Paris (France) and a Aura Detecting Device supplied by a Hyderabad based scholar.

2. Using *Rudraksha* in various numbers, varying their placements in the body and also changing their directions.

3. Varying the time of usage from just a few minutes in a day to 24 hours.

4. Observing effects on a person who cleans the beads

thoroughly and does Rudraksha abhishek or Shiva
poojan wearing Rudraksha regularly.

5. Comparing results of different mukhis, fresh of the
season or old stock and using Rudraksha from different
regions like Nepal or Indonesia.

Rudraksha are amazing beads of nature and their effects
on human beings shall continue to baffle all of us. On the
basis of our latest search/experience we can say that
Rudraksha should not be considered on the same plane as any
other alternative therapy, or approach like pyramids, gemstones, meteorites, volcano ashes and so on. Rudraksha are
yet to be understood for their benefits and what we know so
far is only a beginning of a very complex yet beneficial
chapter for healing humans — their diseases, sufferings and
worries.

Due to our stand on logic-base coupled with modern
education which believe in only scientific evidence and
endorsement required from a Western mind, followed by our
own fear and shame for believing in these types of mystical
objects; we sometime ignore the truth and miss the
opportunity to take advantage of nature's simple yet highly
beneficial products.

About 2 years back I met a Doctor of nuclear medicine—
a Padma award recipient, in a well known hospital of Mumbai
with an objective to conduct advanced studies on Rudraksha.
I was saddened by his arrogant behaviour with everybody
around him and his approach toward the research (He
suggested that dogs, cows and monkeys should wear
Rudraksha first and if proved beneficial to them, then only he
will believe that these are suitable for humans!) I just ignored
his comments and came to terms with the age old belief that

our past (sanchit) *karmas* also play a role. True we need a constructive and result oriented research work on Rudraksha but the work should be carried out by people with some faith in Indian values and traditions and also respectability for others.

FREQUENTLY ASKED QUESTIONS AND ANSWERS

Q. What are your latest findings on Rudraksha for getting maximum benefits?

Ans: i. Rudraksha beads or mala should be washed with water on a daily basis. Just keep your beads or mala below a water tap for a few seconds and then pad-dry or wear directly. Apply any edible oil once in a month over the beads for better shine and longer life. As these beads work on the principle of touch, physical cleaning and appearance of the beads is also important. If the beads get dried over time, they look lifeless and may not give desired results. Whenever you feel that results expected from Rudraksha are not coming then increase the frequency of washing to twice or even thrice in a day.

   ii. Rudraksha should be worn for longer periods and wear them even at night during sleep, provided your sleep is not disturbed. If wearing a Gaurishankar or Sawar, it must be removed at night otherwise the bead may get damaged. Beads should not be kept far away from you and keep then in a clean box or container at a distance not more than a meter from you. If taken out at night, you may wear them immediately on waking up with chanting of *"Om Namah Shivaya"* or *beej mantra*. Alternatively, you may wear them after taking bath.

iii. It has been observed that if Rudraksha are blessed by regular *abhishek* or *pooja* particularly on special occasions of holy festivals then the wearer gets better results. Whenever you visit a temple or a famous shrine of any religious order, or your Guru's or other divine *ashram*, all charged with devotional energies (like a Gurudwara, Shirdi Samadhi Mandir, Jain temple, dargah, any pilgrim centre, a holy river or mountain or a meditation centre) just concentrate your attention on your Rudraksha and chant *"Om Namah Shivaya"* or *beej mantra* and pray for positive energies to bless you. If permissible wash your Rudraksha with water and touch the energy source to get these blessed.

On a Solar eclipse, after bathing chanting of mantras placing the washed Rudraksha in front of you proves beneficial. Rudraksha-abhishek is not done during eclipse and so mantra chanting is beneficial.

Q. What happens if on wearing Rudraksha I get unusual feelings, get allergies, become stressful or start feeling low?

Ans: Rudraksha do not cause any discomfort or negative feelings, however, if such a situation arises then the Rudraksha may be removed and kept at a safe clean place. After a day or two wear again, preferably in a temple and do mantra recitation for a few minutes.

In most cases such feelings disappear.

In some cases, particularly males with hair on the chest are sensitive and feel discomfort on wearing Rudraksha mala, particularly with metal caps. Such persons can wear the Rudraksha, around the wrist or as an armlet or try wearing them without any metal caps or chain.

Q. How much time is required to sense a change in body, mind, status or a given situation after wearing Rudraksha?

Ans: Aura becomes powerful soon after a Rudraksha comes in contact with the body, in other words it becomes sharp and bigger. As we know all the three layers of the body starting from bones, muscles/ flesh and skin, get disturbed aura if affected by any disease or negative emotions. When Rudraksha comes in contact with the body, these aura layers become stabilized almost immediately, however, long lasting results and recovery from diseases, if any, may take place after some time. Correct selection and proper wearing of Rudraksha helps in balancing of *chakras*. Various trials and effort is required to balance these *chakras*, including chanting of proper mantras or by getting blessing of different Gods/ Goddesses who bless the specific chakras.

It can be said that for physical disorders a minimum time of 20 days is required to feel and experience the change, and for reducing level of anxiety or stress about 40 days are optimum. For change of luck and removal of obstacles one needs to constantly wear a *Rudraksha,* for 60 days to notice its positive effects. Anxiety and fear is diminished and effects of evil eye, jealousy and black magic almost disappear immediately.

The above time frame is just approximate and varies from person to person and is grossly dependent on situations. These beads are not magical, however the wearer starts taking thoughtful decisions and thus starts reaping its benefits within the specified time frame. If no effects are visible then one should try using more number of recommended beads or using higher mukhi and powerful beads. Through this process of trial we try to invoke divine blessings using Rudraksha. Thus the wearer has to conduct experiments with himself.

Q. Should I continue to keep fake Rudraksha even after their identification?

Ans: Not only Rudraksha but if you keep imitation jewellery, fake paintings, non-functioning clocks/ watches, dead persons' statue and stuffed animals/ birds etc at home particularly at a place most frequented by you, certainly you will feel depressed, Fake and damaged Rudraksha should be thrown away in water bodies(river/pond or sea).

Only exception being as has been narrated earlier, if such a fake bead had been given to you by your Guru, then you may accept it as Prasad (blessings) from him/her and need not destroy it.

Q. Can I use Rudraksha to destroy or harm my enemies?

Ans: Rudraksha with 9, 10, 16 ,19 mukhis and Trijuti are known for being used for Vair Samvardhan, Maran and destruction, if invoked the tantric way. People are known to practice these *vidyas* by using the above mentioned mukhi Rudrakshas, particularly by conducting rituals on Friday nights. Some go to a funeral ground or to a *devi* temple on dark nights and do *tantric mantra jap* to achieve their goals. We have been against such practices and instead of harming others we advice people to pray for self protection and for leading a safe fearless life. Beads like 9, 10, 11 and 19 mukhis are excellent for protection from any type of enemy or their practices.

Q. For meditation and self control which type of Rudraksha should be chosen?

Ans: A *kantha* of 5 mukhi large sized beads (above 28 mm India) is good for meditation. This should be beaded in wool with 28, 32 or 36 number of beads. A powerful *kantha* beaded in copper wire without any metal caps is also a good option.

As per *Akshmalakopnishad*, three types of wires (copper, silver and gold) woven to a single strand, and stringing a mala using this wire will help one to achieve a higher level of meditative power. There is no need for metal caps.

For a higher level of meditation and to reach a near zero thought level of meditation, a combination using large sized beads of 3M (2 beads), 5M (21 beads), 9M (1 bead), 11M (1 bead), 14M (1 bead), Gaurishankar (1 bead) and 1 M (1bead) should be used to make a higher level Dhyan Yog mala.

Long-term usage of a 14 mukhi over the forehead, particularly during meditation is said to give excellent concentration (see Fig 29).

Rudraksha mala is like a store house of energy, which helps you in keeping powerful *Urja* arising out of meditation or good deeds within yourself. Mention of several kinds of meditation dresses has been made in our scriptures (Ref to Chap. 7) for details or read *Shivpuran* and *Devibhagwatam*. You have to evaluate a practical way of handling or wearing it and also to see the level at which you would like to operate.

Q. What is the most optimum way of doing *pooja* of Rudraksha at home, whether first time or at any time?

Ans: Arrange following items to prepare *Panchamrit (Panchtirtha)*

Pure water (preferably mixed with small amount of Ganges or other holy river water) 50 ml, Milk 50 ml, Ghee (clarified butter) 20 ml and a lamp to light it (diya or deepak), Curd (yoghurt plain) 20 ml, Honey 20 ml.

Mix all the above to make *Panchamrit*

Also arrange small quantities of the following:

Camphor, Sandalwood powder or paste, Rice grains Flowers, preferably white, and Water.

Steps to be followed:

Sit facing East or North in a comfortable posture.

Light the lamp with Ghee.

Wash Rudraksha, using water and then wipe it clean with a cloth. Place Rudraksha in a tray.

Pour *Panchamrit* over Rudraksha using a spoon, and chant with each pouring *Om Namah Shivaya*. Finish all *panchamrit* in this way.

Wash Rudraksha with water and clean using a cloth. Prepare a clean tray and put petals of flowers on the tray. Place Rudraksha on the tray and then chant the following mantra:

"Sadyojat mantra"

Aum sadyojaatam prapadyaami
sadyojataaya namo namah
bhave bhavenaati bhave,
bhavasmaam bhavodbhavaye namah

Offer Sandalwood paste to Rudraksha and then light incense sticks and camphor and offer flowers to Rudraksha. Now, chant the following mantra:

"Aghor mantra"

Aum aghorebhyo agh ghorebhyo
ghor ghor tarebhyo,
Sarvebhyah sarve sharvebhyo namaste
astu rudra rupebhyah

Offer rice to the Rudraksha and chant the following mantra:

"Tatpurush mantra"

Aum tat purushaye vidhmahe,
mahadevaye dheemahi
Tanno rudraha prachodayat

Now chant **"Om Namah Shivaya"** *11 times or chant Rudraksha beej mantra* of each mukhi (if available with you) and then wear Rudraksha. Pray to Lord Shiva and express your wish, if any.

Q. Whether Nepal beads are better than Indonesian beads?

Ans: Physical characteristics and experience shows that Indonesian beads of 1 mukhi, 2 mukhi and 3 mukhi are effective and can be used comfortably if Nepal variety is not available or is out of reach due to cost considerations. (1 mukhi Indonesian is the only and the best option considering 1 mukhi Nepal variety which is difficult to get).

Beyond 3 mukhi the clarity of lines and distribution of inner compartments start getting jumbled up and effectiveness may be questionable. One can wear higher mukhi Indonesian beads in a symbolic way in large number and some wearers have testified them for good results also.

Another advantage of higher mukhi Indonesian beads is their purity as it is not easy to duplicate an Indonesian Rudraksha as the lines are only on the surface of the bead. Nepal beads have deeper lines and can be carved artificially which is a common practice in case of higher mukhi Rudraksha (beyond 8 mukhi), unless these are sourced from a reliable supplier.

Q. Is wearing of Rudraksha advisable to a non-vegetarian, or a person taking alcoholic drinks or a couple during physical relationships?

Ans: Logically there is no need to take off the Rudraksha from the body during any of the above activity. *Shastra* like *Shivpuran* prohibit eating of non-vegetarian food or taking of alcohol or even eating of onion, garlic etc. for the wearer. Other scriptures are silent about it.

However, a compromised suggestion is to take the mala off the body during any of the above activity and wear it again after the activity is over. Most people follow this advice, although not fully convinced with the argument.

Author's assumption is that if Rudraksha powder or extract is being taken orally by any person, as a herbal medicine, then the above restrictions imposed have some basis but for simply wearing Rudraksha over the body this restriction may not apply. However, tradition always overtakes logic and hence there is no harm in following the age old advice — take it off while doing these activities.

One argument in favor of abstaining from Non-vegetarian food or alcohol etc is their coming in the category of *Rajasi* food (in contrast to spiritually desirable *Satvik* food) One who takes *Rajasi* food may become slave of his/her body senses and cannot focus on meditation or pure stable thought process. As Rudraksha is used for *jap* and *dhyan yog,* intake of *Satvik* food is always recommended, even based on logic.

Some wearers have experienced that after wearing Rudraksha, they have switched to strict vegetarian diet and even avoid alcohol.

Q. Should one wear Rudraksha while having bath or while going to toilet.

Ans: Yes. However, bracelet should be removed if going to the toilet. Our scriptures have not mentioned any restriction in this regard.

Q. Can Rudraksha be worn while going to a funeral ground?

Ans: There is no restriction imposed by any of our holy scripture However, as per the tradition prevailing, all articles symbolising power or having source of energy should be taken off the body (like gemstones, Rudraksha, yantras etc) while visiting places like a funeral ground.

Q. For testing the facets of beads, your method of testing by X-ray technique is catching up, but in higher mukhi beads the compartments are difficult to see.

Ans: It is true that in case of higher mukhi beads compartments are overlapped and need services of a radiologist and also may require use of a CT-scan to reach correct conclusion. Normally over 8 mukhi one gets only 50% or even less, fully grown or developed compartments or seeds. A properly nurtured fruit, ripened on the tree itself normally yields a seed which should be visible in an X-ray but even here seeds may not be found in all the compartments.

Q. What is the best way to select type of Rudraksha required by a person?

Ans: In spite of best efforts there is no method which can be fully relied upon to exactly match your needs. Problems are sometime complex, their root causes may vary. Astrological predictions may differ from person to person. Pin pointing a disturbed or unbalanced chakra is a futile exercise as no perfect equipment has been invented so far to observe unbalanced chakra. Numerological evaluation also gives multiple options and therefore we have to live with this fact that some variations may be possible while selecting optimum Rudraksha for you. One should keep the mind open to keep on trying different beads. However, make sure to wear a basic 5 mukhi bead and at least one of the following:

7 mukhi, 9 mukhi, 10 mukhi, 11 mukhi and 14 mukhi.

For good health always choose 3 mukhi, 5 mukhi and 12 mukhi for blood pressure, diabetes or cardiac disorders, 7 mukhi for body pain, 6 mukhi, 13 mukhi and Gaurishankar for fertility, 3 mukhi, 9 mukhi and 10 mukhi for fear and anxiety, 4 mukhi, 6 mukhi and

1 mukhi (Indonesian) for mental illness of anykind.

For meditation and *Shiva Bhakti* any or all of the following beads assigned to Lord Shiva should be used:

1 mukhi, 2 mukhi, 5 mukhi, 14 mukhi and Gaurishankar.

For wealth any one or all Rudraksha assigned to Gods/Goddesses of wealth should be used:

1 mukhi (Indonesian or Nepal) 7 mukhi, 8 mukhi, 15 mukhi, 17 mukhi and 21 mukhi.

For keeping the enemy away and/or to win in legal cases use the following:

10 mukhi, 16 mukhi, 19 mukhi.

Siddha Mala which contains all the beads from 1 to 14 mukhi and also has a Gaurishankar and Ganesh Rudraksha; is a good option to get overall success in any business or for professional excellence.

The epics considered here were written at least 3000 years ago although there is no evidence for it. Held in high esteem they contain knowledge about origin of universe, stories about Lord Shiva and other Gods.

SHRIMAD DEVI BHAGWATAM

BOOK XI CHPATER III

Sri Narayan said... Pranayama is called Sagarbha when performed with the repetition of some mantra; are called Agarbha when it is done simply with mere meditation, without repeating any mantra. After the bathing, the Tarpan with its accompaniments, is to be done; *i.e.* the peace offerings are made with reference to the Devas, the Risis, and the Pitris (whereby we invoke the blessings from the subtle planes where the highsouled pesons dwell.) After this, a clean pair of clothes is to be worn and then he should get up and come out of the water. The next things preparatory to practice Japam are to wear the Tilak marks of ashes and to put on the *Rudraksha* beads. He who holds thirty-two *Rudraksha* beads on his neck, forty on his head, six on each ear (12 on two ears), twenty four beads on two hands (twelve on each hand) thirty-two beads on two arms (sixteen on each), one bead on each eye and one bead on the hair on the crown, and one hundred and eight beads on the breast, (251 in all) becomes himself Maha Deva. One is expected to use them as such. O Muni! You can use the *Rudraksha* after tieing, stringing together with gold or silver always on your Sikha, the tuft of hair on the head or on your ears. On the holy thread, on the hands, on the neck, or on the belly (abdomen) one can keep the *Rudraksha* after one has repeated sincerely and with devotion the five lettered mantra of Shiva, or one has repeated the Pranava (Om). Holding the *Rudraksha* implies that the man has realised the knowledge of Shiva-Tattva. O Brahman! The *Rudraksha* bead that is placed on the tuft or on the crown hair represents the Tara tattva *i.e.,* Om Kara; the *Rudraksha* beads that are held on the two ears are to be thought of as Deva and Devi, (Shiva and Shiva).

22-37. The one hundred and eight *Rudraksha* beads on the sacrificial thread are considered as the one hundred one eight Vedas (signifying the Full Knowledge, as sixteen digits of the Moon completed; on the arms, are consideredias the Dik (quarters); on the neck, are considered as the Devi Sarasvati and Agni (fire). The *Rudraksha* beads ought to be taken by men of all colours and castes. The Brahmanas, Kshattriyas and Vaisyas should hold them after purifying them with Mantras *i.e.,* knowingly; whereas the Shudras can take them without any such purification by the Mantras. *i.e.,* knowingly. *i.e.,* unknowingly. By holding or putting on the *Rudraksha* beads, persons become the Rudras incarnate in flesh and body. There is no doubt in this. By this all the sins arising from seeing, hearing, remembering, smelling, eating prohibited things, talking incoherently, doing prohibited things, etc., are entirely removed with the *Rudraksha* beads on the body; whatever acts. eating, drinking, smelling, etc., are done are, as it were, done by Rudra Deva Himself. O Great Muni! He who feels shame in holding and patting on the *Rudraksha* beads, can never be freed from this Samsara even after the Koti births. He who blames another person holding *Rudraksha* beads has defects in his birth (is a bastard). There is no doubt in this. It is by holding on *Rudraksha* that Brahma has remained stady in His Brahmahood untainted and the

Munis have been true to their resolves. So there is no act better and higher than holding the *Rudraksha* beads. He who gives clothing and food to a person holding *Rudraksha* beads with devotion is freed of all sins and goes to the Shiva Loka. He who feasts gladly any holder of such deads at the time of Shradha, goes undoubtedly to the Pitri Loka. He who washes the feet of a holder of *Rudraksha* and drinks that water, is freed of all sins and resides with honour in the Shiva Loka. If a Brahmana holds with devotion the *Rudraksha* beads with a neeklace and holds, he attains the Rudrahood. O Intelligant One! Wherever whoever holds with or without faith and devotion the *Rudraksha* beads with or without any mantra, is freed of all sins and is entiled to the tattvajnana. I am unable to describe fully the greatness of the *Rudraksha* beads. In fact, all should by all means hold the *Rudraksha* beads on their bodies.

Note: The number one hundred and eight (108) signifies the One Hundred and Eight Vedas, the Brahman, the source of all wisdom and joy.

Here ends the Third Chapter of the Eleventh Book on the glories of the Rudraksha beads in the Maha Puranam Sri Mad Devi Bhagvatam of 18,000 verses by Maharsi Veda Vyasa.

CHAPTER IV

1-11. Narada said... O Sinless one! The greatness of the *Rudraksha* seed that you have described is verily such. Now I ask why is this *Rudraksham* so much entitled to vorship by the people. Please speak clearly on this point. Narayana spoke : "O Child! This is the very question that was asked once by Kartika, the sixfaced One, to Bhagavan Rudra, develling in Kailas'a. What He replied, I say now. Listen. Rudra Deva spoke : "O Child Sadhana. I will dwell briefly on the secret cause of the greatness of the *Rudraksha* seed. Hear. In old days, there was a Daitya called Tripura who could not be conquered by any body. Brahma, Vishnu and the other Devas were defeated by him. They then came to Me and requested Me to kill the Asura. At their request, I called in my mind the Divine Great weapon, named Aghora, beautiful and terrible and containing the strength of all the Devas, to kill him. It was inconceivable and it was blazing with fire.

For full divine one thousand years I remained awake with eyelids wide open in thinking of the Aghora weapon, the destroyer of all obstacles, whereby the killing of Tripurasura might be effected and the troubles of the Devas be removed. Not for a moment my eyelids dropped. Thereby my eyes were affected and drops of water came out of any eyes. (*Note here.* How enemies are to be killed. It requires great thought, great concentration, great yoga and great powers). O Mahasena! From those drops of water coming out of my eyes, the great tree of *Rudraksha* did spring for the welfare of all. This *Rudraksha* seed is of thirty-eight varieties. From My Surya Netra. *i.e.,* My right eye, symbolizing the Sun, twelve yellow coloured (Pingala colour) varieties have come; and from my left eye representing the Moon, the Soma Netra, sixteen varieties of white colour and from my third eye on the top, representing Fire *i.e.,* the Agni Netra, ten varieties of black colour have come out. Of these the white *Rudrakshams* are Brahmins and they are used by the Brahmanas; the red coloured ones are the Kshatriyas and should be used by the Kashatriyas and the black ones are Sudras and should be used by the Vaisyas and the Sudras.

12-19. One faced *Rudraksha* seed is the Shiva Himself,

made manifest and rendered vivid; even the sin incurred in killing a Brahmana is destroyed thereby. Two faced or two headed *Rudraksha* is like the Deva and the Devi. Two sorts of sins are destroyed thereby. The three faced *Rudraksha* is like fire; the sin incurred in killing a woman is destoyed in a moment. The four faced *Rudraksha* seed is like Brahm and removes the sin of killing persons. The five faced *Rudraksha* is verily an image of Rudra; all sorts of sins, e.g. eating prohibited food, going to the ungoables, etc., are destoyed thereby. The six faced *Rudrasha* is Kartikeya. It is to be worn on the right hand. One becomes freed of the Brahmahatya sin. There is no doubt in this. The seven faced *Rudraksha* is named Ananga. Holding this frees one from the sin of stealing gold, etc., O Mahasena! The eight faced *Rudraksha* is Vinayaka. Holding this frees one from the sin of holding an illicit contact with a woman of a bad family and with the wife of one's Guru, etc., and other sins as well. It enables one to acquire heaps of food, cotton, and gold; and in the end the Highest Place is attained.

20-35. The fruit of holding the eight faced *Rudrakshsa* seed has been said. Now I will talk of the nine-faced *Rudraksha*. It is verily the Bhairava made manifest. On the left hand it should be worn. By this, the people get both Bhoga (enjoyment) and Moksya (liberation) and they become poweful like Me and get themselves freed at once, without the least delay, of the sins incurred by committing thousands of abortions, hundreds of Brahmahattyas (killing the Brahmanas). Holding the ten faced *Rudraksha* is verily wearing Janardana, the Deva of the Devas. The holding of which pacifies the evils caused by planets, Pisachas, Vetalas Brahma Raksasas, and Pannagas. The eleven-faced *Rudraksha* is like the Eleven Rudras. The fruits, the efficacy of which I now describe. Hear. The fruits obtained through the performance of one thousand horse sacrifices, one hundred Vajapeya sacrifices, tand making gifts of one hundred thousand cows are obtained thereby.

If one wears the twelve-headed *Rudrakshas* on one's ear, the Adityas get satisfied. The fruits of performing Gomedha and Asvamedha sacrifices are obtained thereby. No fear comes from horned buffaloes, armed enemies and wolves and tigers and other murderous animals. Also the several diseases of the body never come to him. The holder of the twelve-faced *Rudraksha* seed feels always happy and he is the master of some kingdoms He becomes freed of the sins incurred in killing elephants, horses, dear, cats, snakes, mice, frogs, asses, foxes and various other animals.

O Child! The thirteen faced *Rudraksha* is very rare; if anybody gets it, he becomes like Kartikeya and gets all desires fulfilled; and the eight siddhies are under his graps. He learns how to make gold, silver and other metals; he attains all sorts of enjoyments. There is no manner of doubt in this. O Sadhanana! If anybody holds the thirteen faced *Rudraksha*, he becomes freed from the sins incurred in killing mother, father and brothers.

O Son! If one holds on one's head the fourteen faced *Rudraksha* always, one becomes like Shiva. O Muni! What more shall I speak to you! The Devas pay their respects to one holding the fourteen faced *Rudrakshas* and he in the end attains the Highest Goal, the state of Shiva. His body becomes verily the body of Shiva.

36-40. The Devas always worship the *Rudraksha* seed; the highest goal is attained by wearing the *Rudraksha*. The

Brahmanas should hold in their heads at least one *Rudraksha* is to be made and tied on the head. Similarly a rosary of fifty seeds is to be worn and suspended on the breast; sixteen each on each of she two arms; twenty-four *Rudraksha* to be worn on the wrists, twelve on each. O Sadhanana! If a rosary be made of one hundred and eight, fifty or twenty-seven *Rudrakshams* and if japam be done with that, immeasurable merits are obtained. If anybody wears a rosary of one hundred and eight seeds, he gets at every moment the fruit of performing the Asvamedha sacrifices and uplifts his twenty-one generations and finally he resides in the shiva Loka.

Here ends the Fourth Chapter of the Eleventh Book on the Greatness of the *Rudraksham* in the Mahapuranam Sri Mad Devi Bhagvatam of 18,000 verses by Maharsi Veda Vyasa.

CHAPTER V

1-14. Isvara said... "O Kartikeya! Now I will speak how to count the Japam (repetition of the mantra) with the rosary. Hear. The face of *Rudraksha* is Brahma; the upper summit point is Shiva and the fail end of *Rudraksha* is Vishnu. The *Rudraksha* has two-fold powers: It can give Bhoga (enjoyment) as well as Moksha (liberation). Then string ro tie together, like a cow's tail, and like the snake's coiling a body,twenty-five five face *Rudraksha* seeds, thorny and of red, white, mixed colours bored through and through. The rosary is to taper as a cow's tail tapers down. In stringing the beads into a rosary, it should be seen that the flat face of one *Rudraksham* is in front of the flat face of another *Rudraksha*; so the tail, the pointed end of one, must come in front of the tail or the narrower end of another. The Meru or the topmost

bead of the string must have its face turned upwards and the
knot should be given over that. The rosary, thus strungs,
yields success of the mantra (mantra-siddhi). When the rosary
is strung, it is to be bathed with clear and scented water and
afterwards with the Panchagavya (cow-dung, cow urine, curd,
milk, and ghee); then wash it with clear water and sanctify it
with the condensed electrical charge of the Mantra. Then
recite the Mantra of Shiva (Six limbed, with "Hum" added
and collect the rosaries. Then repeat over them the Mantra
"Sadyojata, etc., and sprinkle water over it one hundred and
eight times. Then utter the principal mantra and place them
on a holy ground and perform Nyasa over it, *i.e.,* think that
the Great Cause Shiva and the World-Mother Bhagavati have
come on them. Thus make the Samskara of the rosary (*i.e.,*
purify it) and you will find then that your desired end will be
attained successfully. Worship the rosary with the Mantra of
that Devta for which it is intended. One is to wear the
Rudraksha rosary on one's head, neck or ear and controlling
one self, one should make japam with the rosary On the neck,
head, breast, or the ears or on the arms, the rosary should he
held with the greatest devotion. What is the use in saying
about it so often? It is highly meritorious and commendable
to holds always the *Rudraksha.* Especially on such occasions
as taking baths making gifts, making japams, performing the
Homas, or sacrifices to Visve Devas, in performing the
Poojas of the Devas, in making Prayaschittams (penances), in
the time of Sradha and in the time of initiation, it is highly
necessary to hold *Rudraksha.* A Brahmin is sure to go to hell
if he preforms any Vaidik act without wearing any *Rudraksha.*
Note: It would be offering an insult to Shiva!

15-29. It is advisable to use the true *Rudraksham* with gold
and jewel, on the head, neck or on one's hand. Never use the

Rudraksha worn by another. Use *Rudraksha* always with devotion; never use it while you are impure. Even the grass that grows with the air in contact with the *Rudraksha* tree, goes verily to a holy region for ever. Jabala Muni says in the Sruti: If a man wearing *Rudraksha* commits a sin, he gets deliverance from that sin. Even if animals hold *Rudraksha*, they become Shiva; what of men! The devotees of Sri Rudra should always use at least one *Rudraksha* on the head. Those great devotees, who with *Rudraksha* on take the name of the Highest Self Sambhu, get themselves freed of all sorts of sins and pains. Those who are ornamented with *Rudraksham* are the best devotees. It is highly incumbent on those who want their welfare to wear *Rudraksha*. Those who hold *Rudraksha* on their ears, crown hair, neck, hands and breast, get Brahma, Vishnu, and Maheshvara under them as their Vibhutis (manifestations, powers). The Devas and all those Rishis that started the Gotra, the Adipurusas (the first chief men in several families), held with reverence the *Rudraksha*. All the other Munis, that descended from their families, the ardent followers of Srauta dharma, the pure souled, held the *Rudraksha*. It may be, that many might not like at first to hold this *Rudraksha*, the visibile giver of liberation and so well written in the Vedas; but after many births, out of the Grace of Mahadeva, many become eager to take the *Rudraksha*. The Munis' that are the Jabala Sakhis are famous in expounding the inestimable greatness of *Rudraksha*.

The effect of holding *Rudraksha* is well known in the three worlds. Punyam (great merit) arises from the mere sight of *Rudraksha*; ten million times that merit arises by its touch; and by wearing it, one hundred Koti times the fruit arises and if one makes Japam every day, then one lakh koti times the punyam arises. There is no manner of questionings in this.

30-36. He who holds in his hand, breast, neck, ears, head, the *Rudraksha*, becomes an image of Rudra. There is no manner of doubt in this. By holding *Rudraksha*, men become invulnerable of all the beings, become respected, like Mahi Deva, by the Devas and Asuras and they roam on the earth like Rudra. Even if a man be addicted to evil deeds and commits all sorts of sins, he becomes respected by all, on holding *Rudraksha*. By this men are freed of the sin of taking Uchhista and of all the other sins. Even if you suspend a *Rudraksha* rosary on the neck of a dog and if that dog dies in that state, he gets liberation! Then what to speak of others! By holding *Rudraksha*, men even if they be devoid of Japam and Dhyanam, become freed of all sins and attain the highest state. Even if one holds merely one *Rudraksha* seed purified and sucharged with Mantra Sakti, he uplifts his twentyone generations, gets to Heaven and resides there with respect. I am speaking now further of the Greatness of *Rudraksha*.

Here ends the Fifth Chapter of the Eleveth Book on the Rudraksam rosaries in the Maha Puranam Sri Mad Devi Bhagvatam of 18,000 verses by Maharsi Veda Vyasa.

CHAPTER VI

1-21. Isvara said... "O Kartikeya! Kusagranthi, Jivapattri and other rosaries cannot compare to one-sixteenth part of the *Rudraksha* rosary. As Vishnu is the best of all the Purusas, the Ganga is the best of all the rivers, Kasyapa, amongst the Munis, Uchchaishrava amongst the horses, Maha Deva amongst the Devas, Bhagvati amongst the Devis, so the *Rudraksha* rosary is the Best of all the rosaries. All the fruits that occur by reading the stotras and holding all the Vratas, are obtained by wearing the *Rudraksha* bead. At the time of making the Aksaya gift, the *Rudraksha* bead is capable of giving high merits. The merit that accrues by giving *Rudraksham* to a peaceful devotee of Shiva, cannot be expressed in words. If anybody gives food to a man holding the *Rudraksha* rosary, his twenty one generations are uplifted and he ultimately becomes able to live in the Rudra Loka. He who does not apply ashes on his forehead and who does not hold *Rudraksha* and is averse to the worship of Shiva is inferior to a chandala. If *Rudraksha* be placed on the head then the flesh-eaters, drunkards, and the associates with the vicious become freed of their sins. Whatever fruits are ontained by performing various sacrifices, asceticism and the study of the Vedas are easily attained by simply holding the *Rudraksham* rosary. Whatever merits are obtained by reading the four Vedas and all the Puranas and bathing in all the Tirthas and the results that are obtained by immense practise in learning all are, obtained by wearing *Rudraksha*. If at the time of death, one wears *Rudraksha* and dies, one attains Rudrahood. One has not to take again one's birth. If anybody dies by holding *Rudraksha* on his neck or on his two arms, he uplifts his twenty-one generations and lives in the Rudra Loka. Be he a Brahman or a Chandala, be he with qualities or without qualities, if he applies ashes to his body and holds *Rudraksha*, he surely attains Sivahood. Be he pure or impure; whether he eats uneatables or be he a Mlechha or a Chandala or a Great Sinner, any body if he holds *Rudraksha* is surely equal to Rudra. There is no doubt in this.

If any body holds *Rudraksha* on his head he gets Koti times the fruit; on his ears ten Koti times the fruit, on his neck, one hundred Koti times the fruit, on his holy thread, ayuta times the fruit; on his arm, one lakh Koti times the fruit and if one wears *Rudraksha* on one's wrist, one attains Moksha.

Whatever acts, mentioned in the Vedas be performed with *Rudraksha* on, the fruits obtained are unbounded. Even if a man be without any Bhakti and if he wears on his neck the *Rudraksha* rosary though he does always vicious acts, he becomes freed of the bondage of this world. Even if a man does not hold *Rudraksha* but if he be always full of devotion towards the *Rudraksha*, he attains the fruit that is got by wearing the *Rudraksha* and he attains the Shiva Loka and is honoured like Shiva. As in the country of Kikata, an ass which used to carry *Rudraksha* seed got Sivahood after his death, so any man, whether he be a Jnani (wise) or Ajnani (unwise), gets Sivahood if he holds *Rudraksha*. There is no doubt in this.

22-28. Skanda said... "O God! How is it that in the country of Kikata (Bihar), an ass had to carry *Rudraksha*, who gave him the *Rudraksha!* And what for did he hold that?

Bhagvan Isvara said... "O Son! Now hear the histry of the case. In the Bindhya mountain one ass used to carry the load of *Rudraksha* of a traveller. Once the ass felt tired and became unable to carry the load and fell down on the road and dies. After his death the ass came to Me by My Grace, becoming Mahesvara with trident in his hand and with three eyes. O Kartikeya! As many faces as there are in the *Rudraksha*, for so many thousand Yugas the holder resides with honour in the Shiva Loka. One should declare the greatness of *Rudraksha* to one's own disciple never to disclose its glories to one who is not a disciple or devotee of *Rudraksha* nor to him who is n illiterate brute. He be a Bhakta or not a Bhakta, be he low or very low, if he holds *Rudraksha*, then he is freed from all sins. No equal can be to the merit of him who holds the *Rudraksha*.

29-30. The Munis, the seers of truth, describe this holding on of *Rudraksha* as a very great vow. He who makes a vow to hold one thousand *Rudraksha*, becomes like Rudra; the Devas bow down before him. If thousand *Rudraksha* be not obtained, one should hold at least sixteen *Rudraksha* on each arm, one *Rudraksh* on the crown hair; on the two hands, twelve on each; thirty-two on the neck; forty on the head; six on each ear and one hundred and eight *Rudraksha* on the breast; and then he becomes entitled to worship like Rudra. If any body holds *Rudraksha* together with pearls, Prabala, crystal, silver, gold and gem (lapis lazuli), he becomes a manifestation of Shiva. If a body, through laziness even, holds *Rudraksha*, the sin cannot touch him as darkness cannot come near light. If any body makes japam of a mantram with a *Rudraksha* rosary, he gets unbounded results. Such a merit giving *Rudraksha*, if one such *Rudraksha* be not found in any one's body, his life becomes useless, like a man who is void of Tripundrak (three curved horizontal marks made on the forehead by the worshippers of Shiva). If any body simply washes his head all over with *Rudraksha* on, he gets the frut of bathing in the Ganges. There is no doubt in this. One faced *Rudraksha*, the five faced, eleven faced and fourteen faced *Rudraksha* are highly meritorious and entitled to worship by all. The *Rudraksha* is Sankara made manifest; so it is always worshipped with devotion. The greatness of *Rudraksha* is such as it can make a king out of a poor man. On this point, I will tell you an excellent Puranic anecdote.

40-49. There was a Brahmin, named Girinatha in the country of Kosala. He was proficient in the Vedas and Vedamgas, religious and very rich. He used to perform sacrifices. He had a beautiful son named Gunanidhi. The son gradually entered into his youth and looked beautiful like

Kandarpa, the God of Love. While he was studying at his Guru Sudhisana's house, he, by his beauty and youth captivated the mind of his Guru's wife named Muktavali. The Guru's wife became so much enchanted by his extraordinary beauty that she, being unable to control herself, mixed with him and for some time remained with him in secret enjoyment. Then feeling inconveniences, due to the fear of his Guru, to enjoy her freely, used poison to the Guru, killed him and then he began to live freely with her. Next when his father, mother came to know about this, he put to death instantly his father and mother, administering poison to them. He became addicted to various pleasures and his wealth was exhausted gradually. He began to steal in Brahmans' houses and became addicted very much to drinking. His relatives outcasted him from the society for his bad behaviour and banished him outside the town. He then went into a dense forest with Muktavali; and he begn to kill the Brahmins for their wealth. Thus a long time passed away; when at last he fell into the jaws of death.

50-54. Then to take him to the region of Death, thousands of the Yama's messengers came; at the same time the Shiva's messemgers came; from Shiva-Loka. O Kartikeya! A quarrel then ensued between both the parties of Yama and Shiva," The Yama's messengers, then, said: "O Servers of Sambhu! What are the merits of this man that you have come to take him? First speak to us of his merits." Shiva's messengers spoke"— Fifteen feet below the ground where this man died, there exists the *Rudraksha*. O Yama's messengers! By the influence of that *Rudraksha*, all his sins are destroyed; and we have come to take him to Shiva." Then the Brahmin Gunaridhi assumed a divine form and, getting on an aerial car went with Shiva's messengers before Shiva.

"O One of good vows! Thus have described briefly to you the greatness of *Rudraksha*. This is capable to remove all sorts of sins and yield great merits.

Here ends the Sixth Chapter of the Eleventh Book on the Greatness of *Rudrakshams* in the Mahapuranam Sri Mad Devi Bhagavatam of 18,000 verses by Maharsi Veda Vyasa.

CHAPTER VII

1-4. Sri Narayana said... "O Narda! When Girisa thus explained to Kartikeya the greatness of *Rudraksha*, he became satisfied. Now I have spoken to you of the glories of the *Rudraksha* as far as I know. Now, as to our subject of right way of acting, I will now speak on other things that ought to be known. Listen. The seeing of *Rudraksha* brings in a lakh times of Punyam and koti times merit; again if one makes the japam of a Mantra with that *Rudraksha*, one obtains merit one hundred lakh koti times and one thousand lakh koti times the merit. The merit in holding the *Rudraksha* is far superior to that in holding Bhadraksam. The *Rudraksha* seed that is of the size of an Amalaki is the best; which is the of the size of a plum, is middling; and which is of the size of a gram is the worst this is my word and promise. The *Rudraksha* tree is of four kinds: Brahmana, Kshattriya, Vaisya, and Shudra. The white colour is Brahmana; the red colour is Kshattriya; the yellow colour is Vaisya and the black coloured *Rudraksha* seed is Shudra. The Brahmanas are to use the white coloured *Rudraksha*; the Kshattriyas, the red coloured ones, the Vaisyas, the yellow coloured ones; and the Shudras, the black ones. Those *Rudraksha* seeds that are nicely circular, smooth, hard, and whose thorns or points are distinetly visible, are the best. Those that are pierced by insects, broken in parts, whose thorns are not clearly visible, with swells and holes and those

that are coated over, these six varieities of *Rudraksha* are
faulty. Those *Rudraksha* that have their holes by nature
running through and through are best; and those that have
their holes pierced by men are middling. The *Rudraksha* seeds
that are all of uniform shape,, bright, hard, and beautifully
circular should be strung together by a silken thread. How to
test the *Rudraksha* seed? As gold is tested by a touch stone; so
the *Rudraksha* is tested by drawing lines on it; those on which
the lines are most uniform, bright and beautiful are the best
and they should be worn by the Shivas. One should hold one
Rudraksha on the crown hair, thirty on the head, thirty six on
the beck; sixteen on each arm, twelve on each wrist, fifty on
the shoulders, one hundred and eight *Rudraksha* in the place
of the sacrificial thread; and the devotee should have two or
three rounds on the neck. On the earrings, on the crown of
the head, the head, on bracelets, on armlets, on necklace, on
the ornament worn on the joins one should hold Rudraksham
always, whether one sleeps or eats. Holding three hudred
Rudraksha is the lowest; holding five hundred is middling;
holding one thousand *Rudraksha* is the best; so one ought to
wear one thousand *Rudraksha*. At the time of taking
Rudraksha, on one's head, one should utter the Mantra of
Isana; the mantra of Tat Purusa while holding on one's ears;
Aghora mantra on one's forehead and heart; and the vija of
Aghora mantra *i.e.,* "hasau" while holding on one's hands.
One should wear the rosary of fifty *Rudraksha* seeds,
suspended up to the belly, uttering the Vamadeva mantra *i.e.,*
Sadyojatat, etc., the five Brahma mantras, and the six-limbed
Shiva mantra. One is to string every *Rudraksha* seed, uttering
the root mantra and then hold it One-faced *Rudraksha* reveals
Paratattva (the highest Tattva); when worn, the knowledge of
the highest Tattva arises; the Brahma is seen then. The two-

faced *Rudraksha* is Ardhanarisvara, the Lord of the other half which represents woman (in the same person); if worn, Ardhanarisvara Shiva is always pleased with that man who holds it. The three faced *Rudraksha* is Fire God manifest; it destroys in a moment the sin of killing a woman.

The three-faced *Rudraksha* is the three Agnis, Daksinagni, Garbapatya, and Ahavaniya; Bhagavan Agni always pleased with that man who wears the three-faced *Rudraksha*. The four-faced *Rudraksha* in Brahma Himself. The wearer gets his prosperity enhanced, his diseases destroyed, the divine knowledge springs in him and his heart is always pleased. The five-faced *Rudraksha* is the five-faced Shiva Himself; Mahadeva gets pleased with him who holds it. The presiding Deity of the six faced *Rudraksha* is the seven Matrikas, the Sun and the seven Risis. By putting on this, the prosperity is increased, health and the pure knowledge are established. It should be put on when one becomes pure. The Presiding Deity of the eight-faced *Rudraksha* is Brahmi, the eight Matrikas. By holding this, the eight Vasus are pleased and the river Ganges is also pleased. The putting on of this makes the Jivas truthful and pleasant-minded. The Devata of the mine-faced *Rudraksha* is Yama; holding this puts off the fears of Death. The Devata of the eleven-faced *Rudraksha* is ten quarters. The ten quarters are pleased with him who wears the ten-faced *Rudraksha*. The Devata of the eleven mouthed *Rudraksha* is the eleven Rudras and Indra. Holding this enhances happiness. The twelve-faced *Rudraksha* is Vishnu made manifest; its Devatas are the twelve Adityas; the devotees of Shiva should hold this. The thirteen-faced *Rudraksha*, if worn, enables one to secure one's desires; he does nowhere experience failures. The Kama Deva becomes pleased with him who wears this. The fourteen-faced

Rudraksha destroys all diseases and gives eternal health. While holding this, one ought not to take wine, flesh, onion, garlic, Sajna fruit, Chalta fruit and the flesh of the boar which eats excrements, etc., During the Lunar and Solar eclipses, during the Uttarayana Samkranti or the Daksinayana Samkranti, during the full Moon or the New Moon day, if *Rudraksha* be worn, one becomes instantly freed of all one's sins.

Here ends, the Seventh Chapter of the Eleventh Book on the greatness of one faced etc., *Rudraksham* in the Maha Puranam Sri Mad Devi Bhagavatam of 18,000 verses by Maharsi Veda Vyasa.

Reproduced is translated by Swami Vijnananda "The Srimad Devi Bhagwatam" Munshiram Manoharlal Publishers Pvt. Ltd. New Delhi.

THE SHIVA-PURANA
CHAPTER XXIII

(*The glorification of the Rudraksha and of the names of Shiva*)

The sages said...

1-2. O Suta, Suta the fortunate disciple of Vyasa, obeisance to thee. Please explain again the glorification of the holy ashes, of the *Rudraksha* and of Shiva's names. Lovingly explaining the three, please delight our minds.

Suta said...

3-4. It is good that you have referred to this matter that is highly beneficient to the world. You are blessed, holy and ornaments to your families since you own Shiva as your sole great favourite deity. The anecdotes of Shiva are dear to you all for ever.

5. Those who adore Shiva are blessed and content. Their birth is fruitful and their family is elevated.

6. Sins never touch those from whose mouth the names Sadashiva, Shiva etc. comes out for ever, as they do not touch the burning charcoal of the khadira wood.

7. When a mouth utters "Obeisance to Thee, holy Shiva" that mouth (face) is on a par with holy centres destroying all sins.

8. It is certain that the benefit of making pilgrimages to holy centres accrues to one who lovingly looks at His holy face.

9. O Brahmins, the place where these three are found is the most auspicious one. A mere contact of the place accords the benefit of taking a holy dip in the sacred Triveni.

10. Shiva's name, the ashes and the *Rudraksha* beads— the three are very holy and are on a par with Triveni* (the confluence of the three holy rivers).

11. The sight of the persons who have these three in their bodies is a rare occurrence. But when obtained it removes all sins.

12. There is no difference at all between these two—a sight of the holy man and a bath in the Triveni. He who does not realise this is undoubtedly a sinner.

13. The man who has no ashes on his forehead, has not worn *Rudraksha* on his body and does not utter names of Shiva shall be shunned as one does a base man.

---

* The place of confluece (Prayaga, now Allahabad) of the Ganges with the yamuna and the subterranean Sarasvati.

14. As said by Brahma, Shiva's name on a par with Ganga, the ash is equal to Yamuna and *Rudraksha* destroys all sins (and is equal to Sarasvati).

15-16. Brahma wishing to bestow beneficence weighed one against the other. He put on one side the benefit achieved by a person in whose body the three things were present. On the other side he put the blessedness achieved by those who took their bath in the holy Triveni. Both were found equal. Hence scholars shall wear these always.

17. From that time onwards Brahma, Vishnu and other Devas wear these three. Their very sight dispels sins.

The Sages said...

18. O righteous one, you have explained the benefit of the three things: Shiva's name etc. Please explain it vivdly.

Suta said...

19. O brahmanical sages, you are all good devotees of Shiva, gifted with knowledge and great intellect. You are the foremost among the wise. Please listen with reverence to their greatness.

20. O Brahmins, it is mysteriously hidden in sacred texts, Vedas and Puranas. Out of love for you I reveal the same to you now.

21. O foremost among the brahmins! Who ever does know the real greatness of the three except Shiva who is beyond all in the whole universe?

22. Briefly I shall explain the greatness of the names as prompted by my devotion. O brahmins, do you lovingly listen to his greatness: the destroyer of all sins.

23. Mountainous heaps of great sins are destroyed as in a blazing forest fire when the names of Shiva are repeated. They are reduced to ashes without any difficulty. It is true, undoubtedly true.

24. O Saunaka, different sorts of miseries with sins as their roots can be quelled only by mutterna Shiva's names, and not by anything else entirely.

25. The man who is devotedly attached to the Japas of Shiva's names in the world, is really a follower of the Vedas, a meritorious soul and a blessed scholar.

26. O sage, instantaneously fruitful are the different sacred rites of those who have full faith in the efficacy of the Japas of Shiva's names.

27. O sage, so many sins are not committed by men in the world as are and can be destroyed by Shiva's names.

28. O sage, Shiva's names repeated by men, immediately destroy the countless heaps of sins such as the slaughter of a brahmin.

29. Those who cross the ocean of worldly existence by resorting to the raft of the names of Shiva do definitely destroy those sins that are the root-cause of worldly existence.

30. O great sage, the destruction of sins that are the roots of worldly existence is certainly effected by the axe of Shiva's names.

31. The nectar of Shiva's names shall be drunk by those who are distressed and scorched by the conflagration of sins. Without it, the people who are scorched by the conflagration cannot have any peace.

32. Those who are drenched by the nectarine downpour of Shiva's names never feel ill at ease even in the middle of the conflagration of worldly existence.

33. The noble souls who have acquired great devotion to the names of Shiv, and those like them, attain perfect liberation instantaneously.

34. O lord of sages, devotion to the names of Shiva, that destroys all sins can be acquired only by him who has performed penances in the course of many births.

35. Salvation is easy of access only to him who has extraordinary and unbroken devotion for the names of Shiva. I believe in this.

36. Even if he has committed many sins, a person who has reverence for the Japa of Shiva's names, becomes certainly free from all sins.

37. Just as the trees in a forest are burnt and reduced to ashes by the forest fire, so also are the sins destroyed by Shiva's names.

38. O Saunaka, he who regularly sanctifies his body by the holy ashes and who performs the Japa of Shiva's names crosses even the terrible ocean of worldly existence.

39. A person who undertakes the Japa of Shiva's names is not sullied by sins even after misappropriating a brahmin's wealth and killing many brahmins.

40. After going through all the Vedas it has been decided by our ancestors that the noblest means of crossing the ocean of worldly existence is the performance of the Japa of Shiva's names.

41. O excellent sages, why should I say much? By means of a single verse I shall mention the greatness and efficacy of the names of Shiva or the destruction of all sins.

42. The power of the names of Shiva in destroying sins is more than the ability of men of commit them.

43. O sage, formerly the king Indradyumna who was a great sinner, attained the excellent goal of the good through the influence of Shiva's names.

44. O sage, similarly a brahmin woman too of very sinful activities attained the excellent goal of the good through the influence of Shiva's names.

45. O excellent brahmins, thus I have told you about the surpassing excellence of the names. Now please listen to the greatness of holy ashes, the most sacred of all.

CHAPTER XXV

(The greatness of Rudraksha)

Suta said...

1. O sage Saunaka, highly intelligent, of the form of Shiva, noble-minded, please listen to the greatness of Rudraksha. I shall explin it briefly.

2. Rudraksha is a favourite bead of Shiva. It is highly sanctifying. It removes all sins by sight, contact and Japas.

3. O sage, formerly the greatness of Rudraksha was declared to the Goddess by Shiva, the supreme soul, for rendering help to the worlds.

Shiva said...

4. O shiva, Mahesani, be pleased to hear the greatness of

Rudraksha. I speak out love for you from a desire for the benefit of the devotees of Shiva.

5-7. O Mahesani, formerly I had been performing penance for thousands of devine years. Although I had controlled it rigorously, my mind was in flutter. Out of sport, I being self-possessed just opened my eyes O Goddess, from a deisre of helping the worlds. Drops of tears fell from my beautifyl half-closed eyes. From those tear-drops there cropped up the *Rudraksha* plants.

8. The became immobile. In order to bless the devotees they were given to the four Varnas devoted to the worship of Vishnu.

9-10. *Rudraksha* grown in Gauda[1] land became great favourites of Shiva. They were grown in Mathura, Lanka, Ayodhya, Malaya,[2] Sahya[3] mountain, Kasi and other places. They are competent to break asunder the clustered sins unbearable to the others, as the sacred texts have declared.

11. At my bidding they were classified into Brahmins, Kshatriyas, Vaisyas and Shudras. These *Rudrakshas* are of auspicious nature.

12. The colours of the four types of *Rudrakshas* are respectively white, red, yellow and black. All people shall wear the *Rudraksha* of their own Varna.

---

1. Gauda desa, according to Skandapurana, was the central part of Bengal extending from Vanga to the borders of Orissa:
2. Malaya: a mountain range on the west of Malabar, the western ghats, a bounding in sandal trees.
3. Sahya: It is one of the seven principal ranges, the other six being Mahendra, Malaya, Suktimat, Riksha, Vindhya and Paripatra or Pariyatra.

13. If they desire their benefit, namely worldly pleasures and salvation and if the devotees of Shiva wish to gratify Shiva they must wear the *Rudraksha*.

14. A *Rudraksha* of the size of an Emblic myrobalan (Dhatriphala) is mentioned as the most excellent; one of the size of the fruit of the jujube tree (Badariphala) is spoken of as the middling.

15. O Parvati, lovingly listen to this from a desire for the benefit of the deovtees. The meanest of *Rudrakshas* is of the size of a gram according to this excellent classification.

16. O Maheshvari, even the *Rudraksha* which is only of the size of the fruit of the jujube accords the benefit and heightens happiness and good fortune.

17. That which is of the size of the emblic myrobalan is conducive to the destruction of all distresses. That which is of the size fo a Gunja (the berry) is conducive to the achievement of the fruit of all desire.

18. The lighter the *Rudraksha*, the more fruitful it is. Each of these is fruitful and that of a weight of one tenth is considered by scholars as the most fruitful.

19. The wearing of *Rudraksha* is recommended for the sake of destroying sins. Hence that which is conducive to the achievement of every object has to be worn certainly.

20. O Paramesvari, no other necklace or garland is observed in the world to be so auspicious and fruitful as the *Rudraksha*.

21. O Goddess, *Rudrakshas* of even size, glossy, firm, thick and having many thornlike protrusions yield desires and bestow wordly pleasures and salvation for ever.

22. Six types of *Rudrakshas* shall be discarded: that which is defiled by worms, is cut and broken, has no thornlike protrusions, has cracks and is not circular.

23. That which has a natural hole from end to end is the most excellent; that which is bored through by human effort is the middling one.

24. The wearing of *Rudraksha* is spoken of as conducive to the destruction of great sins. If eleven hundred *Rudrakshas* are worn on the person, the man assumes the form of Rudra.

25. Even in hundredsof years, it is impossible to describe adequately the benefit derived by wearing eleven hundred and fifty *Rudrakshas*.

26. A devout man shall make a coronet consisting of five hundred and fifty *Rudrakshas*.

27. A person of pious nature shall make three circular strings in the maner of the sacred thread, each having three hundred and sixty beads.

28. O Mahesvari, three *Rudrakshas* must be worn on the tuft and six in each of the ears right and left.

29-30. Hundred and one *Rudrakshas* shall be worn round the neck; eleven *Rudrakshas* shall be worn round each fo the arms, elbows and wrists. Devotees of Shiva shall have three *Rudrakshas* in the sacred thread and round the hips five *Rudrakshas* shall be tied.

31. O Paramesvari, the person by whom so many *Rudrakshas* are worn is worthy of being bowed to and adored by all like Mahesa.

32. Such a person while in contemplation shall be duly

seated and addressed "O Shiva." Seeing him, every one is freed from sins.

33. This is the rule regarding eleven hundred *Rudrakshas*. If so many are not availble, another auspicious procedure. I Mention to you.

34-36. One *Rudraksha* shall be worn on the tuft, thirty on the head, fifty round the neck; sixteen in each of the arms; twelve round each of the wrists; five hundred on the shoulders, and three strings each having hundred and eight in the manner of the sacred thread. He who wears in all a thousand *Rudrakshas* and is of firm resolve in performing rites is bowed to by all Devas like Rudra himself.

37-39. One *Rudraksha* shall be worn on the tuft, forty on the forehead, thirty-two round the beck; hundred and eight over the chest; six in each of the ears; sixteen round each of the arms; O lord of sages, according to the measurement of the forearms, twelve or twice the number shall be worn there. A person who wears so many out of love, is a great devotee of Shiva. He shall be worshippped like Shiva. He is worthy of being always honoured by all.

40. It shall be worn on the head repeating Isana mantra; on the ears with Tripurusa mantra; round the neck with Aghora mantra and on the chest also likewise.

41. The wise devotee shall wear the *Rudraksha* round the forearms with Aghora Bija mantra. A string of fifteen beads shall be worn on the stomach with Vamadeva mantra.

42. With five mantras—Sadyojata etc. three, five or seven garlands shall be worn. Or all beads shall be worn with the Mula mantra.

43. A devotee of Shiva shall refrain from eating meat, garlic, onion, red garlic, potherb, Slesmataka, pig of rubbish and liquors.

44. O Uma, daughter of the mountain, the white *Rudraksha* shall be worn by the brahmin, the red by the Kshatriya, the yellow by the Vaisya, the black by the Shudra. This is the path indicated by the Vedas.

45. Whether he is a householder, forest-dweller, ascetic or of any Order, none shall go out of this secret advice. Only by great merits can be opportunity to wear the *Rudraksha* be obtained. If he misses it he will go to hell.

46. The *Rudrakshas* of the size of an Emblic myrobalan and those of lighter weight but depressed with thorns, those eaten by worms or without holes and those characterized by other defects shall not be worn by those wishing for auspicious results. They shall avoid small ones of the size of gram. O Uma, *Rudraksha* is an auspicious complement to the my phallic image. The small one is always praiseworthy.

47. People of all Varnas and Asramas even women and Shudras can wear *Rudrakshas* at the bidding of Shiva. The ascetics shall wear it with the Pranava Om).

48. If any one wears it during the day he is freed from sins committed during the night; if he wears it during the night he is freed from the sins committed during the day. Similar is the result with its wearing during morning, midday or evening.

49. Those who wear Tripundra the matted hair and the *Rudraksha* do not go to Yama's abode.

50-52. (Yama's directive to his attendants): "Those who wear at least one *Rudraksha* on their heads, Tripundra on the

forehead and repeat the five-syllabled mantras shall be
honoured by you all. They are indeed saintly men. You can
bring the man here who has no *Rudraksha* on his person, and
no Tripundra on his forehead and who does not utter the
five-syllabled mantra. All those who have the ash and
Rudraksha shall be honoured always by us after knowing their
power. They shall never be brought here."

53. Yama commanded his attendants like this. They too
remained quiet agreeing to it. In fact they were surprised.

54. Hence Mahadevi, the *Rudraksha* as well as the person
who wears it is my favourite. O Parvati, even if he has
committed sins he becomes pure.

55. He who wears *Rudraksha* round the hands and arms
and over the head cannot be killed by any living being. He
shall roam in the world in the form of Rudra.

56. He shall be respected by the Gods and Asuras always.
he shall be honoured like Shiv. He removes the sin of any one
seen by him.

57. If a person is not liberated after meditation and
acquisition of knowledge he shsll wear *Rudraksha*. He shall be
freed from all sins and attain the highest goal.

58. A mantra repeated with *Rudraksha* is a crore times
more efficacious. A man wearing Rudraksha derives a
hundred million times more merit.

59. O Goddess, as long as the *Rudraksha* is on the person
of a living soul he is least affected by premature death.

60. One shall attain Rudra on seeing a person with
Tripundra, his limbs covered with *Rudraksha* and repeating
the Mrtyunjaya mantra.

61. He is a favourite of the five deities the five deities referred to here are: the sun, Ganesha, Goddess Durga, Rudra and Vishnu. Cp. and a favourite of all gods. O beloeved, a devotee shall repeat all mantras wearing a garland of *Rudrakshas* (or counting on the beads).

62. Even the devotees of Vishnu and other deities shall unhesitatingly wear the *Rudraksha*. Especially the devotee of Rudra shall wear *Rudrakshas* always.

63. *Rudrakshas* are of various types. I shall explain their different classifications. O Parvati, hear with great devotion. These *Rudrakshas* bestow wordly pleasures and salvation.

64. A *Rudraksha* of a single face is Shiva Himself. It bestows worldly pleasures and salvation. The sin of brahmin-slaughter is washed off at its mere sight.

65. Where it is adored, Fortune cannot be far ooff. Harms and harassments perish. All desires are fulfilled.

66. A *Rurdraksha* with two faces is Isa, the lord of devas. It bestows the fulfilment of all desires. Especially that *Rudraksha* quickly quells the sin of cow-slaughter.

67. A *Rudraksha* with three faces always bestows means of enjoyment. As a result of its power all lores become firmly established.

68. A *Rudraksha* of four faces is Brahma Himself. It quells the sin of man-salughter. Its vision and its contact instantaneously bestow the achievement of the four aims of life.

69. A *Rudraksha* with five faces is Rudra Himself. Its name is Kalagni. It is lordly. It bestows all sorts of salvation and achievement of all desired objects.

70. A five-faced *Rudraksha* dispels all sorts of sins such as accrue from sexual intercourse with a forbidden woman and from eating forbidden food.

71. A *Rudraksha* with six faces is Kartikeya. A man who wears it on the right arm is certainly absolved of the sins of brahmin-slaughter and the like.

72. A *Rudraksha* with seven faces, O Mahesani, is called Ananga. O Devesi, by wearing it even a poor man becomes a great lord.

73. A *Rudraksha* with eight faces is called Vasumurti and Bhairava. By wearing it a man lives the full span of life. After death he becomes the Triden-bearing lord (Shiva).

74. A *Rudraksha* with nine faces is also Bhairva. Its sage is Kapila. Its presiding goddess is Durga of nine forms, Mahesvari Herself.

75. That *Rudraksha* shall be worn on the left hand with great devotion. He shall certainly become Sarvesvara like me.

76. O Mahesani, a *Rudraksha* with ten faces is Lord Janardana Himself. O Devesi, by wearing it, the devotee shall achieve the fulfilment of al desire.

77. O Paramesvari, a *Rudraksha* with eleven faces is Rudra. By wering it one becomes victorious everywhere.

78. One shall wear the twelve-faced *Rudraksha* on the hair of the head. All the twleve Adityas (suns) are present therein.

79. A *Rudraksha* with thriteen faces is Visvedeva. By wearing it, a man will attain the realisation of all desires. He will derive good fortune and auspisiousness.

80. A *Rudraksha* with fourteen faces is the highest Shiva. It

shall be worn on the head with great devotion. It quells all sins.

81. O daughter of the king of mountains, thus I have explained to you the different types of *Rudrakshas* based on the number of faces. Please listen to the mantras with devotion.

On Hreem obeisance (Om Hreem namah)		*Single faced*
Om namah	:	2
Kleem namah	:	3
Om Hreem namah	:	4
Om Hreem namah	:	5
Om Hreem Hum namah	:	6
Om Hum namah	:	7
Om Hum namah	:	8
Om Hreem Hum namah	:	9
Om Hreem namah	:	10
Om Hreem Hum namah	:	11
Om Kraum Ksaum Raum namah	:	12
Om Hreem namah	:	13
Om namah	:	14

82. For the achievement of all desired objects, the devotee shall wear the *Rudraksha* with mantras. He shall have great devotion and faith. He shall be free form lethargy.

83. The man who wears the *Rudrakshas* without mentra falls into a terrible hell and stays there during the tenure of fourteen Indras.

84-85. On seeing a man with the garland of *Rudrakshas*, all evil spirits, ghosts, Pisacas, witches like Dakini and Sakini, other malignant spirits, evil charms and spells etc. fly away suspecting a quarrel.

86. Seeing a devotee with the garland of *Rudrakshas*, O Parvati, Shiva, Vishnu, Devi, Ganapati, the sun and all the Gods are pleased.

87. Thus realising its greatness the *Rudraksha* must be worn well, O Maheshwari, repeating the mantras the devotion to make virtues flourish.

88. Thus, the greatness of ash and *Rudraksha* that bestow worldly pleasures and salvation, was explained to Girija by Shiva, the supreme soul.

89. The person who apply ash and wear *Rudraksha* are great favourites of Shiva. Enjoyment of worldly pleasures and salvation are certainly due to their influence.

90. He who applies ash and wears *Rudraksha* is called a devotee of Shiva. A person devoted to the Japa of the five syllabled mantra is a perfect and noble being.

91. If Mahadeva is worshipped without the Tripundra of ash and without the garland of *Rudraksha*, he does not bestow the fruit of cherished desire.

92. Thus, O lord of sages, whatever has been asked has now been explained. The greatness of ash and *Rudraksha* bestows the luxuriant fulfilment of all desires.

93. He who regularly listens to the highly auspicious greatness of ash and *Rudraksha* with devotion shall attain the fulfilment of all desires.

94. He will enjoy all happiness here. He will be blessed with sons and grandsons. In the next world he will attain

salvation. He will be a great favourite of Shiva.

95. O lordly sages, thus the compendium of Vidyesvara-samhita has been narrated to you all. As ordered by Shiva it bestows achievement of everything and salvation.

Translation reproduced from "The Shiva Purana" by 'A book of scholars' published by Motilal Banarsidass Publishers Pvt. Ltd. New Delhi.

RUDRAKSHA JABALOPANISHAD

Let all my body parts grow and be healthy, speech, breath, eyes, ears, strength and all organs should develope to full potention. All upnishads are supreme God like (Brahma-swaroop). Neither I should feel separated from Brahma nor Brahma may let me away. This way by feeling close to Atma (soul) let me be blessed by the Dharma (duties) as narrated in Upnishad. All teachings of Upnishad Dharma may assimilate within me Om Shantih Shantih Shantih.

Once upon a time Bhusanda asked Kalagni Rudra "How *Rudraksha* got produced? What are the advantages of *Rudraksha* wearing?"

Kalagni Rudra replied "To kill demon Tripurasur I closed my eyes (in meditation). As a result of this, the water (tears) which fill from my eyes on the earth got converted to *Rudraksha* trees and *Rudraksha* got produced from them. As obliged for welfare & all, I have to state that even taking the name *"Rudraksha"* blesses the speaker with results equivalent of donating ten cows. By seeing and touching *Rudraksha*, the benefits are doubled. (In fact) I have no stamina to explain further (about benefits). In this regard the following are the verses.

Q : Where are these found? What are their names? Why people wear them? How many facets they have? How and by which mantras they are to be worn?

Ans : By keeping the eyes open for one thousand divine years, during the meditation, some water drops fell on the earth.

These drops (tears) converted to great *Rudraksha* trees an to bless the devatees got stablished (stay-fixed) by wearing these *Rudraksha*, sins committed day and night get absolved. By looking at *Rudraksha* it gives hundred thousand times benefits and by wearing hundred lac (koti) times.

The wearer gets not hundred lac (koti) times but hundred koti (arab) times. By wearing and doing japam on *rudraksha* mala the benefit are thousand lac-koti times and lac-koti in hundred multiple times, respectively. *Rudraksha* of amla size (size of dhatriphal or myrobalan) is the best. The (smaller) berry size is medium. The (smallest) size of a gram (chana size) is lowest or meanest Now I explain further.

By Lord's order these divine beads got classified as Brahmin, Kshatriya, Vaisya and Shudra (Division of castes according to work nature). Brahmins should wear white, kshatriya red, vaisya yellow and shudras black.

Beads of equal size, round, smooth, strong (hard), big and thorny are considered auspicious. Those eaten by insects, broken or damaged without thorns, infested with insects and which do not appear good are the six types which are unauspicious (and should not be worn). If *rudraksha* has a natural hole at the appropriate place then it is the best. If the hold is made by force then it is medium quality *rudraksha*.

The equal size, smooth, hard and strong *rudraksha* should be strung using silk thread and worn. *Rujdraksha* should be good in appearance, sober and equal in size. The bead lines should appear like gold lines on a pumice stone (kasauti). Such *rudraksha* is better and only such a mala should be worn by Shiva devotees. One *rudraksha* on the tuft of hair (crown) and thirty around the head should be worn. Thirty-six around neck, sixteen each on the arms, twelve on each wrist and fifteen on the shoulder should be worn.

A mala of one hundred eight should be worn like the sacred thread (yagnopaveet). Two round, three round, five round or seven round *rudraksha* mala should be used around throat. *Rudraksha* should be used as a crown over head, like ear-rings (kindal) on eas and also like a rosary around ear.

Rudraksha should be used continuously while sleeping or awake around arms and waist in the form of threaded rosary. Three hundred *rudraksha* are inauspicious, five hundred medium and one thousand the best for wearing. *Rudraksha* should be worn by chanting Ishana mantra over the head, Tatpurush mantra over the throat and Aghor mantra over the heart.

The intelligent one will use *rudraksha* on both the hands chanting Aghor mantra. *Rudraksha* beads should be strung and sanctified (blessed) by a (अ) to ksha (क्ष) Fifty letters (of the sanskrit language), then by chanting panchakshari mantra (Namah Shivaya) the mala should be blessed. Then by chanting seed mantras the beads should get invoked (for its divine powers) and then in three, five or seven rounds may be worn around the neck.

Bhusund asked. Lork Kalagni Rudra again — what are the different properties of *rudraksha* according to different properties of *rudraksha* according to different facets (mukhis)? I want to know the powers of different facets to remove the inquspicous and to gain fruit ful reslts.

(Kalagni Rudra replies) There is a shloka (verse) about this:

One mukhi represents the supreme Lord and by wearing this the wearer having won over the senses assimilates with Lord Shiva (Shiva Tattva) O Muni!

Two mukhi represents Ardhanareshwar and by wearing this always Lord Ardhanareshwar Shiva pleases.

Three mukhi *rudraksha* represents three forms of Agni (fire) and by wearing this the four headed Lord is pleased.

Four mukhi *rudraksha* represents Lord Brahma (Creator) and by wearing this the four headed lord is pleased.

Five mukhi *rudraksha* repsents five face lord (Shiva as Panch Mahadev). It is symbolises supreme God (Brhma) also. By wearing this *rudraksha* the sin of killing a person gets absolved.

Six mukhi symbolises Kartikeya (Elder son of Lord Shiva) by wearing which Mahalaxmi gets pleased and good health is also obtained. Intellgent people consider this *rudraksha* as a form of Lord Ganesh and use to get intelligence, education, for wealth (Mahalaxmi), and also for purity.

Seven mukhi *rudraksha* represents seven mother (Brahmi etc.). Its wearing gives great wealth and good health. By wearing it with purity one would get vast knowledge and wealth.

Eight mukhi *rudraksha* symbolizes eight mothers. It is dear to eight vasus also. Ganges also pleases with the wearer. All the three please with the wearer.

Nine mukhi represents nine powers. By wearing this all the nine powers (shakti) get pleased.

Ten mukhi is symbolises Yamdev (Lord of Death). By seeing and wearing it leads to peace of mind. There is no doubt about it.

Eleven mukhi is eleventh rudra himself. It is a good luck provider.

Twelve mukhi *rudraksha* symbnolises (Lord Vishnu). It is also considered as twelve Suryas (Dwadash Adityas), and these are worn by its worshippers.

Thirteen mukhi *rudraksha* is for fulfilment of desires and gives successes. It is auspicious. Lord cupid gets pleased with the wearer.

Fourteen mukhi *rudraksha* has specially got formed from Lord rudra's eyes. It is for removal of all diseases and for giving perpetual good health.

Wearer of *rudraksha* should abstain from taking alcohol, meat, onion, sahijan (Shigni), Lisoda (Shleshmatak), vidvarah etc. which are not compatible for normal eating.

Rudraksha wearer becomes free from all sins if *rudraksha* are worn on any eclipse day, meeting point of day & night, at the time of solar cycle: ayan-change (Uttarayan, Dakshinayan), dark moon day or fal moon day, the last day of lunar month. The main body part of *rudraksha* bead is considered as Vishnu, the bottom part (where the mukhs end) as Brahma and the top part (from where the mukhs originale) as Shiva. On all its points reside various devas. Sonatkumar then asked Lord Kalagni... Rudra O Lord! please tell us the method for wearing *rudraksha*.

At that time (several rishis) like Nidadh, Sadbharat, Dattateya, Katyayan, Bharadwaj, Kapil, Vashishtha, Pippalad etc., sat all round Lord Kalagni Rudra and when asked by Lord Kalagni Rudra why they are here told that we all want to hear the *rudraksha* wearing procedure.

Then Kalgni Rudra said... Due to its origin from Rudra's eyes the name *Rudraksha* is known in the entire universe. At the time of ending the universe Lord Shiva used to slightly open and close the eyes (open for shortime and close for most of the time). *Rudraksha* has produced from such eyes. The *rudraksha* properly of rudraksha is proven.

If the word *rudraksha* is spoken hundred times at gives benefit euqal to donating ten cows. The same *rudraksha* is also called "Bhasma Jyoti" *rudraksha*. If such a *rudraksha* is touched by hand and worn it gives benefit equal to two thousand cow donation. The same *rudraksha* if worn on the ears give benefit equal to donating eleven thousand cows and the wearer gets the form of eleventh rudra. Such a *rudraksha* if worn on forehead gives fruits equal to that of donating hundred lac cows. Out of all the places wearing on the ear is most fruitful and cannot be discribed.

(*Rudraksha* desciption ends here)

Rending of *Rudraksha* Jabalopanishad is considered quspicous for all and give benefit to all.

Translated by the author

PADMA PURAN
SRUSHTI KHAND CHAPTER 57
(Description of Rudraksha glory)

Amongst all living beings, any one wearing *rudraksha* is of the highest order and even a sight of such a being washes away all the sins. One who wears *rudraksha* touching his/her body througout the day wanders like the one who has achieved salvation. The one wearing *rudraksha* over forhead, chest and arms, that person becomes like Ishaan (like Shiva) and remains present at all places where Yajnas (Homams) are performed. The province or area becomes holy and acclaimed where any such person lives.

Persons who see or touch another person wearing *rudraksha* become free from all negativities and faults. Performing jap, tarpan (offering water of chanting mantras), giving donations, doing worship, taking bath or walking around holy objects become perpetual and abundant if conducted with *rudraksha* as an objective. The blessings of *rudraksha* is like divine blessings from major pilgrim centres.

By wearing (*rudraksha*) over the body a person becomes free from sins and becomes entitled to stay in heaven (apavargabhak). By accepting the *rudraksha* mala and by wearing mala having brahma-knots (between the beads) if someone does jap or give donation, chant prayers and a mantras or make offerings to Devatas (Gods), all such acts become perpetual and immortal and also absolves the person of all the sins.

O great twice born (Dvij)! I shall now narrate properties of the mala which please listen. After learning about these one can attain the path of salvation (Nirvan).

A bead without lines, eaten by insects, having broken protrusions, and the beads goint with other bead should not get a place in the mala.

Mala should be knotted by the wearer him/her self and the beads should be strung over each other properly. Mala made by shudra (one having mean thoughts or having negativities) are considered impure. It should be rejected after knowing this.

After stringing twenty-seven beads in snake-shaped manner, the mala should get a meru (central) bead. There should be a knot between the beads and the entire mala should be impressive and balanced. Intelligent people should do jap on such mala.

Such a mala, made in purified way should be used with thumb as a base and beads coming inward (towards the person) — a person should do jap with the middle finger (as the main counting finger) as the main acting medium.

By the movement of a fingers, reach the meru (central bead) and (without jumping over the bead) reverse and start counting again. Always use the same fixed numbers for jap. Jap with undefined or unlimited numbers is not beneficial.

Jap for all devatas can be done with own mala. If jap is done at a pilgrim centre (teertha sthaan) then he/she gets the benefit several crore times.

On a pure land, at the root of a tree determined for performing a yagna (or at the roots of a khair tree), at a cow-yard, on a four-way cross road, or inside the house if Vishnu mantra, Shiva-mantra, Ganesh-mantra or Sun-mantra is used for jap then one gets unlimited results.

If jap (counting of mantras) is performed at neutral place (in caves of mountains or away from habitats), inside a Shiva temple, at the cremation ground, or at a four-way cross lane, the jap performer shall get immediate results of Siddhi (to fullfil all desires). All vedic, Paurnanik and Tantrik mantras are chanted with *rudraksha* mala and such counting gives desired results and gives nirvaan (moksha) also which is ultimate of human objectives. One should get drenched with water over head which came in contact with *rudraksha*.

By *rudraksha* one gets purified from all sins (committed earlier) and (he/she) gets perennial divine results. On each *rudraksha* bead, a God resides. Any person wearing *rudraksha*, even if belinging to this earthly bodies, gets entitled to a level higher than the Devalok (location of the heavenly Gods).

The Twice-born (Dvijas) said: where *rudraksha* grows, or where does it go on the tree of yagnas, why does it place itself over earth as a rigid tree. Also who has promoted this tree (as *rudraksha?*)

Vyas said: O Dvijas! In olden times a demon named Tripurasur eixted at the time of Krityug (Satyayug — a divine age). He killed Devatas and went to the galaxies (Antarikshapura). After the destruction of all dwellings (Lokas of human, para-human or super-human varieties) he sat like Brahma (the Supreme). At this time Lord Shiva heard the atrocities committed by this demon and the condition of the Devatas. Lord Shankar saw through his fire-filled eyes and then using his "agavagam" — Pinaka (the bow of Lord

Shiva). He killed the demon by forming himself as Kaal (the time God).

This demon (Tripurasur) fell like meteorite. The tired "rudra" God (Shiva) had swed which fell over the earth immediately from these drops of swed grand *rudraksha* trees grew. The living beings do not know the secrets of this fruit.

Skand bowed the head over the peak of mt Kailash for the supreme God (Mahadeva-Shiva) and said: O Lord Shiva! I would like to know about the *rudraksha* fruit deeply (1 would) also like to know about jap, wearing, sighting and touching it? How does it benefit?

Lord Shiva said: "By seeing it if you get a hundred thousand times of a blessing (punya) then by touching ten million (crore) times. A person who wears it get ten crore times divine benefits.

A hundred million times and thousand million times divine blessings are available by doing jap. There is no need to think (for an alternative) to this.

A socially bycotted person living with all kinds of prohibited deeds or a person full of sins (and abnormal unholy deeds) can also become free of all sins by wearing *rudraksha*.

Even a dog can achieve 'rudratva' (Shivahood) if it dies wearing *rudraksha* around neck then what is there to discuss about human beings?

Even if worn without the aim of meditation and still higher level (of dharana etc.) then also the wearer attains the supreme divinity (after death) freeing (him/her) self from all sins.

Kartikeya said: Ek mukhi, two mukhi, three mukhi, four mukhi, five mukhi, six mukhi, seven mukhi, eight mukhi, nine mukhi, ten mukhi, eleven mukhi, twelve mukhi, thirteen mukhi, fourteen mukhi, are all Shiva formlike as told by Lord Shiva.

O Lord! tell us about different gods of these mukhi *rudraksha*. How are their goods points or negative points (doshas)?

If you feel I am obliged then please let me know the truth and that (secret).

Lord said:

Ek mukhi (one facet) is Lord Shiva incarnate, it absolves the sin of committing murder of a Brahmin (Brahma-Hatya). It must be therefore worn over body and this (action) absolves the person of all the sins committed.

Thereafter, the wearer of one mukhi *rudraksha* goes to Shiva lok (the abode of Lord Shiva) and lives happily with Lord Shiva himself. This requires kind patronage of Lord Shiva to get such a resultant situation (after several events).

O Shadanan (six headed one)! A dying person wearing one mukhi *rudraksha* gets the "nirvan" (gets out of cycle of birth & death).

O God of Gods! a wearer of two mukhi *rudraksha* absolves him/her self of all the sins committed, even that of killing a cow, wearing two mukhi paves the way to attain perpetual heaven which exists without any decay.

Two mukhi *rukdraksha* is like fire. The body of a person wearing this bead gets purified from all sins accumulated since birth just like fire destroys all things as fuel. Sins like killing of a woman, Brahma-hatya (killing of a Brahmin) and of similar killings, get washed away on wearing this *rudraksha*. The fruits (benefits) one gets by worshipping fire, or by offering ahutis (feeding the devas during fire worship during Yajna) are obtained by the brave person and he attains a place in the heaven.

On the earth, if one wears a three mukhi *rudraksha* then he/she becomes like Brahma (supreme God), In several birth-cycle later all sins committed through the body get absolved.

The three mukhi wearer does not come to a womb again (do not take birth), does not suffer from any disease and do not lead an in disciplined life. He is never defeated (his/her) house never catches fire get destroyed.

All the above and beyond any and above all difficulties get resolved by three mukhi *rudraksha*. No bad omen occurs for a three mukhi *rudraksha* wearer.

Four mukhi *rudraksha* is Brahma Himself. Any person as a Dvij who wears it becomes an accomplished person knowing all Shastras, Vedagya and becomes acceptable and gets worshipped. If this *rudraksha* gets placed in the body of any wearer of this *rudraksha*, this Dvij (twice born — from any caste) becomes knowledgable for all epics, Vedas and becomes acceptable. He attains Brahminisam through Dvijitva. (This was the acceptable practice in ancient times and anyone could become Brahmin through Dvijitva route).

A person (wearing four mukhi) becomes knowledgeable of the absolute meanings, knower of smriti and puranas. All sins created out of killings of humans or of lower level gets absolved immediately.

Five mukhi *rudraksha* is rudra itself. It is known as 'Kalagni rudra.'

By wearing five mukhi *rudraksha*, one gets freed from sins of committing adultery with forbidden persons and eating forbidden foods. There is no doubt about this.

Lord Shiva always gets pleased with this (wearer). It becomes like a protective shield of all persons. All different forms of Lord Shiva: Sadyojaat, Ishaan, Tatpurush, Aghor and Vaamdev all reside in the five mukhi *rudraksha*. Due to this the five mukhi is available on the earth in plenty.

It is the soul of rudra (Atmaj roop). Therefore, all knowledgable people should wear it. In front of Shiva, this *rudraksha* is worshipped by Devatas and Asuras (negative forces-rakshasas) for several thousand crore years and hundred-crore worth of universal cycle. On earth it is omnipresent and in a Shiva temple it is full of divine light.

Therefore, by all means the five mukhi *rudraksha* should be worn.

Five mukhi *rudraksha* is Kartikeya himself (Shan mughan or Subramaniam). It should be worn on the right arm. By wearing this one gets absolved of killing a Brahmin (Brahma hatya) and similar other sins — there is no doubt about this. Even till the end of the earth cycle a person remains brave. He/she never gets defeated and roams full of great virtues. The wearer also obtains status of Lord Shiva's son (Kumaratva).

A Brahmin wearing six mukhi *rudraksha* is worshipped by Kings, a Kshatriya (warrior-class) obtains victory and Vaishya-Shudras remain full with wealth & luxury. For these people

Gauri (Parvati) is blissful and remains available like mother. Therefore, the male wearer of six mukhi becomes a victorious prson of the world by his physical power. He becomes great in oratory and keeps patience. In an assembly, at King's place and during discussions he remains a great articulater (& debator) having patience. He never becomes a pity or remains a weakling. He definitely not gets Shafer or broken. All these virtues and other similar virtues are in six mukhi *rudraksha* by wearing it.

Seven mukhi *rudraksha* are "mahasen, anant, naagraat (kartikeya, Vaasuki and Naagraaj) in (seven snake) form." In its each mukh one snake resides (or offers its blessing or power through it.) Anant, Karkat, Pundareek, Tatkshak, Visholwan, Kaarosh, and Shankhachooda are the seven great poweful snakes which reside at the seven mouths of this *rudraksha*.

The wearer of this bead does not get effected by the poison. Lord Shankar remains pleased with the wearer the same way he remains happy in the company of snakes.

Due to the happiness & blessings the wearer becomes free from all committed sins by each passing day. Sins like Brahmanicide, drinking of alcohol, stealing, adultery with own teacher's wife, get condoned by the wearer. He then definitely enjoys the luxury of all the three lokas (abodes) as enjoyed by the Devatas.

Eight mukhi *rudraksha* is like "Mahasen (Kartikeya) and Ganesh". Now listen to the divine benefits by wearing this *rudraksha*.

He will never be a fool (or a person unable to understand difference between good or bad). He will not be wihout intellect (he/she) do not face obstacles in any work they pursue (the wearer) remains excellent in writing and gets success in handling big jobs. Success remains foremost in all the works initiated by such a person.

The one who uses half lies and cheats during transactions of measurements (like weighing etc.) or takes shelter of lies and dishonesty, the one who touches teacher's wife for intercourse, touching her stomach or by hand to embrace or any similar sins. If committed by a person then wearing of eight mukhi *rudraksha* absolves all the sins perpetuated by such acts. Then such a person after getting blessings of the three Gods (Brahma-Vishnu-Mahesh) and after enjoying heavenly perpetual bliss gets salvation. All these benefits come from wearing eight mukhi *rudraksha*.

Nine mukhi *rudraksha* is considered as Bhairav. It should be worn in the arm.

By wearing this light yellow coloured *rudraksha* which offers salvation also, any person becomes strong like me. If a person commits several killings of human beings then also his all sins get washed away by wearing nine mukhi *rudraksha*. He is worshipped in the heaven by Devatas and Rudra.

Wearing of ten mukhi *rudraksha* removes the fear of snake bite. It is pure like Shankar himself at Lord Shankar's residing place and it is also like Ganesh. There is no doubt about this.

By wearing eleven mukhi *rudraksha* one should understand eleven rudras. It should be worn on the centre of the tuft. Now listen to its benefits. The benefits one gets by performing one thousand Ashwamedha Yajana and one-hundred-crore yajnas and by donating hundred thousand cows, are obtained immediately by wearing eleven mukhi *rudraksha*. In this lok (planet earth) he becomes like Shankar and does not get rebirth.

Wearing twelve mukhi *rudraksha* around throat region. Lord Aditya (Sun) gets pleased. He establishes himself in the twelve mukhi *rudraksha*. The results obtained by performing Yajnas of Gomedh and Narmedh are available immeidately (to the wearer). He gets protection from any of the world's hardships (thunder, snowfall etc.). The wearer does not get fear from fire and does suffer from illness. He gets material wealth and gets pleasure and become Ishwar (owner). He is not touched by poverty. The sins of committing killings of elephant, horse, human being, cat, rat, donkey, snake, pig or fox etc., get absolved for the wearer of twelve mukhi *rudraksha*, there is no doubt on this.

If one obtains thirteen mukhi *rudraksha* which is Rudra himself, then it is for all the good things let this be understood. All the desires get fulfilled and give results, those wanting to taste the necter (Sudha-Rasayan) and engaged in metal processing then O Sadhanan! all there works become fruitful and they remain lucky. One gets perpetual heavenly bliss just like that of Lord Maheshwar.

O Son! If fourteen mukhi *rudraksha* is worn always on forehead or over the arms then the wearer becomes a power source like Shakti-pind (Shakti Peeth and Jyotirling together). There is no need to describe virtues of this *rudraksha* again and again. That person is always worshipped by Gods. Even the blessed ones meet such a person by luck only. Kartikeya said: O Lord! How each mukhi (*rudraksha*) is worn by rituals (nyas), and by chanting of mantras, please tell us.

Ishwar said: O Kartikeya! Listen, I shall describe the

method of performing rituals for each mukh. When *rudraksha* wearing without mantras has so many benefits then if a person on this earth wears *rudraksha* after chanting and blessing by mantras then I do not have stamina to describe the virtues and importance (in this case). Now mantras are being told:

(for mukhi)

Om Rudra ek-vaktrasya	:	1
Om kham dwi-vaktrasya	:	2
Om vum tri-vaktrasya	:	3
Om hreem chatur-vaktrasya	:	4
Om hraam panch-vaktrasya	:	5
Om hroom shad-saktrasya	:	6
Om hrah sapta-vaktrasya	:	7
Om kam ashta-vaktrasya	:	8
Om joom nav-vaktrasya	:	9
Om ksham dash-vaktrasya	:	10
Om shreem ekadash-vaktrasya	:	11
Om hraam dwadash-vaktrasya	:	12
Om kshaum trayodash-vaktrasya	:	13
Om Nraam chaturdash-vaktrasya	:	14

By these mantras the sanctification should be done in (proper) order.

A person wearing mala on the head and heart when walks then for each step he gets benefit equal to that of performing as Ashwamedha Yajna. There is no doubt on this.

Wearing all the mukhis makes a person like myself.

Therefore O Son! one should make all efforts to wear *rudraksha*.

The one who listen to these mantras or the pious virtues then he/she gets the same benefit like that of wearing all the mukhi *rudraksha*. After obtaining all described benefits the person goes to heaven and get salvation (moksha). Any person wearing *rudraksha* if dies then he goes to my blissful abode (Shiva lok) and he is worshipped by all Devatas.

Translated by the author

REFERENCES

1. *Shiva Puran* (Geeta Press, Gorakhpur)
2. *Shrimad Devibhagawatam* (Munsihram Manoharlal Publishers, New Delhi)
3. *Rudraksha Jabalopanishad*
4. *Rudradhyaye* (Geeta Press, Gorakhpur)
5. *Shrimadbhagawadgeeta* (ISCKON)
6. *Shiva Rahasya* (Shiv Dutta Shastri, Savitri Thakur Prakashan, Varanasi)
7. *Skand Puran* (Geeta Press, Gorakhpur)
8. *Padma Puran* (Geeta Press, Gorakhpur)
9. *Mantra Maharnava*
10. *Mahhakaal Samhita*
11. *Shiva* (Science of Spirituality – Vol. 9A, Dr. Jayant Athavale)
12. *Aksha Malakaupanishad*
13. *Rudraksha*, Subas Rai, Ganga Kaveri Publications, Varanasi
14. Meditation and Mantras, Swami Vishnu-Devanand, Motilal Banarsidas Publishers, New Delhi
15. *Rudraksha Dharan Aur Japyog, "Nishant Ketu"* Munshiram Manoharlal, New Delhi
16. J.D. Hooker, "Flora of British India"
17. *Meru Tantra*

18. Ling Puran

19. Rudraksha (Marathi) Vasant Rao Vaidya, Majestic Publications, Mumbai

20. *Guru Charitra*

21. Hymns (Chinmay Publications, Mumbai)

22. *Shiva Lilamrut*

23. A Note on *Rudraksha. Elaeocarpus sphaeicus (Gaertn)* K. Schum by Krishnamurthy T., 1964, Indian Forester 90, 11, 774-776

24. "Action of a fraction of *Elaeocarpus Ganitrus* on Muscles" Bhattachrya S.S. Sarkar, P.R.G. Kar, (Medical College, Kolkata).

25. "Celled Stone of *Elaeocarpus ganitrus* Roxb"- by Oza G. M, Current Science, 41(7): 269, 1972

26. "Further Observations with *Elaeocarpus ganitrus* on Normal and Hhypodynamic Heart", Sarkar P.K., Bhattacharya S.S., Deptt. of Pharmacology, Medical College, Kolkata

27. *Rudraksha* and *Ratna*, "*Rudraksha*" Therapy: Rudra Centre.

28. "More about *rudraksha*" by Joyce Diamanti 2001, The Bead society of Greater Washington Newsletter 18(2):6

29. Notes on botanical identity of beads found under the name − '*Rudraksha*' − By Yelne M.B. Biorhythm, Ayu Academy Series, 44, PP, 39-44, 1955

30. *Rudraksham* by N. Swarnalatha (Journal of Oriental Research Institute, Vol. II, No.1, Oct. 2000

31. *Rudraksha* − a religious tree and its economic importance" By Mitra B., Das Gupta R., Sur P.R. Ethnobot Publishers, Jodhpur, 1992

32. "*Rudraksha* – not just a spiritual symbol but also a medicinal remedy" Dennis T.J. (19993 a) Sachitra Ayurved (*Elaeocarpus ganitrus* Roxb)

33. Coode, M J E (2001). "*Elaeocarpus* in New Guinea - new taxa in the Debruynii subgroup of the Monocera group. Contributions to the Flora of Mt Jaya, V". *Kew Bulletin*, Kew, United Kingdom.

34. *Red Data Book of Indian Plants*. Botanical Survey of India.

35. Zmarzty, Sue (2001). "Revision of Elaeocarpus (*Elaeocarpaceae*) section *Elaeocarpus* in southern India and Sri Lanka" *Kew Bulletin*, Kew, United Kingdom.

36. Power of *Rudraksha* Kamal N. Seetha, 2005, Nagpur

37. Lee, David W.(1998) The biology of rudraksha **Current Science 75 (1):** 26-30.

38. Hui, Gao and Ya, Tang (2006) Typification of **Elaerocarpus decipiens** (Elaeocarpaceae) and its new variety from Taiwan, China. **Novon 16:** 59-60.

39. Images may be seen from:
     www.plantsindia.org/Elaeocarpaceae.html

40. Pharmacognosy 15th Edition by Trease and Evans.

41. Indian *Materia Medica* (K.M. Nadkarni) Popular Prakashan Pvt. Ltd., Mumbai.

42. Saligram Nighantu (Lala Saligramji Vaishya) Khemraj Shrikrishandas, Mumbai (Page 531).

43. Dravya Gun Vigyan (Professor Priyavrat Sharma) Chaukhambha Bharati Academy, Varanasi.

44. Ras Yog Sagar (Vaidya Pt. Hariprapannaji) Krishandas Academy, Varanasi.

NOTE

The extensive and elaborate knowledge provided by the learned author in this book shall enable the readers to:

1. Choose suitable rudraksha according to their profession and needs.

2. Distinguish between fake and genuine rudraksha.

To learn more about *The Power of Rudraksha*, write to the author at:

kamalseetha@gmail.com
Mobile: 9373106326
Overseas callers may dial: 00-91-9373106326
www.rudralife.com

JAICO PUBLISHING HOUSE
Elevate Your Life. Transform Your World.

ESTABLISHED IN 1946, Jaico Publishing House is home to world-transforming authors such as Sri Sri Paramahansa Yogananda, Osho, the Dalai Lama, Sri Sri Ravi Shankar, Sadhguru, Robin Sharma, Deepak Chopra, Jack Canfield, Eknath Easwaran, Devdutt Pattanaik, Khushwant Singh, John Maxwell, Brian Tracy, and Stephen Hawking.

Our late founder Mr. Jaman Shah first established Jaico as a book distribution company. Sensing that independence was around the corner, he aptly named his company Jaico ('Jai' means victory in Hindi). In order to service the significant demand for affordable books in a developing nation, Mr. Shah initiated Jaico's own publications. Jaico was India's first publisher of paperback books in the English language.

While self-help, religion and philosophy, mind/body/spirit, and business titles form the cornerstone of our non-fiction list, we publish an exciting range of travel, current affairs, biography, and popular science books as well. Our renewed focus on popular fiction is evident in our new titles by a host of fresh young talent from India and abroad. Jaico's recently established translations division translates selected English content into nine regional languages.

Jaico distributes its own titles. With its headquarters in Mumbai, Jaico has branches in Ahmedabad, Bangalore, Chennai, Delhi, Hyderabad, and Kolkata.

SINCE 1946